Light in the Darkness

Light in the Darkness

African Americans and the YMCA, 1852-1946

NINA MJAGKIJ

THE UNIVERSITY PRESS OF KENTUCKY

Publication of this volume was made possible in part by a grant from the National Endowment for the Humanities.

Scholarly publisher for the Commonwealth,
serving Bellarmine University, Berea College, Centre College of Kentucky, Eastern Kentucky University, The Filson Historical Society, Georgetown College, Kentucky Historical Society, Kentucky State University, Morehead State University, Murray State University, Northern Kentucky University, Transylvania University, University of Kentucky, University of Louisville, and Western Kentucky University.

Editorial and Sales Offices: The University Press of Kentucky
663 South Limestone Street, Lexington, Kentucky 40508–4008

03 04 05 06 07 5 4 3 2 1

Library of Congress Cataloging-in-Publication Data

Mjagkij, Nina, 1961–
Light in the darkness : African Americans and the YMCA, 1852-1946 / Nina Mjagkij.
p. cm.
Includes bibliographical references and index.
ISBN 0-8131-1852-2 (cloth: alk. paper)
ISBN 0-8131-9072-X (pbk: alk. paper)
1. YMCA of the USA. 2. Afro-Americans—Segregation. 3. Race relations—Religious aspects—Christianity. I. Title.
BV1190.M43 1993
267'.3973'0899073—dc20 93-19857

This book is printed on acid free recycled paper meeting the requirements of the American National Standard for Permanence in Paper for Printed Library Materials.

Manufactured in the United States of America.

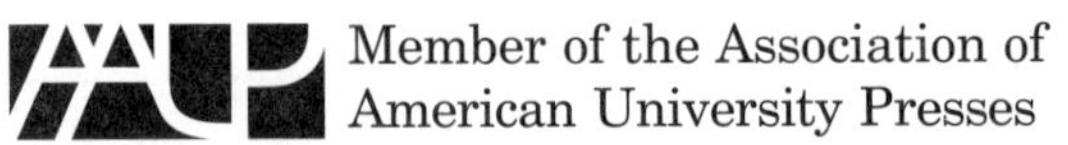
Member of the Association of American University Presses

Meinen Eltern
Anatolij und Brigitte Mjagkij gewidmet

Contents

Acknowledgments

I WISH to express my gratitude to the institutions and organizations that supported my research. The Fulbright Commission of the Federal Republic of Germany provided a travel grant that funded my initial visit to the United States. The American Historical Association gave me a Beveridge Grant, and the Rockefeller Archive Center, a Research Grant. The University of Cincinnati supported me with two Summer Research Fellowships, a Neff Fellowship, and a Taft Fellowship, and Ball State University assisted me with a New Faculty Research Grant.

I have received generous help from the staffs of the Moorland-Spingarn Research Center, Howard University; the Library of Congress; the Rockefeller Archive Center; the YMCA of the USA Archives, University of Minnesota Libraries, Minnesota; the Amistad Research Center, Tulane University; and the interlibrary loan departments of the University of Cincinnati and Ball State University. I am particularly indebted to Esme E. Bhan, Howard University; David J. Carmichael, Dagmar K. Getz, and Andrea Hinding, YMCA Archives; Thomas Rosenbaum, Rockefeller Archive Center; Michael Spangler and Debra Newman Ham, Library of Congress; and Andy Simons, Amistad Research Center.

Many friends and scholars inspired, challenged, and encouraged me. I owe special thanks to Kriste Lindenmeyer, Robert Earnest Miller, Thomas Winter, and Theresa Ruth Eisenberg for reading parts of the book and to Cindy and Frank Surett, who opened their home and hearts to a perfect stranger. I would also like to thank Reinhard R. Doerries and Günter Moltmann, who first introduced me to American history at the University of Hamburg.

I have also benefited from the insightful comments and suggestions of Clarke A. Chambers, Willard B. Gatewood, Jr., James R. Grossman, Bruce Levine, Joanne Meyerowitz, Abraham J. Peck, and Jeffrey C. Stewart. I owe an enormous debt to Roger Daniels, who read more drafts of the book than either of us cares to remember. Most important, though, he challenged and inspired me. Last but not least, I would like to thank my parents, Brigitte and Anatolij Mjagkij. They never understood my fascination with history, but they always encouraged and supported me.

Introduction

IN 1949 Carl Murphy, president of the Baltimore *Afro-American*, complained to the National Council of the Young Men's Christian Association that he could not "get a cup of coffee or a piece of pie" in the cafeteria of the city's Central YMCA. Humiliated and outraged, Murphy suggested that the YMCA "take the 'C' out of the YMCA sign and put it into practice."[1] Murphy was but one of a growing number of African Americans who challenged the YMCA to end its long-standing jim crow policy. The YMCA had excluded blacks from membership in white associations since its emergence in the United States in 1852. Despite this exclusion, the YMCA encouraged African Americans to establish their own associations and join the Christian brotherhood on "separate-but-equal" terms. During the late nineteenth and early twentieth centuries many African Americans, particularly the educated elite, responded with enthusiasm.

The black elite welcomed the YMCA's mission to develop "the whole man—body, mind and spirit," particularly at a time when white society refused to recognize African-American men fully as men.[2] They embraced the YMCA's character-building programs as a means for racial advancement and led in the establishment of separate black associations under black leadership. By the early twentieth century they had created a virtually autonomous African-American YMCA. After nearly a century of segregation, and under growing pressure from African Americans, the American YMCA passed a resolution urging white associations to end jim crowism in 1946. The resolution represented a crucial turning point and signaled the beginning of the end of segregation in the YMCA.

This book traces the history of African Americans in the YMCA from 1852 to 1946, examining the changing racial policies and practices of the North American YMCA as well as the evolution of African-American associations. During the first century of its existence in the United States, the YMCA followed the lead of the nation in its treatment of African Americans. The Christian brotherhood did not challenge racism, discrimination, or segregation but embraced jim crowism. Nevertheless, African Americans joined the YMCA in large numbers: they built their own associations and staffed them with black leaders. After establishing control over their associations, African Americans challenged jim crowism and pressured the YMCA to desegregate all of its facilities.

In the early 1850s, when the Confederation of North American YMCAs first emerged, most African Americans lived in slavery. The white founders of the YMCA did not even consider the possibility of having African Americans join them. The YMCA was dedicated to building character in men, and African-American slaves were, after all, property. Only one group of free blacks, in Washington, D.C., established a YMCA before the Civil War. That organization, however, was short-lived because of its lack of money.

From the beginning the Confederation of North American YMCAs was troubled by the debate over slavery. The Canadian YMCAs challenged the confederation to live up to its Christian ideals and to speak out in opposition to slavery. Confederation leaders, however, afraid to alienate white southerners, made a conscious effort to avoid addressing the issue. The Canadian associations, appaled by the YMCA's acquiescence, resigned from the confederation before the Civil War. The confederation's attempt to shield the association from entanglement in sectional politics was not entirely succesful. During the 1850s branches in the North were increasingly plagued by factional feuds over slavery.

With the onset of the Civil War, the YMCA could no longer evade the issue. Associations in the North condemned salvery and denounced southern branches for their defense of the peculiar institution. Not surprisingly, the Confederation of North American YMCAs disintegrated. Only two southern associations operated continuously throughout the Civil War. Many of the northern associations, however, remained active. They established the U.S. Christian Commission to provide relief services to the soldiers of the Union army. Wartime efforts strengthened the ties between northern branches. Following the war these branches led in the reorganization of the Confederation of North American YMCAs, and their members dominated the highest-ranking positions in the association.

The Civil War also helped to create a change in the YMCA's racial policy. During Reconstruction the YMCA began to encourage African Americans to organize their own branches. Separate black associations emerged in the North and in cities and towns in South Carolina, where African Americans constituted a large proportion of the population. The African-American associations founded during Reconstruction had only an ephemeral existence. This was in part because of the limited financial resources of many black communities as well as a lack of financial and administrative support from the national YMCA. The Confederation of North American YMCAs functioned as an umbrella organization for autonomous, self-supporting associations. It did not provide financial assistance to any local branches—black or white.

Following Reconstruction the YMCA embarked on a new policy. Beginning in 1876 the YMCA appointed the first international secretary to promote association work among African Americans in the South. Between 1876 and 1891 two white men served successively as international secretaries for African-American YMCA work. George D. Johnston, a southerner, visited communities in the South to introduce African Americans to YMCA work and to enlist white support. Johnston's endeavors remained unsuccessful, and in 1879 he was succeeded by Henry Edwards Brown, a former abolitionist from the North. Brown took a different and more effective approach. He visited black colleges and universities in the South and introduced African-American students to the YMCA. Brown hoped that after graduation these students would carry the idea of association work into their local communities. Brown's successful strategy laid the foundation for the transition from white supervision of African-American YMCA work to black leadership.

In 1888 the black association in Norfolk, Virginia, had raised enough money to hire a full-time professional YMCA secretary. The man chosen for the position was William A. Hunton, a black Canadian who had been active in the Ottawa YMCA. Hunton's employment signaled the beginning of the shift to black leadership. The shift was completed in 1891, when Hunton succeeded Brown as international secretary and became the highest-ranking African-American YMCA official in the United States.

During the 1890s Hunton laid the foundation for the emergence of a semiautonomous African-American YMCA. Without the prospect of financial assistance from the national YMCA, Hunton advocated racial solidarity and self-help. He consolidated the black YMCAs and organized regional conferences. When he launched the *Messenger*, a monthly newspaper, he further strengthened the ties between African-American associations. Hunton's dynamic leadership resulted in the formation of numerous black YMCAs in cities and on college campuses. In response to the growing number of African-American associations, the American YMCA employed an additional black international secretary. In 1898 Jesse E. Moorland, a Howard University graduate, became Hunton's assistant. Under the leadership of Hunton and Moorland, the number of African-

American YMCAs continued to increase throughout the early twentieth century.

As the number of black YMCAs and the membership in them grew, Hunton and Moorland started to search for competent and reliable men willing to become professional YMCA secretaries. They were particularly eager to recruit college graduates interested in and capable of performing a broad range of tasks. YMCA secretaries had to serve as janitors, librarians, teachers, preachers, counselors, accountants, fund-raisers, athletic instructors, and song leaders. They also had to assist men in finding housing and employment. Hunton and Moorland faced the problem of recruiting men into a new profession that required hard work and long hours in exchange for little pay and no job security.

The training of these YMCA secretaries presented yet another problem. Many secretaries had been members of YMCA student branches, but they lacked specialized training. Moorland tried to assist the newly recruited secretaries with the publication of the *Secretarial Letter*. The newsletter, published between 1902 and 1937, provided the secretaries with a forum to exchange information about various branches, membership activities, and fund-raising strategies. Similar to the short-lived *Messenger*, the *Secretarial Letter* served as a medium of communication and strengthened the ties between the black secretaries.

The *Secretarial Letter*, however, provided no formal instruction in YMCA work. In the late nineteenth century the American YMCA had opened training schools for professional YMCA secretaries in Springfield, Massachusetts, and Chicago, but these schools virtually excluded African Americans. In response, Hunton and Moorland established a separate training school for black YMCA secretaries in 1908. The Chesapeake Summer School operated in various locations throughout the late 1940s. The school offered African-American secretaries instruction in YMCA work and also helped to maintain a sense of unity and solidarity among them.

Meanwhile, Moorland also became concerned about securing competent African-American men to succeed him and Hunton on the International Committee. While all black secretaries had to be role models for African-Americans and positive examples for whites, Moorland believed that the international secretaries represented the elite of African-Americans in the YMCA. Thus, Moorland was especially selective in his choice of international secretaries. He carefully assessed each candidate's educational background, personal conduct and appearance, and ability to cope with racism. The ideal secretary was of "sterling character," neither a John Brown nor an

Uncle Tom, but a "well-trained, refined, yet vigorous and forceful gentleman."[3]

The demand for trained black secretaries further increased when African Americans in the YMCA secured the financial assistance of white philanthropists. During the first three decades of the twentieth century, George Foster Peabody, John D. Rockefeller, Sr., and especially Julius Rosenwald contributed matching funds to black YMCA fund-raising campaigns. With the support of white philanthropists, African Americans obtained twenty-six YMCA buildings, largely in northern cities. While some black critics charged that the support of white philanthropists perpetuated segregation in the YMCA, the fund-raising campaigns also helped to foster a sense of racial solidarity among African-Americans. Cutting across class and gender lines, the fund-raising campaigns mobilized people from all walks of society in an effort to raise money to match promised donations from benefactors. Moreover, the buildings, equipped with swimming pools, gymnasiums, cafeterias, reading rooms and classrooms, employment bureaus and dormitories, enabled the black YMCAs to expand their programs.

African-American YMCA work continued to grow when the United States entered World War I. During the war African-American YMCA secretaries accompanied the nearly four hundred thousand black soldiers to camps in the United States and France. In so-called Y-huts, the secretaries offered religious, recreational, and educational programs to the African-American troops. The secretaries also staffed and managed two military vacation resorts for black soldiers in France.

African-American participation in World War I did not change the YMCA's racial policy. Following the war, however, many white association leaders began to foster interracial dialogue and cooperation. Whites in the YMCA had taken an interest in social justice in response to the Social Gospel, the Progressive reform movement, and the democratic rhetoric of the war. More important, many white YMCA officials feared that the demobilization of African-American troops would exacerbate racial tensions, and they hoped to avert violence through interracial work.

Although whites in the YMCA increasingly sought dialogue with their black coworkers, they did not challenge the association's jim crow policy. They were convinced that they could improve segregation by making "separate but equal" truly equal. African-American YMCA leaders welcomed the growing interest in interracial work but carefully guarded their autonomy within the YMCA as long as the association denied them true equality.

During the 1930s black association leaders faced new challenges. The depression reduced the incomes of African-American YMCAs drastically, forcing them to dismiss staff and cut salaries in order to continue operating. At the same time attendance at the YMCAs increased, as an ever-growing number of unemployed African Americans sought the services of the associations. Despite financial problems, almost all African-American YMCAs survived the depression with the help of the federal government. New Deal agencies, such as the Works Progress Administration and the National Youth Administration, assigned personnel to black associations. The government workers helped to renovate YMCA buildings and to fund educational and work programs at the associations.

While African-American association leaders tried to cope with the financial crisis, they also sought new strategies of attacking jim crowism in the YMCA. Channing H. Tobias, who succeeded Moorland as senior secretary of the Colored Work Department in 1924, appealed to the World's Conference of YMCAs to exert pressure on the American association. The conference repeatedly condemned segregation during the 1930s, but it lacked the power to enforce its resolutions.

Nevertheless, the conference became an important ally of African-American association leaders, who used the international gatherings as a forum to expose segregation in the American YMCA and to embarrass white delegates from the United States.

The YMCA finally reexamined its racial policy in response to growing African-American protest during World War II. Inspired by the rhetoric of the war, African Americans challenged the YMCA to live up to the democratic ideal that American troops were defending around the world. Disillusioned with the results of two decades of interracial dialogue and cooperation, black association leaders renounced accommodationism and embraced the goals of the "Double V" movement. They demanded the elimination of segregation and started to collaborate with civil rights groups.

White YMCA officials responded to the pressure. Some white association leaders were concerned about the discrepancy between the association's jim crow policy and the nation's defense of democracy, and others were embarrassed by a YMCA study that compared racism in the United States to anti-Semitism in Germany. The national leadership of the YMCA, however, feared to divide the association during the war and delayed the decision to desegregate until afterward. In 1946 the YMCA dissolved the Colored Work Department, abolished all racial designations from its publications, and urged local associations to desegregate.

Many white associations, particularly in the South, refused to implement the resolution. They claimed that the national YMCA had no authority to enforce such a resolution, since all associations had complete autonomy. Similarly, African-American associations were faced with the prospect of surrendering their autonomy. Thus the 1946 resolution represented merely the beginning of the end of jim crowism in the YMCA. The process of the YMCA's desegregation, however, is a story for another book.

This book examines the history of African Americans in the YMCA before 1946. Like the African-American experience itself, this book is about racism, prejudice, and discrimination in American society. It is about the humiliation, pain, and agony that African Americans suffered when YMCAs denied them membership or even a cup of coffee. Yet this book is not about victims.

The history of African Americans in the YMCA is the story of the struggle for racial advancement. It is the story of black communities overcoming class, gender, religious, and personal differences and uniting to raise funds for the creation of public spaces not controlled by whites. It is the story of the educated elite who created safe havens where African-American men could "build true manhood."[4] Faced with emasculation through lynchings, disfranchisement, race riots, and jim crow laws, the educated elite established YMCAs as sanctuaries where African-American men could be men and African-American boys could become men. This is a story of hope and success in the face of adversity. Although separate black YMCAs were the product of discrimination and segregation, for many African Americans they represented "a light in the darkness" of racism.[5]

1

The Origins of Racial Divisions in the YMCA, 1852-1875

DURING the 1850s the debate over slavery threatened to tear the United States apart. The Compromise of 1850 had provided a temporary sectional truce, but it satisfied neither North nor South. White southerners insisted that the territorial expansion of slavery was essential for the survival of the peculiar institution. White northerners hoped to keep new territories open for free white labor. Abolitionists were particularly critical of the passage of a stringent new Fugitive Slave Act, which touched off a mass exodus of African Americans to Canada. Antislavery sentiments in the North reached new heights following the publication of Harriet Beecher Stowe's *Uncle Tom's Cabin* in 1852.

In the same year the first Young Men's Christian Association was established in the United States. Like the nation, the YMCA was torn by the debate over slavery during the 1850s. Initially, YMCA leaders tried to avoid a discussion of slavery in order to maintain a unified organization. When the Civil War started, however, the Confederation of North American YMCAs disintegrated. All but two YMCAs in the South ceased to exist, while associations in the North organized the U.S. Christian Commission and offered relief services to the Union army. Following the war the northern associations reorganized the Confederation of North American YMCAs. They encouraged African Americans to join them, but in separate associations. Several self-supporting black YMCAs emerged, but they only had an ephemeral existence, largely because African Americans lacked the necessary financial resources to maintain the associations.

The YMCA was founded in London in 1844 by a group of twelve young merchants under the leadership of George Williams. Williams had left his rural home in Somerset to find employment in London. He shared the experience of many single young men who had come to London during the Industrial Revolution.[1] Throughout the week the men were "working from early morning to late at night . . . eating and sleeping in cramped rooms above or below the business premisses."[2] The city taverns often provided their only diversion during spare time and on Sundays. Williams was appalled by these conditions, and in 1844 he established a prayer group "to improve the spiritual condition of young men" employed in houses of business.[3]

Many young men of different Protestant denominations greeted Williams's idea enthusiastically. For the first meetings Williams gathered a handful of men in his bedroom. Soon their numbers grew, and the group moved into St. Martin's Coffee House and then into Radley's Hotel. On June 20, 1844, the group adopted a constitution and the name Young Men's Christian Association.[4] The YMCA pledged itself to improve the spiritual and intellectual conditions of its members and launched prayer meetings as well as public lectures.[5] In early 1845 the YMCA hired its first full-time secretary, and three years later the group moved to its first furnished quarters on Gresham Street. The concept of Christian fellowship groups for young men spread to other cities and to other countries. By 1851 sixteen cities in England, Scotland, and Ireland reported having YMCAs, and four years later delegates from around the world gathered in Paris to establish an international alliance.[6]

Americans first encountered the YMCA during the 1851 World's Fair in London. Some Americans who had visited the fair launched similar associations after their return to the United States.[7] Around midcentury, American cities had begun to attract a growing number of young men, and many city dwellers were concerned about the potential "moral hazards" the single male newcomers to the cities faced.[8] The middle-class particularly embraced the YMCA as "a viable urban alternative for the web of supportive moral institutions" the young men from the countryside had left behind.[9]

Organized YMCA work emerged in the United States when the *Christian Watchman and Reflector*, a Boston weekly, published the European travel accounts of George M. Van Derlip, a New York University student, on October 30, 1851. Van Derlip's article contained a description of the Gresham Street YMCA in London, which he had visited during the World's Fair. The article inspired Thomas V. Sullivan, a retired sea captain "doing missionary work among young men on the waterfront," to form a similar organization in Boston. In early 1852 Sullivan called a meeting of interested men, and the newly formed YMCA elected its officers. The Boston association rented rooms, opened a library, and offered its members an employment bureau, a boardinghouse register, prayer meetings, and lectures. From its inception, the Boston YMCA aggressively promoted its work, sending copies of its constitution to clergymen throughout the country.[10]

In the same year a group of young businessmen, under the leadership of George H. Petrie, who had also visited the London YMCA during the World's Fair, established a YMCA in New York City. The YMCA in New York emulated the Boston association and instructed its members to seek out "young men taking up their residence in New York and its vicinity and endeavour to bring them under moral and religious influences by aiding them in the selection of suitable boarding places and employment . . . securing their attendance at some place of worship on the Sabbath, and by every means in their power surrounding them with Christian associates." In the fall of 1852 the New York group opened a reading and meeting room at 659 Broadway.[11]

Also in 1852 other groups established associations in various American cities, including Washington, D.C., where William Chauncey Langdon, an examiner in the Patent Office, organized the city's first YMCA.[12] Langdon was also the moving force behind the organization of a unified North American YMCA. As early as 1852 he proposed a plan for such a unification. It took two years, however, before his plan materialized. On February 28, 1854, Langdon invited representatives from the thirty-two YMCAs known to him to a meeting in Buffalo, New York. Delegates from nineteen YMCAs in the United States and Canada attended the meeting in June 1854. They insisted on the autonomy of local groups but agreed to form a voluntary Confederation of North American YMCAs. The men present appointed a Central Committee that had no governing function or authority over local branches, but was merely responsible for organizing the confederation's annual conventions.[13]

From the outset the Confederation of North American YMCAs was troubled by the issue of slavery. At the first meeting in Buffalo, John Holland, president of the Toronto association and the only Canadian representative, attempted to force the convention to address the question. Holland asked the delegates to recognize that "in Christ Jesus, there is neither bond nor free" and presented a resolution inviting "all Christian young men, of whatever degree or condition in life, to an equal participation."[14] Langdon, general secretary of the newly formed Central Committee, recalled that he "instinctively felt that this was, perhaps, the true crisis of the Confederation."[15] Langdon feared that even the discussion of the resolution would alienate southern associations and threaten the existence of the confederation. Thus, the Central Committee tried to avoid addressing the issue and referred the Holland resolution to the Business Committee, which never reported back.[16]

The Toronto association ratified the proceedings of the Buffalo convention and joined the confederation, although it "viewed with misgivings the reluctance of the Confederation to take a clear position on the slavery question." Charles R. Brooke, secretary of the Toronto YMCA and the only Canadian representative on the Central Committee, continued to urge the committee "to incorporate into the organic law of the Confederation some provision equivalent to the resolution offered at Buffalo by Mr. Holland." Brooke pointed out that he asked the YMCA not to condemn slavery but to recognize "the rights of Christian slaves to become members of the Association."[17] Langdon, however, continued to fear that any official statement regarding slavery would result in the premature death of the Confederation of North American YMCAs.

Langdon had experienced the divisiveness of the slavery issue while working with the Washington, D.C., YMCA. In the fall of 1852 a "Southern member" of the Washington branch had proposed to ban the *National Era*, an abolitionist newspaper, from the YMCA's reading room.[18] The Board of Managers of the Washington branch bowed to southern pressure and issued a declaration stating that "no political or partisan paper shall be admitted into the library, without having been reported and approved" by the board.[19] Langdon, although he was opposed to slavery, believed that a similar statement could save the confederation, "now that the danger came from the opposite direction."[20]

On November 9, 1854, the Central Committee met to discuss Brooke's proposal. Again it avoided taking a clear position on slavery. Instead, the Central Committee explained that it acknowledged the autonomy of local YMCAs and therefore had no authority to issue binding policies on slavery or any other issue. Anticipating an end of the controversy, one YMCA official congratulated Langdon: "You have check-mated Toronto and saved us all trouble."[21]

The Central Committee's decision to evade the issue of slavery seems to have satisfied American YMCAs, since they continued to join the confederation. The Toronto association, however, withdrew from the confederation in protest in April 1855.[22] Brooke explained Toronto's decision:

> It was thought desirable that our delegate should present a resolution to the Convention, not on the subject of Slavery, but on the right of all to the privileges of the Alliance not withstanding any social differences. You may think this in-

> expedient, *we* think otherwise. . . . When it was known here that the resolution had been suppressed, it was with difficulty that the Association was brought to accept the basis of the Alliance. They did so, however, in the hope that the Committee . . . would have accommodated the matter, by either adopting such a sentiment in their constitution . . . or by some sentence in one of their circulars. . . . *that hope proving groundless*, there was only one course to pursue, that of withdrawing from the Alliance.[23]

Langdon sharply criticized Toronto's decision to withdraw from the confederation in a report to the first world convention of YMCAs in Paris in 1855. Moreover, at that meeting the Reverend Abel Stevens, the spokesman for the American delegation, unsuccessfully tried to convince the convention to adopt a constitution that would eliminate further discussion of slavery in the American YMCA.[24]

While the Toronto association refrained from attending further annual meetings of the confederation until 1864, its decision apparently had little impact on American YMCAs. American associations generally avoided a discussion of slavery in favor of strengthening the newly created confederation. Only the Providence, Rhode Island, YMCA withdrew from the confederation, and some members of the Pittsburgh association "made it a condition of attending the coming Convention, that they should be free to bear their conscientious testimony against what they believed to be a national sin."[25]

The Central Committee, fearing that Pittsburgh's antislavery faction would use the second annual convention as a forum to discuss slavery, acted fast. In July 1855, when the Central Committee sent out invitations to the annual convention, it assured its members that it had no intention of infringing upon the autonomy of local associations, explaining that "the confederated existence is intended, *in no way, at no time, under no circumstances, and in no relation*, whether as a Convention or as a Central Committee, to advance upon the local character *of any Association.*" Despite the committee's attempt to remove the slavery debate from the confederation, the controversy continued to have a divisive impact on some local groups.[26]

The New York City YMCA was torn by an ongoing debate over slavery that began when the Library Committee banned Harriet Beecher Stowe's *Uncle Tom's Cabin* from the reading room in 1853. The Board of Directors supported the decision, explaining that it had a moral obligation to protect young men from controversial literature: "It is not deemed proper that this library should contain all works from the press. Theories and opinions of every shade are freely spread upon the printed page—so that youth is compelled to pass an ordeal which, though it may possibly strengthen and expand the mind of a few, will prove fatal to others." The decision represented a setback for the antislavery faction, but opposition to slavery continued to grow within the ranks of the members of the New York City YMCA.[27]

In 1854 leading members of the New York City association signed a petition protesting the passage of the Kansas-Nebraska Act.[28] Two years later some members, convinced that "there could be no legitimate divorce between religion and politics when moral issues were at stake," organized a Young Men's Republican Union and campaigned for presidential candidate John C. Frémont and the newly organized Republican party.[29] The controversy over slavery resulted in an "explosion dividing the ranks of the membership" of the New York City YMCA. In August 1856 George P. Edgar, chairman of the Library Committee, cancelled the association's subscription to the *New York Express* following the paper's criticism of a parade in support of Frémont in which some of the YMCA members had marched. The Board of Directors demanded Edgar's resignation, and in response his supporters asked the members of the board to resign. Eventually the incident resulted in the mass resignation of supporters of each group annoyed over the internal quarrel.[30]

The controversy in the New York City YMCA reflected the growing tensions that the slavery issue caused throughout the nation and within the Confederation of North American YMCAs. Members of the Central Committee had hoped that the 1855 resolution would end the debate over slavery. In 1856, however, the issue of slavery continued to disrupt the confederation. That year the Central Committee decided to hold the third annual convention in Richmond, Virginia. Protesting southern slavery, the Montreal YMCA refused to send delegates and then resigned from the confederation, explaining that it could not approve of "Southern Associations which reject Christian young men of colour."[31]

The withdrawal of the last Canadian association from the Confederation of North American YMCAs did not end the controversy. As the nation itself became increasingly divided, the debate over the YMCA's position on slavery apparently intensified. In 1859 the confederation adopted a policy designed to pacify the contending sides: "Any difference of opinion on other subjects, however important in themselves, but not embraced by the specific designs of the Associations, shall not interfere with the harmonious relations of the Confederated Societies."[32] This resolution was the YMCA's final attempt to evade a clear-cut position on slavery before the Civil War.

During the 1850s the YMCA tried to shield itself from sectional strife in the interest of maintaining its frail confederation. Like America's political leadership, YMCA leaders were willing to compromise on the issue of slavery in order to save their union. When the Civil War started and sectional loyalties divided the nation, however, the Central Committee was forced to retreat from its policy of evasion. Northern associations began to take strong pro-Union and antislavery positions and denounced southern YMCAs for their support of the slave system. Meanwhile, southern associations urged YMCAs in the North to accept the political division of the country. The YMCAs in Richmond and New Orleans sent letters to northern associations defending the South. The Richmond YMCA blamed "the distorting medium of the press" for the "misunderstanding between the North and the South" and urged YMCAs in the North to accept the secession. The Richmond association explained that "the separation of the South from the North is irrevocable, and the sooner this great fact is acknowledged by the nations of the earth the better it will be for the interests of humanity." Northern YMCAs responded with their own set of letters, explaining that they could no longer tolerate slavery on moral grounds. Noble Heath, Jr., corresponding secretary of the New York City YMCA, wrote: "Slavery is wrong, you have determined to defend that wrong. You have counted no cost in defending it even before it was assailed but have been willing even to destroy our government for fear it might be. May God forgive you; your position is utterly false and my heart bleeds that men calling themselves Christians can connect themselves with so wicked a cause. . . . Your Christians will meet ours in battle."[33] YMCAs in the North now began to agitate against the South. They sponsored lectures condemning southern slavery and held the South responsible for "this fratricidal war."[34]

Sectional allegiances during the Civil War thus ended the first Confederation of North American YMCAs. Similarly, the slavery conflict had divided Methodists, Baptists, and Presbyterians, while other denominations that did not formally separate suffered internal tensions. The Civil War not only severed the relationships between northern and southern associations but also reduced the membership in and number of American YMCAs. Associations in the North and South were drained of their constituencies when many of their members joined the armies of the Union and the Confederacy. Before 1861, 240 associations existed in the United States; by the end of the Civil War only 60 were still in operation. Because of the war most YMCAs in the South ceased to exist. Only two southern associations—those in Richmond, Virginia, and Charleston, South Carolina—survived the hostilities.[35]

While YMCAs in the South did not try to organize a southern federation, many YMCAs in the North disbanded their regular activities and devoted much of their energy to the organization of relief work for soldiers.[36] In November 1861 delegates from fifteen YMCAs in the North held an emergency meeting in New York and organized the U.S. Christian Commission, "to promote the spiritual and temporal welfare of the soldiers in the army and the sailors in the Navy." The relief activities for soldiers established a new bond among the members of the 111 YMCAs in the North who organized army committees to assist the U.S. Christian Commission. Although reduced in number and membership, YMCAs in the North not only survived the war but, through their cooperation in the U.S. Christian Commission, emerged with strengthened ties and became the leading force in the reorganization of the postwar YMCA.[37]

These northern associations under the leadership of the Central Committee made their first efforts to reestablish a Confederation of North American YMCAs in 1863. That year the Central Committee declared its dissolution and issued a call, "inviting *all* the Associations of the loyal States and British Provinces to send delegates" to a convention in Chicago.[38] The emerging new confederation, consisting of YMCAs from the North and from Canada, established an Executive Committee to replace the prewar Central Committee.

In 1864, when the delegates of the new confederation met in Boston, they discussed for the first time the possibility of YMCA work for African Americans. Joseph A. Pond, acting president of the convention, expressed the YMCA's interest in assisting African Americans, particularly former slaves, and emphasized that the YMCAs had a "duty to the fugitive thousands whom the continued advance of our armies is sending to the North. . . . let them come, where their humbled manhood may lift itself erect! Let them come where they may find sympathy, relief, education and salvation."[39] Pond's statement signaled the beginning of a new phase of YMCA work, characterized by the confederation's interest in association work for African Americans.

The following winter the U.S. Christian Commission constructed and staffed thirty buildings for the use of the Twenty-fifth Corps, "the largest single organized body of black soldiers." In these buildings, agents of the U.S. Christian Commission offered religious and educational services. The army did not oppose the instruction of black troops but saw it as a means of maintaining morals and morale. The army noted that the commission's efforts among black soldiers served as a means of social control. Chaplains and officers praised the U.S. Christian Commission, because those who were taught "were more obedient and respectful to their officers; discipline was improved; habits of vice were checked, and in many cases genuine religious interest was excited."[40] The educational and religious programs for black soldiers remained the only form of organized association work the YMCA offered African Americans during the Civil War.

In the decade following the war the YMCA began to encourage African Americans to organize associations and send delegates to the annual conventions. Moreover, at the 1867 convention the Executive Committee called upon whites to "promote the formation of Young Men's Christian Associations among the colored brethren throughout the United States and the British provinces." Nothing came of this appeal. In 1869, when the convention met at Portland, Maine, the Executive Committee urged the delegates once more "to aid in the formation of colored Associations throughout the South." This time "a lady in the gallery . . . sent down $10.00 for the freedmen," making the first official contribution for YMCA work among African Americans. Two white YMCA officials, Richard C. Morse, editor of *Association Monthly*, and Cephas Brainerd, chairman of the Executive Committee, donated a library to a YMCA that African Americans had established in Charleston, South Carolina, in 1866. In addition, the delegates drafted a statement in response to a letter from members of a black YMCA. The convention delegates greeted African Americans as "co-workers in the same great cause" and encouraged them to join the confederation and to send delegates to future conventions: "We hail you in the spirit of Christian fraternity and equality. We rejoice in every new right or privilege which you obtain in every new movement of an educational, religious or philanthropic character in which you engage and shall both pray, and labor for your prosperity."[41] Although the confederation promised to pray and labor for black YMCAs, it made no effort to assist them.

Despite the lack of support from the confederation, African Americans began to launch separate associations. In 1870, when the confederation met at Indianapolis, George A. Hall, a white YMCA official, reported that African Americans in South Carolina had begun to organize several associations. Hall urged the delegates to assist the black YMCAs in South Carolina because of their limited resources and reminded the convention that it was "the plain duty of the associations represented in this convention to make ample provision for the prompt prosecution of the general work of visitation of all young men, without distinction of color." Brainerd, chairman of the

Executive Committee, affirmed Hall's statement and added: "As regards both races, it challenges our sympathy and demands our aid. . . . the helping hand of every brother at the South, be he white or black, is needed."[42] While Hall and Brainerd called for the inclusion of African Americans in the YMCA, they neither suggested integrating existing associations nor proposed specific plans for the promotion of association work among African Americans.

When the confederation met the following year in Washington, D.C., B.W. Arnett, a delegate from Toledo, asked how the YMCA intended to promote black association work. Several resolutions concerning "labor among the colored race" were introduced but were reported back "with the recommendation that it is not expedient to adopt them in their present form." Instead the 1871 convention proclaimed that the YMCA "has no politics and knows no distinction among men except those who love Christ and those who love Him not." Thus, in the postwar years whites in the YMCA became increasingly aware of the possibility of black membership. The confederation acknowledged the right of African Americans to join the association and encouraged them to establish their own branches and participate in the annual conventions. During Reconstruction, however, the YMCA's support of African Americans "barely went beyond convention oratory."[43]

A major obstacle limiting YMCA assistance of black associations was inherent in the organization's confederated structure. The YMCA consisted of autonomous, self-supporting groups, and the central body did not provide financial assistance to any of its local affiliates. YMCA work for African Americans therefore depended almost entirely on the initiative and ability of African Americans to organize groups of young men and to raise sufficient funds among their own people. While the YMCA encouraged black association work, it failed to address the major problem black communities faced: hampered by the lack of financial resources, African Americans needed more than inspiring words.

Nevertheless, African Americans struggled to establish their own associations. Anthony Bowen, a former slave from Maryland, established the first YMCA for African Americans in Washington, D.C., in 1853.[44] As a slave, Bowen had received some education from his owner's daughter-in-law. Later he obtained permission to hire himself out during his free time, and Bowen was able to purchase his freedom on October 21, 1830. At age twenty-one Bowen moved to Washington, where he secured a government position. He soon rose to become the first black clerk in the U.S. Patent Office. During the 1840s "Bowen sponsored and obtained permits for free blacks in the

District to conduct meetings at what became known as 'The Colored People's Meeting House' located at 7th and D Streets, NW." In 1845 and 1847 Bowen opened Sunday schools for African Americans and offered instruction in reading, writing, and Bible studies.[45]

Through his work at the Patent Office, Bowen probably met William Chauncey Langdon, the founder of Washington's white YMCA. It is possible that Langdon introduced Bowen to association work and perhaps even assisted him in the establishment of a YMCA for African Americans.[46] In December 1853, one year after the establishment of Washington's white YMCA, Bowen organized an association for African Americans and became its first president. The black YMCA owned no facilities and met in Bowen's home on Sunday afternoons. Limited by lack of funds and restricted by laws regulating the personal freedom of free blacks, the first African-American YMCA in the United States offered its members no more than Bible study meetings.[47] The black association in Washington, D.C., continued to exist throughout the Civil War but "never evolved beyond club status." No record of other African-American YMCAs before the Civil War has been found.[48]

In the years following the Civil War, African Americans established a number of YMCAs despite a chronic lack of financial resources. In 1866 African Americans organized YMCAs in New York City, Charleston, South Carolina, and Harrisburg, Pennsylvania. In 1867 a black YMCA began activities in Philadelphia. A group of young African-American men under the leadership of the Reverend James A. Handy also reorganized and revitalized Washington's black YMCA in December 1866. The constitution these men in the capital drew up indicates that African Americans embraced YMCA work for different reasons than whites did. Whites viewed the YMCA as an organization that safeguarded the morals of young uprooted men in the city by surrounding them with a proper and wholesome environment. The leaders of the black YMCA in Washington shared this concern, but most important, they regarded association work as a means for racial advancement. They proclaimed that their goal was "the mental, moral and spiritual improvement of our race." The founders of the black YMCA were convinced that the "wholesome" influence of the association would enable African Americans to reach "mental, moral and Christian equality." Moreover, they hoped that the YMCA would prove useful in producing role models for other African Americans. They discouraged YMCA members from spending "evenings where no good comes to you, but where your precious time, money and health are given to those whose characters, in many instances, you cannot even respect."[49] The success of the black YMCA in Washington is difficult to assess because few records documenting the work of any of the early black associations have survived.

Unlike the Washington YMCA, the black branch in New York City was sponsored by the city's white association and continued as an auxiliary from 1866 to 1871.[50] New York City's black YMCA was the first to send an African-American delegate, E.V.C. Eato, to an annual convention.[51] Led by Eato, who attended the convention in Montreal in 1867, African-American delegates attended most of the subsequent annual meetings of the YMCA and were usually "given the same courtesy of the floor as other delegates."[52] Eato "was received with greatest enthusiasm by the Convention."[53] Asked to report on the work of the black branch in New York City, Eato outlined an ambitious plan for association work among African Americans in the South:

> We feel . . . that the practical work of reform and reconstruction for our brethren of the South must be done through this kind of labor, and by Christian young men. We have been enabled to see such good results from the efforts of our own Association, that we desire to form similar ones outside of the City of New York. The politicians of the country may do much to reconstruct society and ensure the freedom of the sons of Africa; but we need the refining processes of Christianity to make of them good, true, noble citizens and worshippers of God.[54]

Eato's plan to send African Americans from the North to the South in order to assist in the Christianization of the former slaves did not materialize, probably because of a lack of money.

Apparently African Americans in the South did not need the inspiration or guidance of their northern brothers. They established their own YMCAs. During the early 1870s black association work boomed in South Carolina. African Americans established twenty-three YMCA branches and initiated annual state conventions, which met at Columbia (1870), Charleston (1871), Winnsboro (1872), and Newberry (1875).[55]

Eato had hoped that the YMCA could turn the former slaves into "good, true, noble citizens and worshippers of God," but African Americans in the South embraced association work for a different reason. The tremendous growth of black YMCAs in South Carolina was part of a larger struggle of the freedmen to obtain education.[56] During slavery, education had been an important means of resistance; following emancipation, it became the key to racial advancement. The freedmen embraced education to define their freedom and to control their lives and resist "racial and class subordination." During the war South Carolina's African Americans "opened schools at their own expense" and with the assistance of freedmen's aid societies. Beginning in 1865 the Freedmen's Bureau became a major agent of education, and many northern churches sent teachers to South Carolina to satisfy the African-American population's seemingly "unquenchable thirst for education."[57]

African Americans in South Carolina took advantage of these educational opportunities, but they also used their newfound political power to provide the legal foundations for a statewide public education system.[58] In 1868 seventy-six African Americans were members of South Carolina's constitutional convention that called on the state to establish public schools.[59] The convention created a Committee on Education chaired by Francis L. Cardozo, a black delegate, to provide South Carolina with its first state-funded school system. Despite the lack of financial resources, the lack of "suitable schoolhouses, scarcity of good teachers, and the apathy and opposition to the new system," South Carolina's African Americans persisted in their struggle to obtain education. In 1869, 8,200 black children were enrolled in South Carolina's public schools, and by 1876 the number had grown to 70,800.[60]

While the public schools provided education for children between six and sixteen years of age, the Freedmen's Bureau and the freedmen's aid societies offered schooling to African Americans of all ages.[61] After 1870, however, the Freedmen's Bureau had only a nominal existence, and the northern missionary societies began to shift their support to academic and vocational training for African Americans. South Carolina's black churches continued to display an interest in educating adults, but they "sought only to teach the Negro masses their special versions of Christian morality and to educate a chosen few for the pulpit."[62] While the black churches were limited by their sectarian appeal, the work of South Carolina's black YMCAs was interdenominational and aimed at involving the African-American community at large. This helps explain the tremendous popularity of YMCA work among African Americans in South Carolina.

In 1870 twenty delegates from nine YMCAs, as well as Methodist and Baptist ministers from local churches, gathered for the first state convention of African-American YMCAs in Columbia.[63] The main focus of the convention was education. The delegates insisted that education was "of the most vital importance to the future success of the rising generation."[64] In order to provide African Americans throughout the state with educational facilities, the YMCA convention recommended the creation of "day and night schools" and urged every member "to contribute a small sum of money monthly for the purpose of establishing reading rooms, and procuring . . . books and periodicals." The delegates also advised YMCA members to assist all those willing to become teachers. Within two years the black YMCAs in South Carolina established five reading rooms, and seven associations reported the existence of lecture programs. Moreover, the black YMCAs operated forty-seven schools, with an attendance of nearly five thousand students.[65] The South Carolina YMCAs most likely used churches or private homes, since African Americans in the South lacked sufficient funds to purchase buildings.

From their first convention on, the delegates also encouraged the expansion of African-American YMCA work. They invited representatives of black newspapers to attend the conventions and publicize their activities. They urged existing branches to conduct public meetings to increase membership. The convention delegates also recommended that all members cooperate with local ministers in the formation of "auxiliary societies in every village where they may find a door opened to receive them."[66] For the promotion of YMCA work in rural areas, the convention suggested that "the most active, vigilant and persevering young men . . . go forth as missionaries." Funds for this field work were to be raised through subscriptions from local residents. Throughout their existence the African-American YMCAs in South Carolina reported a general increase in membership, and they saw the establishment of sixteen new branches by 1875.[67]

While the African-American YMCA leaders viewed their work as a community effort and sought the cooperation of local black churches, they warned the ministers not to politicize the YMCA. The delegates tried to place black YMCA work apart from political Reconstruction in order to avoid any partisan affiliation. African-American association leaders objected to "ministers of the gospel . . . entering into politics," proclaiming that they "have lost their spiritual power and influence as ministers . . . and became corrupt demagogs [*sic*] and politicians."[68]

The attack on ministers involved in Reconstruction politics was most likely a comment on the activities of Richard Harvey Cain. Cain, an African Methodist Episcopal minister and editor of the Charleston *Missionary Record*, had been an outspoken delegate to the South Carolina constitutional convention. Afterward, he "passed immediately into the State Senate." Between 1870 and 1871 Cain continued as a lobbyist in Columbia, and as a minister he was also active in the black YMCA conventions. In 1871 Cain was attacked for his real estate speculations, and later he was indicted for fraud.[69]

The black YMCAs in South Carolina, however, seem to have been less troubled by political scandals than by the lack of money. In 1875 the South Carolina delegates met for the last time. By then it was obvious that the African-American associations were unable to raise the funds necessary for their survival. Henry W. Thomas, secretary of the black YMCA in Charleston and chairman of the convention, reminded the delegates: "Now, brethren, do you expect this work to go on without money? It is impossible." Lack of money was a major cause for the failure of successful black YMCA work in South Carolina: only the Charleston branch operated continuously to the end of the nineteenth century.[70]

Another factor contributing to the demise of South Carolina's African-American YMCAs was the changing political climate. Although South Carolina was not officially "redeemed" until 1877, white opposition to black political leadership had undermined the success of Reconstruction from the start. Since the end of the Civil War, whites had tried to discredit South Carolina's Reconstruction governments, charging them with corruption, fraud, and ignorance. In addition to agitation, whites resorted to violence in asserting their opposition to black political leadership. Racial violence culminated in the Ku Klux Klan riots of 1870-71 and led to the formation of white military clubs in the fall of 1875.[71] While white southern opposition paved the way for the failure of Reconstruction, "the inability of the Forty-third Congress . . . to agree on a policy toward the South" marked the end of the era.[72]

The end of Reconstruction also brought to an end the first twenty-five years of the YMCA's existence in North America. During the YMCA's pioneering years in the United States, the association's racial policy followed the lead of the nation. In the 1850s the North and the South desperately sought to compromise on the issue of slavery. Similarly, the YMCA tried to evade a discussion of slavery in the interest of maintaining its fragile union. When the Civil War divided the nation, associations in the North finally denounced slavery, and the YMCA disintegrated. Following the war the northern associations dominated the leadership ranks of the North American YMCA and encouraged African Americans to join the association. The YMCA's interest in Christian manhood, however, did not translate into Christian brotherhood. Instead, the YMCA urged African Americans to organize separate associations.[73]

African Americans, embracing the idea of association work as a means of racial advancement, established a number of YMCAs. Their efforts were hampered, however, by the black communities' lack of financial resources. The short-lived existence of black YMCAs during this period illustrates that despite local interest African Americans were unable to raise sufficient funds.

While the YMCA acknowledged the initiative of African Americans and urged its affiliates to support black associations, it provided no financial or administrative aid. The lack of assistance was in part the result of the YMCA's loose, confederated structure. Lack of commitment on the part of white YMCA leaders also proved to be an obstacle for the establishment of African-American associations before, during, and after the Civil War. Not until the end of Reconstruction did the YMCA move away from its laissez-faire policy and begin to assist African-American associations systematically.[74]

2

White Supervision of African-American YMCA Work, 1875-1891

DURING the 1870s federal troops withdrew from the South, and white southerners returned to power, ushering in a new era of race relations. White redeemers attempted to reestablish the racial order of the Old South and systematically excluded African Americans from political participation through legal means, intimidation, and physical violence. They devised a set of laws that provided for the physical and social separation of the races and trapped African Americans in a system of segregation and subordination. White southerners reversed nearly all gains that blacks had made during Reconstruction. African Americans were free, but since they were deprived of political power and caught in a system of economic dependence, their freedom had little meaning.

While the country turned its back on African Americans, the YMCA began to assist them following Reconstruction. In 1875 the YMCA's Executive Committee discussed the possibility of aiding African-American associations, and in 1876 it appointed a traveling secretary for black association work in the South.[1] From 1876 to 1891 two white men, George D. Johnston and Henry Edwards Brown, served successively as traveling secretary for African-American YMCA work. Johnston and Brown were aware of the lack of financial resources in black communities, so they did not establish YMCA branches. Instead they visited southern communities to promote YMCA work and to recruit association leaders among black ministers, teachers, and college students. The Executive Committee's decision to foster association work among African Americans in the South was a response to pressure from three different groups in the YMCA: those interested in missionary work who hoped to recruit African Americans for service in Africa, former abolitionists from the North who were concerned about the status of the freedmen, and white southerners who wanted to maintain "racial harmony."[2]

The YMCA's interest in missionary work emerged in response to concerns for immigrant groups of various ethnic and racial backgrounds. In the late 1860s the YMCA established separate branches for Germans and Chinese, in the 1870s for Dutch and Scandinavians, and in the 1880s for French Canadians and American Indians. The YMCA's concern for immigrants helped pave the way for increasing support of association work for African Americans.[3] In the 1880s the YMCA also began to venture into missionary work abroad. The YMCA sent secretaries to Japan in 1888 and to India in 1889. In 1889 the YMCA established a Committee on Work in Foreign Mission Lands, and during the following decade the association sent missionaries to Brazil, Mexico, China, and Africa.[4] Stimulated by the YMCA's work abroad, a growing number of association members began to consider the recruitment and training of African Americans for missionary work in Africa.[5]

Another group of YMCA members who supported systematic assistance of association work for African Americans were former abolitionists from the North. Many of them were members of the New York City YMCA who also dominated the ranks of the Executive Committee. Cephas Brainerd, director of the New York City YMCA, chaired the Executive Committee from 1867 to 1892 and played a leading role in transforming the committee from an advisory to a supervisory agency. Brainerd also used his influential position to advocate YMCA work among African Americans.[6]

The third group of YMCA members supportive of association work on behalf of African Americans were paternalistic white southerners. Following Reconstruction they tried to revive the image of the Old South that romanticized slavery but also encouraged noblesse oblige. This image of paternalistic racial benevolence was spurred by fears that political chaos would erupt if African Americans were not educated to "use the ballot intelligently and in harmony with Southern whites."[7]

The leading exponent of white southern support for African-American association work was Joseph Hardie, a merchant and banker from Selma, Alabama. After the Civil War Hardie was elected to the YMCA's Executive Committee, on which he served for thirty years. Hardie played an important role in rebuilding southern YMCAs during Reconstruction as well as supporting YMCA work for African Americans in the South. Born near Huntsville, Alabama, on June 26, 1833, Hardie received his bachelor's degree from Princeton in 1855. In the same year he moved to Selma, where he worked as a clerk in a grocery store. The following year he became a partner in the firm, and in 1859, sole proprietor. In 1861 Hardie enlisted in the Fourth Alabama Infantry. Following the war he settled in Selma.[8]

Hardie believed in paternalistic benevolence as a means of achieving "racial accommodation and harmony." While he accepted black freedom and suffrage, he was convinced that white southerners needed to protect their interests by educating African Americans in voting. Hardie believed the YMCA could serve this purpose, and he urged its members to support association work among African Americans. Hardie explained that "it is not a question that only appeals to me as a Southern man, but it is one in which we are all interested, because it appertains to the welfare of our common country. These people are citizens wielding the power of the ballot, shaping your laws, moulding your institutions."[9] Although Hardie supported YMCA assistance for African-American association work as a means of social control, his Presbyterian upbringing also made him a strong believer in the Protestant self-help ethic. Hence, Hardie favored limited assistance, which he hoped would enable African Americans to help themselves and would make further aid from whites unnecessary.[10]

The YMCA embarked on its new racial policy during the annual convention in 1875. When the YMCA delegates gathered that year in Richmond, there was no indication of increased support for African Americans. On the contrary, the first convention held in the South since the Civil War erupted in controversy when Robert T. Wheeler, the first black student delegate, from the YMCA at Howard University, asked to be seated. The local program committee ruled against Wheeler's admission, but the "full committee voted to receive him."[11] Following this controversy, the seating of black delegates at YMCA conventions was apparently never again challenged. The annual YMCA meetings welcomed African-American delegates, but the convention hotels often barred them or presented them with inferior rooms and services.[12]

Despite the initial dispute, the 1875 convention represented a turning point in the history of African Americans in the YMCA. This change was triggered by the ministers of Richmond's black churches, who petitioned the convention to promote association work among African Americans. Joseph Hardie, who had been appointed by the Executive Committee to chair the convention because of sectional considerations, responded to the appeal. Hardie urged the delegates to assist African Americans, explaining that "there is a great work to be done amongst the colored people of the South. I place it upon your hearts and your consciences here to-night. . . . God will bless the colored young men of this country, and they may be rescued from the inroads of disease and corruption, and the many evils which they are surrounded by." Hardie then announced that he would begin to look for a man willing to work among African Americans in the South. In January 1876 Hardie convinced the Executive Committee to employ the Reverend G.S. Pope of Selma, Alabama, for a three-month trial period.[13] The Executive Committee, however, raised no funds toward Pope's salary, and he was apparently never hired.

In July 1876, when the YMCA convention met in Toronto, Hardie again urged the delegates to support association work among African Americans in the South. Hardie pointed out that during "the past twelve months comparatively little [had] been done." Robert R. McBurney, chair of the convention, explained that a lack of funds was responsible for the YMCA's "inaction." He assured the delegates that the members of the Executive Committee were not opposed to association work for African Americans and "wanted with all their hearts to enter upon it."[14]

Forcing the delegates to make a decision, Hardie explained that he had found "a suitable man" who would be willing to organize African-American YMCAs in the South if $500 could be raised for his services. Dr. Stuart Robinson, a delegate from Louisville, moved by Hardie's appeal, offered the first subscription of $50. Within a few minutes the convention raised $700 in pledges, including $155 from the Canadian delegates and $100 from George Williams, the founder of the YMCA.[15]

After the 1876 convention the Executive Committee authorized Hardie "to obtain a suitable person to engage in the colored work . . . at the rate of $1,500. a year for a time as an experiment." The members of the Executive Committee chose to employ a white man, hoping not to alienate southern white supporters of African-American YMCA work. In October 1876 Hardie recommended General George D. Johnston, from Tuscaloosa, Alabama, as traveling secretary for African-American association work in the South.[16]

Johnston was born on May 30, 1832, in Hillsborough, North Carolina. In 1852, upon receiving his law degree from Cumberland University, Johnston moved to Marion, Tennessee, where he practiced law. In 1856 he became the city's mayor, and in 1857 he was elected to the Tennessee legislature for a two-year term. When the Civil War broke out, Johnston joined the Confederate army and served with the Fourth and Twenty-fifth Alabama regiments. Through his service in the Fourth Alabama Infantry, Johnston met Hardie, who was adjutant of the regiment. After the war Johnston returned to Marion. He practiced law there until 1871, when he was appointed commandant of cadets at the University of Alabama, a post he held until 1873.[17]

In January 1877 Johnston began his work as traveling secretary for black YMCA work in the South. He surveyed the "conditions and needs" of African Americans in Alabama, Georgia, Tennessee, South Carolina, and Virginia. Johnston visited African-American churches, hoping to stimulate interest in YMCA work, and he met with members of white associations, trying to enlist their support for black YMCA work. Johnston followed no systematic plan. Instead he adapted his methods "to the circumstances and wants of each locality." In Augusta, Georgia, for example, Johnston visited white ministers and YMCA officials, who then met with representatives from the African-American churches and Sunday schools to discuss association work. In addition, some white YMCA members volunteered to visit Sunday schools operated by African Americans in order to introduce association work to the black population. Initially, Johnston encountered no opposition, and he claimed that his activities "received a cordial endorsement" from whites as well as from blacks. Some members of the white YMCAs in Charleston and Augusta, however, urged Johnston to discontinue his visits to South Carolina and eastern Georgia because "the political excitement was so great."[18]

At the 1877 YMCA convention in Louisville, Johnston was officially introduced "as visiting agent of the young [black] men of the South." Pointing to the YMCA's missionary interest abroad, Johnston and Hardie challenged the delegates to continue their support of African-American association work. They explained that it was "hypocritical to be praying for the Chinese, Indians, and others and appealing for funds to send missionaries to them while we turn our backs on the godly men at home who are teaching christianity and call them 'nigger teachers.'" The delegates voted to authorize the continuation of Johnston's work but appropriated no permanent funds. Johnston continued as traveling secretary until 1878, but his success was limited. As one black YMCA official later recalled, Johnston "was not a failure but it was soon apparent to Mr. Hardie that the General could not get anywhere near the colored young men on whose behalf the work was supposed to be." The reasons for the discontinuation of Johnston's work remain unclear. Lack of funds as well as the inability of the former Confederate general to communicate with African Americans were probably determining factors.[19]

One year after Johnston left the YMCA, Hardie recommended another white man, Henry Edwards Brown, to succeed Johnston as traveling secretary for African-American association work. Brown, unlike Johnston, was a northerner. Born in Ridgefield, Ohio, in 1839, he attended school in Ripley and in 1854 left for preparatory school at Oberlin Academy. Brown graduated three years later and entered

Oberlin College, where he received his bachelor's degree in 1861. While studying at Oberlin, Brown was influenced by its abolitionist president Charles G. Finney, and he decided to devote his life to working among African Americans. Brown later recalled that he was deeply moved by the assassination of Abraham Lincoln: "I went to my room and pledged myself to God that if He would give me opportunity, I would work for the uplifting of the colored man."[20]

During the Civil War, Brown served for a brief time in the U.S. Christian Commission. In 1864 he enrolled in Andover Theological Seminary, from which he graduated two years later. In 1867 Brown went to Talladega, Alabama, to help establish a school for African Americans under the sponsorship of the American Missionary Association. Brown served Talladega College as principal, teacher, and minister from 1867 to 1870. In 1871 he received a theological degree from Oberlin and established Talladega's theological school, where he taught until 1875. That year Brown left Talladega to work as minister and traveling evangelist in Michigan. Hardie knew of Brown's work at Talladega and in February 1879 convinced him to join the YMCA as traveling secretary for African Americans in the South.[21]

Brown's interest in YMCA work for African Americans was based on his abolitionist convictions.[22] Brown believed that the YMCA could play a vital role in transforming the former slaves into responsible citizens, thereby guaranteeing the survival of "a free republic." Despite his abolitionist upbringing, however, Brown shared the paternalistic views of many white southerners. While Brown fostered racial uplift, he believed that white southerners were better qualified to work with African Americans. Brown claimed that the "southern white has an *affection* for his 'brother in black' which is not common in the white from the North." Brown particularly criticized some of the missionaries from the North who went South during Reconstruction. He characterized them as too rational to assist African Americans, who, according to Brown, were "overflowing in . . . emotional nature" and unable to relate to "the cold intellectual religion of the philosophers we were bringing to them." Brown admitted that he, who had gone South under the auspices of the American Missionary Association, was no exception.[23]

Unlike many white southerners, who attributed the condition of African Americans to innate inferiority, Brown blamed socioeconomic circumstances. Long enslavement, he pointed out, had resulted in a lack of property holding, which explained the "constant burden of debt." Moreover, Brown explained, many African Americans lived in a "hot, damp, malarious climate," which exposed them to diseases that were exacerbated by their lack of proper nutrition. These conditions, Brown argued, hampered black association work. He urged continued white assistance until African Americans were able to support their own YMCAs independently.[24]

Two months after Brown accepted the position of traveling secretary, for which the Executive Committee paid him one hundred dollars a month, he presented his first report to the 1879 YMCA convention. Brown explained that, like his predecessor, Johnston, he did not attempt to establish separate YMCA branches for African Americans in the South. Instead Brown tried to lay the foundation for a network of African Americans who would provide the leadership for black YMCA work in the future. While traveling through the South, Brown visited black churches and introduced African Americans to the principles of YMCA work. Brown was enthusiastic about his work and proclaimed confidently: "No other present organization can do the work, for none other has the supporting and hearty co-operation of Southern and Northern men, of both political parties, and of all churches." Apparently not all white delegates shared Brown's enthusiasm. Hardie tried to pacify the opposition and asked the delegates to support Brown's work, not for the sake of African Americans in the South but in the interest of the YMCA's missionary work in Africa. Hardie assured the delegates that African Americans trained in YMCA work would have "a grand future in the foreign mission field," and he asked them to consider "the vast multitudes in Africa ignorant of the God whom we worship, we feel under obligation to give them the Gospel of Christ; the colored people of the South, having past [*sic*] through the rude civilization of slavery . . . and now made freemen and lifted up to the rank and dignity of citizenship . . . may go forth . . . clad in the full armor of the Gospel to proclaim the truth . . . throughout this vast missionary field."[25]

Another influential supporter of Brown's work was Cephas Brainerd, chairman of the International Committee, which replaced the Executive Committee in 1879. Brainerd was born on September 8, 1831, in Haddam, Connecticut. In 1853 he moved to New York City to study law, and two years later he was admitted to the bar. In addition to practicing law, Brainerd lectured on international law at the City University of New York and served as recording secretary of the New York Prison Association from 1867 to 1877.[26]

Brainerd's connection with the YMCA began in 1853, when he joined the New York City association. He became an active member and served as the branch's vice-president between 1857 and 1859. During the Civil War Brainerd worked with the U.S. Christian Commission, and in 1862 he became director of the New York City

YMCA, a position he held continuously for forty-two years.[27] Following the Civil War Brainerd made YMCA work "virtually a second career." In addition to serving as director of the New York City association, Brainerd became chairman of the YMCA's Executive Committee in 1867, a position he held for twenty-five years. Under Brainerd's leadership the Executive Committee, and later the International Committee, changed from an advisory to a supervisory body, and Brainerd became "the great and invisible dynamo to which all the wires" ran.[28]

Throughout his period of membership in the YMCA, Brainerd advocated freedom and justice for African Americans. Brainerd had joined the New York City YMCA in 1853, when the controversy erupted over the exclusion of *Uncle Tom's Cabin* from the association's reading room. Brainerd, a member of the Republican party, became a leading force in the association's abolitionist faction. He recruited YMCA members into a Young Men's Republican Union which campaigned for Frémont in 1856 and Lincoln in 1860. In 1861 President Lincoln appointed Brainerd arbitrator of the court for the suppression of the slave trade, and in 1864 Brainerd successfully represented a group of African Americans whose property had been damaged during the New York draft riot.[29]

In 1867, when Brainerd became chairman of the YMCA's Executive Committee, he championed black association work. Brainerd hoped that blacks and whites in the YMCA would eventually work together "without controversy or debate as to the question of race." Brainerd urged Brown to avoid complete segregation and not to "go any further than is necessary in recognizing the separateness, absolute and entire between the two races in Christian work." Brainerd favored white assistance as long as African Americans lacked the resources to finance YMCA work. Yet he cautioned Brown to "keep clear of the idea that the black race is to be dominated and perpetually advised by the white race." African-American YMCA work, Brainerd was convinced, had to be placed in the hands of African Americans.[30]

Unlike white southerners who supported association work for African Americans in order to recruit them for missionary work in Africa, Brainerd believed that YMCA work would aid African Americans in their struggle for racial uplift in the United States. While Brainerd did not publicly criticize whites who advocated the recruitment of African Americans for missionary work, he did so in his private correspondence. In a letter to Brown he bitterly objected that some southerners apparently believed that "niggers Christianized by the institution of slavery are not fit to live as free men in the land of their birth, but they are fit to teach Christianity and industry and self-government to the niggers of Africa." Brainerd was aware of the status of race relations in the South, and he urged Brown to proceed cautiously. He reminded Brown that association work for African Americans was still "experimental" and depended on the YMCA's ability to raise funds and to stimulate support among its members. Hence, Brainerd advised Brown "to keep in harmony with the sentiment of the South" and to seek the cooperation of white associations willing to assist African Americans. Moreover, he urged Brown to be patient and to "see to it that thorough work is done if we but raise one cotton plant we must see to it that [it] is a first class one." Brainerd, aware of the continued need to raise funds for black association work as well as southern white opposition to it, insisted on "quiet work, and no public show." Brainerd hoped to make association work for African Americans a permanent feature of the American YMCA, and he cautioned Brown: "We want things to take shape in the minds of those upon whom we depend for money and real substantial sympathy before we go over much into the papers."[31]

Not only white southerners but also some members of the International Committee did not wholeheartedly support association work for African Americans. Brainerd assured Brown that "none of us do—doubt the value of the work you are doing." Yet he informed Brown that his work was "treading on the very border line of Y.M.C.A. work," because many members did not think that the association's function was to assist African Americans in racial uplift. Consequently, Brainerd urged Brown to be careful not to "get over the line, for the danger will be either that some other phases of our work will suffer, or that in making a choice which may be forced on us the work among Colored young men must be stopped." Despite these warnings, Brown apparently encountered little or no opposition from YMCA members or white southerners. He did, however, face other problems. Brown complained that the lack of appropriate meeting places restricted his work and prevented him from coming into "contact with the masses of the people." To cope with this limitation, Brown initially visited black churches to inform African Americans about YMCA work. In the churches he recruited men who then went out in "twos and threes" and "visited the people at their homes . . . for a short cottage Bible reading." While these "house to house efforts" grew out of necessity, Hardie praised them as a calculated attempt to enable African Americans "to help themselves."[32]

Yet another impediment to Brown's work was the lack of cooperation among the black churches. Religious factionalism, Brown claimed, was exacerbated by some ministers whom he described as "ignorant ranters" more interested in stirring up emotions during religious services than in helping their congregants. Because of this, Brown thought it unwise to attempt to establish separate black YMCAs. Instead he continued to focus on stimulating interest in YMCA work among African Americans, particularly teachers, students, and ministers. In 1882 Brown reported that he had managed to overcome some of the intraracial tensions and that the "pastors in all denominations and teachers in higher schools and colleges [are] beginning to regard a Y.M.C.A. as a desirable help in church and school."[33] This new spirit of cooperation inspired Brown to launch the second phase of association work for African Americans in the South.

In 1882 Brown discontinued his practice of recruiting individuals who could only reach a relatively small number of African Americans through their house-to-house work. Instead he asked black ministers and teachers to organize regional conventions for African Americans interested in YMCA work. From January to June 1882 Brown addressed thirty-five such conventions organized by local black churches. He reported that during these gatherings, attended by approximately 1,600 men, "the walls of separation which they had been so long building" were beginning to crumble and the participants were beginning to feel "the stimulus of a united effort." While the regional conventions helped to stimulate interdenominational cooperation and resulted in growing support from African-American churches and schools, they also had shortcomings, which Brown noted. Organizing the conventions was time-consuming, and ministers and teachers were not always able to attend them because they could not leave their work for several consecutive days.[34]

In 1883 Brown changed his strategy when several African-American colleges and universities invited him to their campuses to talk to the students about YMCA work. Brown realized that the African-American schools provided the ideal setting for his work. At the schools he could reach large numbers of young men without spending much time organizing special conventions. Moreover, the students represented the type of men the YMCA wished to attract: the educated elite. Brown explained that the students were "the teachers, pastors, editors, and other efficient workers of the near future" and were sure to assume influential positions in society. Reflecting the YMCA's disdain for the working class, Brown explained that "waiters, hackmen, barbers, porters, and those who get their living by odd jobs, cannot be depended upon to lead our work in any of the cities. The students . . . are the sure and safe means of promoting our work among this race." In 1883 Brown announced that "the larger part of my work should in the future be in the schools," in order to secure the "intelligent, constant, aggressive power of the young men in these institutions."[35]

At the schools Brown not only aroused the interest of the students but also assisted them in the establishment of YMCA campus branches. In 1883 five African-American schools reported the existence of YMCAs. In the same year eleven new branches were established, and three defunct associations were reorganized. In 1884 African-American students formed nine new branches.[36]

Although Brown was convinced that the black colleges and universities were the ideal recruiting ground for future YMCA leaders, he also noted that the "poverty of most of the students" forced them to earn a living while studying, which left little time for YMCA work. Moreover, he observed that the students' limited financial resources as well as the "long distances between Associations" made regional or state conventions "almost impossible."[37]

Nevertheless, Brown's work among African-American students in the South was successful. Between 1883 and 1888 they established twenty-eight YMCAs on college campuses, although many lasted only a short time. With the prospect of growing black leadership for YMCA branches in cities, Brown also began to assist African-American communities in their efforts to establish YMCAs. In 1883 Brown helped found black YMCAs in Little Rock, Arkansas; McIntosh, Georgia; and Charlotte, North Carolina.[38]

Despite Brown's success, the International Committee still regarded his work as experimental. In 1886 the secretary of the International Committee who was responsible for white YMCA work in the South became ill and was unable to perform his duties. The YMCA sacrificed association work for African Americans and assigned Brown to the post. Forced to devote most of his time to white YMCAs in the South, Brown was unable to visit any black schools and could only correspond with black associations. Nevertheless, that year African-American students organized two new YMCAs.[39]

In 1887 Brown resumed his work on behalf of African Americans, and he visited nearly all of the YMCAs on black college campuses in the South. At the annual convention that year, Brown reported that "the schools promise soon to furnish some good men. . . . many young men in their colleges are being trained in Association methods and work. The day is rapidly approaching when it will be wise to organize branch or independent colored Associations in all cities of the South, and in the larger cities of the North." The convention delegates were apparently impressed with the results of Brown's work. They recommended that the International Committee include association work for African Americans in its annual budget.[40]

The YMCA's decision to set aside an annual budget for work among African Americans was a major victory for Brown, whose work had been considered experimental for nearly a decade. During that time Brown's salary had been raised through donations collected at the YMCA's annual conventions. Brown realized that his work depended on the goodwill of contributors, including white southerners. Conscious of the precarious status of African-American YMCA work, Brown proceeded cautiously. The YMCA's decision to allocate permanent funds for Brown's work allowed him to foster association work among African Americans more aggressively without having to worry about alienating southern contributors.

In the same year Brown convinced the International Committee to recruit an African American to work as full-time secretary for the black YMCA in Norfolk, Virginia. African Americans in Norfolk had established a prayer group in 1871, and four years later they had launched a YMCA. In 1887 Joseph Smithson, an Englishman, visited the city, and impressed with the work of the black YMCA, he suggested the employment of an African-American secretary to the International Committee.[41] Brown visited the Norfolk YMCA, and he assured the International Committee that the city's African-American population had displayed enough interest in an association "to warrant the employment of a colored secretary."[42]

The man chosen for the position was a black Canadian, William A. Hunton, who became the "first salaried employed officer of any race of a Colored Association." Edwin D. Ingersoll, field secretary of the International Committee, had "discovered" Hunton in 1886. Ingersoll attended state and local conferences throughout the United States and Canada in order to recruit men for the secretaryship. In February 1886 Ingersoll interviewed several young men interested in YMCA work at the provincial convention in Hamilton, Ontario. Hunton was among them. Ingersoll was impressed by both Hunton's modesty and his successful work in the Ottawa YMCA. He enthusiastically reported to the International Committee that he had found the man that "possibly was called of God to be the Moses of our day to lead the young men of his race in the entire South of this country out of Egypt and the bondage from which they had been recently delivered."[43]

William A. Hunton was born on October 31, 1863, in Chatham, Ontario. His father, Stanton, was born in Virginia and after purchasing his freedom had reached Canada in 1843.[44] His mother, Mary

Ann Conyer, was a free African American from Cincinnati. She died when William was four years old, and he and his eight brothers and sisters were reared by their father. Stanton, a brickmason, instilled Christian ideals and the values of thrift and industry in his children. William Hunton's wife later recalled that "if chores ran short," Stanton would have his sons move a huge pile of bricks from one section of the yard to another just to keep them busy.[45]

After completing high school, Hunton entered the Wilberforce Institute of Ontario, from which he graduated in 1884. Hunton then worked as a public school teacher in Dresden, Ontario, until he was appointed a probationary clerk in the Department of Indian Affairs in Ottawa in May 1885. In Ottawa he joined the local YMCA and was probably its only black member. He was active in the YMCA's choir, served on the Sunday school staff, and eventually became chairman of the Boy's Work Department.[46]

Ingersoll was convinced that Hunton was an ideal candidate for the secretaryship, but some members of the International Committee had reservations about his employment. Richard C. Morse, general secretary of the International Committee, was concerned that a black Canadian would have difficulties facing American racism. Morse cautioned that Hunton might not be "aware of the social sacrifices that might be involved in his undertaking things very different there [in the South] from what they are at Ottawa, in the way of his social intercourse with white and colored people alike, and the change would involve trial and self-sacrifice on his part." Another obstacle to Hunton's employment was the continued lack of funds. The International Committee offered to pay Hunton's traveling expenses from Ottawa to Norfolk, but his projected annual secretarial salary of eight hundred dollars was to be raised by the members of the African-American YMCA in Norfolk. Brown, confident that Norfolk's black community could raise the necessary funds, assured Hunton, "I have no idea of a failure."[47] In December 1887 Hunton agreed to take the risk and resigned from his post with the Canadian Department of Indian Affairs.[48]

On January 20, 1888, Hunton arrived in Norfolk and became the first full-time secretary of an African-American YMCA. In the following three years Hunton organized debating societies, educational classes, athletic work, a choral club, a Bible study group, and a library in "a few small rooms over a store in Church street." After Hunton completed his first year as secretary of the Norfolk branch, Brown reported that the "experiment has demonstrated the feasibility of such a work," and he urged the YMCA to train African Americans as secretaries and to advance financial support. Brown also noted that African Americans in other cities were asking the International Committee for competent association secretaries and that Howard University, Storer College, and Lincoln University had started to offer special training classes for YMCA secretaries.[49]

In 1889 Hunton attended the YMCA's annual convention and presented the first paper read by a black secretary: "Association Work among Colored Young Men." Hunton complained that the lack of sufficient funds continued to hinder the progress of black association work. He pointed out that "not one of our forty-one Associations has a building of its own, or a gymnasium, or baths, or a lecture-hall capable of seating over 200 people." The funds neccessary for successful black YMCA work, he explained, could not be raised by African Americans, "who have had only twenty-five years of growth in education and money-making."[50]

Supporters of black association work doubted that white southerners would help to finance YMCAs for African Americans. Brainerd was pessimistic and predicted a "very dark" future for the African-American YMCAs: "Personally I do not believe the Southern whites mean to do the least thing, a few may help a little, but the body of the whites, will do all they can to hinder."[51] Despite Brainerd's concern about southern white opposition, he handed the national supervision of black YMCAs over to Hunton.

In 1890 Brown was unable to visit African-American YMCAs in the South because of poor health, and he informed the International Committee that Hunton would assume his responsibilities. Brainerd cautioned Brown not to act too quickly and "franchise [Hunton] all around" until the Norfolk work was successful. But Brainerd had faith in Hunton's ability and hoped that he would serve as a role model and convince white southerners of the benefits of black association work. Brainerd also hoped that Hunton would recruit capable secretaries, whom he considered essential for the organization of YMCAs in African-American communities. Brainerd, always aware of possible opposition from white southerners, insisted that the black secretaries "must be of a far higher average" than secretaries employed by white associations.[52]

Hunton's visits to the African-American student YMCAs in the South convinced him that the method of annual visitation was no longer sufficient. He urged more aggressive recruiting as well as systematic training for the secretaryship in order to stimulate interest in YMCA work among black students. After his return to Norfolk, Hunton suggested to the YMCA a plan for the training of black secretaries: "In a short visit, the most likely men might be picked out, set apart, and directed in a course of study and line of work. Afterwards . . . the best available Association worker might be sent to each of the points named, or at which a class had been set apart, to spend two, three or even four weeks, as the case may require, in inspiring, instructing and encouraging the candidates." The International Committee was pleased with Hunton's work. When Brown's health declined, the group appointed Hunton as international secretary for "Colored Work" on December 16, 1890. Hunton accepted the position, admitting that he had "met with many difficulties and discouragements" but insisting that "not once have I had the desire to give up Y.M.C.A. work, but I have ever felt like pushing forward." In January 1891 Hunton assumed his new position and became the first African-American secretary employed by the International Committee of the YMCA.[53]

Hunton's appointment to the International Committee marked the end of white supervision and the beginning of African-American leadership in the YMCA. While Hunton's employment represented a victory for those who had advocated black leadership for black associations, it also provided for the complete separation of blacks and whites in the YMCA. The YMCA's racial policy had come full circle: after a brief period of paternalistic benevolence during the 1870s and 1880s, the association returned to benign neglect in the last decade of the nineteenth century. The International Committee continued to pay Hunton's salary, but beyond that it advanced no financial or administrative assistance.

Unless otherwise indicated, all photos are from the Moorland-Spingarn Research Center, Howard University.

In 1888, Canadian-born William A. Hunton became the first full-time black YMCA secretary in the United States. During the 1890s he supervised black association work nationwide and laid the foundation for a semi-autonomous African-American YMCA. YMCA of the USA Archives, University of Minnesota Libraries.

When Jesse E. Moorland joined the YMCA's International Committee in 1898, he launched nationwide fundraising campaigns for the construction of black YMCA buildings.

In the early 1900s Hunton and Moorland recruited several additional secretaries. The men were carefully chosen to be role models for black men and boys. Clockwise from top left: Channing H. Tobias, John B. Watson, Max Yergan, and R.P. Hamlin.

Racism and lack of money prevented African Americans from attending training schools for white YMCA secretaries. In 1915 new black recruits gathered for secretarial training at Storer College in Harpers Ferry, West Virginia. In the front row, second and third from right, are Channing H. Tobias and Jesse E. Moorland.

Julius Rosenwald, president of Sears Roebuck, became a major financial supporter of black YMCAs in 1910, offering challenge grants. American Jewish Archives, Hebrew Union College.

The 1915 fundraising campaign of these men in St. Louis led to construction of the Pine Street YMCA in 1919.

Above, African-American YMCAs often sponsored father and son dinners to strengthen family ties and give boys proper role models. Below, YMCA reading rooms provided access to books, magazines, and newspapers, and also afforded many African-American men a place to establish professional and personal contacts.

Above, YMCA dormitory rooms offered clean, affordable housing for visitors and newcomers to a city. Below, Bible study groups such as this were an integral part of YMCA work, but association leaders carefully avoided identification with any particular church.

African-American YMCAs gave members the opportunity to participate in team sports (above) in order to teach fair play and the value of cooperation. Below, swimming pools offered recreation and exercise, and teachers and students often used them for physical education classes.

World War I saw important African-American YMCA work with black soldiers. Above, a YMCA secretary teaches a class at the Y-hut at Camp Travis, Texas. Below, troops congregate in front of the Y-hut at St. Nazaire, France, in July 1917. Both from YMCA of the USA Archives, University of Minnesota Libraries.

African Americans attended national YMCA meetings but also organized their own conventions, allowing black delegates to maintain a sense of racial solidarity.

Below, the staff of the YMCA's Colored Work Department in 1925. Front row, left to right: Robert P. Hamlin, Channing H. Tobias, and Robert B. DeFrantz. Back row: L.K. McMillan, William C. Craver, John H. McGrew, Ralph W. Bullock, and Frank T. Wilson. YMCA of the USA Archives, University of Minnesota Libraries.

3

Growth and Centralization under African-American Leadership, 1891-1898

DURING the last decade of the nineteenth century, race relations in the United States deteriorated until they reached a nadir. African Americans in the South were deprived of the ballot, jim crow laws established legal segregation in nearly all aspects of life, and lynchings "attained the most staggering proportions ever reached in the history of that crime."[1] Many African Americans did not openly challenge jim crowism but instead began to advocate racial solidarity and self-help. They hoped that through intraracial cooperation and self-improvement African Americans "would gain the respect of white men and thus be accorded their rights as citizens."[2] Booker T. Washington's call for accommodationism and gradualism epitomized this general trend in African-American thought.[3]

Accommodationism and gradualism also became the course of action for African Americans in the YMCA. William A. Hunton challenged the association's racial policy as disgraceful and un-Christian but found that he was unable to end the YMCA's jim crowism. Instead, Hunton focused on building a sense of community among African-American YMCAs. He continued his predecessors' strategy of promoting YMCA work at colleges and universities in order to recruit African-American association leaders. Hunton also began to assist African Americans in the establishment of YMCAs in urban communities. Most important, though, he systematically consolidated black associations during the 1890s. Hunton organized African-American YMCAs into regional conferences and provided them with a medium of communication. In 1896 he launched a monthly newspaper, the *Messenger*, which served as a clearinghouse for information about the work and progress of African-American YMCAs and offered its readers advice on various aspects of association work.[4] Furthermore, when the Spanish-American War started, Hunton raised funds to provide YMCA services for black troops.

In 1891, when Hunton began his career as international secretary, the prospect of successful YMCA work among African Americans was bleak. Growing racial tensions made Hunton's work "more difficult than it had been earlier, and in some areas made it virtually impossible." Even staunch supporters of African-American association work, such as Joseph Hardie, were now convinced that separate black YMCAs could not be successfully organized because of the racial climate. Cephas Brainerd concurred, noting that the situation "was never more grave, or has not been for many years, than at the present time."[5] The deterioration of race relations and the tightening of the color line had a marked impact on the YMCA. In 1891 the YMCA convention officially acknowledged the long-established de facto segregation of African Americans. In the past, the YMCA had encouraged African Americans to organize separate branches, but it had never endorsed segregation or advised white associations to exclude African Americans from membership. Based on the YMCA's recognition of branch autonomy, the decision to admit African Americans or deny them membership in white associations was made on the local level. White branches in the South did not admit African Americans, and in the middle and northern States white associations often pigeonholed the applications of blacks in an attempt to prevent them from joining. By the 1890s five white associations in the North—in New York, Chicago, Boston, Brooklyn, and Springfield, Massachusetts—reported having African-American members.[6] Hunton observed that African Americans joined white YMCAs "even under most favorable circumstances" only in small numbers, "seldom, if ever, more than a dozen."[7] They were most likely discouraged by the possibility of discrimination and humiliating treatment. Despite these exceptions, exclusion of African Americans from membership in white branches remained the rule throughout the nineteenth century.

In 1891, in a resolution designed to prevent the duplication of YMCA work on the local level, YMCA convention delegates recognized the legitimacy of "Colored Associations." Hunton vehemently opposed the codification of the YMCA's jim crow policy. He insisted that the only practice "endorsed by the International Committee, is that which accords to colored applicants the very same treatment given to white." Hunton appealed to the YMCA to end this un-Christian practice and urged white members to "look into the disgraceful chasm that yawns between us—the white and colored people of this country—to-day, and then . . . look to Jesus Christ for wisdom and power to bridge it."[8]

Although Hunton criticized segregation in the YMCA, he discouraged blacks and whites from challenging local racial practices. Prejudices, he believed, could only be overcome gradually. If whites learned to accept African Americans as fellow Christians, Hunton argued, the YMCA would need no color line. He explained: "In laboring among the young men of my race, I constantly urge them to learn the lesson of Christian love; to love God and to love all their fellow-men, even their enemies. . . . If you, brethren, will faithfully teach the same lesson of love to the young men of your race, we shall soon join glad hands."[9] In the meantime, though, Hunton asked African Americans to accommodate themselves to existing racial practices and to establish separate branches.

Hunton continued to criticize the YMCA's jim crow policy, but it did not paralyze his work. Hunton focused much of his energy on providing the growing African-American urban population with YMCA branches. Attracted by economic opportunities and better living conditions, young men from rural areas as well as graduates of the African-American colleges were "flocking to the city centers . . . seeking employment." These men, Hunton insisted, "must be protected from the tremendous evils surrounding them." He suggested providing them "with means for physical cleanliness . . . reading-room, library and night school, and the other uplifting influences of a 'Christian home away from home.'"[10]

The black educated elite shared Hunton's concern about "the allurements, pitfalls and fierce temptations" confronting young black men in the cities.[11] Booker T. Washington applauded the "strong, constructive and stimulating influences" of the YMCA among the young men and boys who "are leaving the simple and comparatively healthy life of the plantation and are joining the already overcrowded throngs in the cities." For the African-American elite, the YMCA appeared to offer an attractive alternative to the demoralizing forces of "the gambling den . . . the saloon, the house of vice, and a thousand less flagrant evils" leading young men "to certain moral and spiritual ruin."[12]

Advocates of association work among urban blacks came largely from the ranks of the African-American college students who had been introduced to YMCA work at their schools. Following their graduation, many of these men settled in southern cities and started to organize YMCAs. During the 1890s they increasingly sought Hunton's advice concerning administrative problems, membership drives, and fund-raising campaigns to acquire property.[13]

Although Hunton was interested in promoting association work in cities, he urged African Americans not to rush but to plan carefully and to consider the problems involved in the organization of YMCAs. Hunton's caution was well founded. In the years following the Civil War the "mortality rate" among YMCA branches had been "excessively high." In 1892 the *Era* illustrated the problem in an article describing a "visit to an imaginary burial ground for defunct Y.M.C.A.'s which was said to contain over 3,400 graves."[14]

Hunton attributed the high "mortality rate" among African-American YMCAs to a lack of proper planning. He claimed that "the dry bones of dead Associations lie bleaching in the sun" because too many black YMCAs were hastily established before the founders had secured enough financial support or personal commitment. In 1892 Hunton described what he believed to be the typical scenario for the formation of a black YMCA: "A mass meeting is called, the marvelous results accomplished in other places by Associations are painted in glowing colors . . . a constitution is secured; an organization is effected; and they plunge headlong into the work, into debt, and into a multitude of troubles, which result in the unhappy death of the movement."[15] Hunton feared that this lack of planning would drain local communities of financial resources as well as long-term personal commitment, which he believed to be essential for the successful establishment and continued operation of a YMCA.

Concerned about the negative effects of failing YMCAs, Hunton published a set of guidelines in 1892. This pamphlet, entitled *First Steps*, was designed to help those interested in establishing associations and outlined a plan for the successful formation of YMCAs. Hunton advised African-American men to establish a Young Men's Band and to meet weekly for at least two months to consider the work and problems involved in organizing a YMCA. During this "getting ready to organize period," Hunton predicted, the "half-hearted volunteers" would lose interest and drop out, "leaving a few intelligent and determined Christian workers as excellent material for a good foundation." Hunton recommended that the men consider the employment of a professional YMCA secretary only after the emergence of a determined core group.[16]

Hunton advised the men to seek support from the community following the formation of a YMCA: to hold public meetings and explain the "object, scope and cost of the work" to local residents, and to solicit contributions. No association buildings, Hunton insisted, should be opened until cash and "reliable pledges" had been secured to support the operation of a YMCA for at least one year. Hunton particularly urged the men to consult with the African-American ministers of each city, seeking their approval and assistance. Some ministers apparently fered the YMCA as a competitor for souls as well as for money and actively opposed association work. One of the founders of the YMCA in Danville, Virginia, claimed that the city's "ministers have always fought [the] Y.M.C.A. . . . they killed us in '91, and have done nothing to help us since." A member of the black YMCA in Baltimore recalled that a Baptist pastor told him that the YMCA was "no good" and an "Enemy of the Church." In Chicago, a group of African Americans who tried to organize a YMCA complained about the lack of church cooperation, explaining that "our preachers are not all at unison with each other."[17] Lack of church support or active opposition from ministers were crucial obstacles for many African-American YMCAs in the late nineteenth century.

Most churches, however, supported association work, and ministers were often among those who initiated the formation of YMCAs. The founders of the African-American YMCA in Memphis reported that "pastors of the several denominations are doing all they can to aid us." In Chattanooga the minister of the Leonard Street Presbyterian Church invited the YMCA to use the church "rent free" until the association was able to secure its own quarters.[18]

Although Hunton emphasized systematic planning, community action, and church cooperation as prerequisites for the successful establishment and operation of African-American YMCAs, he also believed that whites had an obligation to provide assistance. African Americans, Hunton explained, had limited funds for association work because they "generally are poorer, and they are already giving liberally for the support and extension of Church and educational work." In addition, he pointed out, African-American fund-raising efforts were hampered by racism. White southerners usually did not support black associations, and secretaries of white branches did not encourage their members to contribute to black YMCAs, afraid to weaken their own treasuries.[19]

The inability of African Americans to raise sufficient funds among the black population and the unwillingness of local white residents to assist them stimulated Hunton to seek help from the YMCA conventions. Hunton repeatedly urged association delegates to support the work of African Americans, claiming it was their Christian duty. "Satan is not waiting for a better time," he reminded the delegates, "but is tearing down upon our young men with a tremendous force of evil. Shall Christians sleep while poisonous tares are being sown in this large portion of our Lord's vineyard?" Moreover, Hunton insisted that the delegates had an obligation to aid African Americans rather than sending missionaries overseas. "If the Young Men's Christian Associations of America have a missionary field anywhere in the world," he claimed, "it is right here at home among colored young men who are struggling against tremendous odds to lift themselves above and beyond the degradation of the past."[20] Despite Hunton's continued appeals, the YMCA conventions did not extend financial support to black associations.

Unable to gain the support of convention delegates, Hunton proposed a plan to the International Committee, hoping to obtain its assistance for African-American YMCAs. In 1893 he suggested a four-step procedure. First, he urged the International Committee to extend financial aid to African-American associations in the South. Second, he recommended supervision of local fund-raising campaigns by a member of the International Committee. This, he hoped, would eliminate fraudulent activities of imposters. In 1892, for example, "King" Albert Mack, self-proclaimed president of the black YMCA in Louisville, had cheated African Americans out of money, claiming he was raising funds for a local YMCA building. Third, Hunton suggested that the fund-raising campaigns of black associations should expand beyond local communities and seek support from northern philanthropists. Finally, his plan called on already existing African-American YMCAs to support each other, encouraging self-help and intraracial cooperation.[21]

The International Committee did not heed Hunton's advice, probably because his plan called for direct financial support to local branches, which would have violated the YMCA's fundamental principle of local autonomy. Hunton doubted that African Americans could establish successful branches without aid from the YMCA, and he concluded that "self-support of existing Associations . . . is yet very difficult. The rapid formation of new organizations is not therefore encouraged until a better development of existing work is assured."[22] Weakened by the lack of funds, Hunton tried to draw strength from racial solidarity. Beginning in 1890 Hunton organized state and regional conferences for African-American YMCAs. From 1890 to 1898 representatives gathered fourteen times in Virginia, Tennessee, North Carolina, and Georgia.[23] Unlike the state conventions of white associations in the South, which often excluded African Americans, the meetings organized by Hunton were open to all YMCA delegates regardless of race. Only a few white representatives, however, attended the African-American YMCA conventions.[24] The object of the conferences, Hunton explained, was "to secure the adoption of effective and uniform methods of work." The delegates discussed common problems as well as strategies to improve association work. Individual branches reported on their ongoing activities, and "weak points were exposed, questionable methods condemned and remedies suggested."[25]

In addition to debating the problems of establishing and maintaining an association, the delegates talked about the YMCA's role in the struggle for racial advancement. The YMCA, the delegates argued, played an important part in providing African-American men with the opportunity to build their manhood, "to think rightly, to feel nobly and, as a consequence, to develop self-respect." S.G. Atkins, a delegate from Winston, North Carolina, explained that schools, churches, and homes were important for the development of character, but they did not adequately meet the needs of young black men. The schools, Atkins claimed, "stop at a point with most of our youth where the danger is greatest," and the churches waste much of their funds for social gatherings and excursions. The homes, Atkins conceded, were "a powerful factor" but failed to provide a stimulating environment. "What ought to be homes among us," he charged, "are largely only places in which to eat and sleep. . . . Many of our so-called homes positively drive the boys out and send them a-drifting."[26] Atkins concluded that the YMCA should provide services complementing those of school, church, and home.

The delegates to the African-American YMCA conventions insisted that their work of building manhood was not restricted to benefiting merely the Talented Tenth. The Reverend Z.D. Lewis, a delegate from Richmond, explained that the association was not "the resort of a favored few." On the contrary, he argued, it was "a rallying point for the rich and poor, educated and uneducated, well-dressed and humbly-clad, in short, for all the young men of the city without respect to possessions, condition or attainment." Charles C. Dogan, secretary of the black YMCA in Norfolk, concurred and pointed out that the association's mission was to serve all men regardless of class.[27]

Despite their call for fraternal cooperation without class distinction, African Americans in the YMCA were very class-conscious. They recruited their leaders among the college-educated elite, convinced that the Talented Tenth would provide proper role models for young men and inspire them "to be Christian gentlemen."[28] Although African-American YMCA leaders patronized lower-class and uneducated members of the race, they nevertheless made special efforts to keep the doors of the association open to rich and poor alike.

While African Americans in the YMCA insisted upon serving all classes of blacks, their concept of racial unity did not include women. In many cities African-American women had formed ladies' auxiliaries in support of YMCA fund-raising campaigns. Association leaders acknowledged the efforts of the auxiliaries and urged African-American mothers and wives "to liberally support" YMCA work.[29] The interest that black women took in the YMCA's work, however, troubled many association leaders, who feared that the presence of women would have a demoralizing impact on the men. The secretary of the African-American YMCA in Norfolk explained that men might come to YMCAs only "for the purpose of escorting ladies." Nevertheless, he encouraged the delegates to make use of the ladies' auxiliaries to "assist in serving light refreshments" during social receptions.[30]

Some local YMCA officials were apologetic about the support of women. The president of the black YMCA in Columbia, South Carolina, explained that "necessity has caused us to organize an auxiliary of Ladies whitch [*sic*] I did not intend to do." John W. Evans, secretary of the Indianapolis association, reported that women were allowed to attend the fund-raising meetings but assured the international secretary that they would be excluded as soon as the YMCA acquired rooms. The Chattanooga YMCA, even more rigid, refused to employ a female janitor "because it would necessitate the constant presence of a woman in the building."[31]

Despite their exclusion from YMCA programs, African-American women actively and enthusiastically supported association work. They did so in the hope that the YMCA's services for men would benefit the entire community. Husbands and sons who participated in wholesome YMCA programs were less likely to spend their time and money in places of ill repute. African-American women frequently attended organizational meetings of YMCAs and at times outnumbered men. In Nashville, for example, only ten men but forty women gathered for a fund-raising meeting. The Baltimore association leaders praised the Ladies Auxiliary for serving refreshments and donating window shades, noting that "they are often more interested in the good of the young men than [are] the young men themselves." African-American women did not protest their exclusion, although at times they complained when the men failed to show proper appreciation for their work.[32]

Hunton tried to overcome class and gender differences by further consolidating African-American YMCAs when he launched a monthly newspaper in 1896. The *Messenger* was edited by YMCA secretaries from Virginia, Pennsylvania, North Carolina, and Washington, D.C., and published by the association in Richmond.[33] The *Messenger* carried news of activities in colleges and in cities, reported about the African-American YMCA conferences, and offered advice on various aspects of association work. The editors of the *Messenger* stressed racial unity and encouraged African-American YMCAs to promote association work "among all classes . . . to improve the mental, moral and spiritual condition of our young men." Moreover, the paper emphasized the YMCA's duty to provide educational programs for all African Americans and not only the educated elite. It proclaimed: "Knowledge is power. Ignorance is a crime." The *Messenger* urged associations to include in their reading rooms "choice books to suit all classes and conditions of men." It also encouraged YMCAs to offer different programs for those who have had "either extensive or limited" schooling as well as "those who have been denied mental training." The paper, however, cautioned African-American YMCA secretaries to offer appropriate instruction without embarrassing those with little or no schooling.[34]

The *Messenger* discontinued publication in 1897, probably because of a lack of funds. The paper was financed entirely through subscriptions from African-American YMCAs, which were fighting for their own economic survival.[35] The paper's brief publication, however, did illustrate the desire of African Americans in the YMCA to consolidate their activities and to stimulate intraracial cooperation.

While Hunton aimed his efforts largely at increasing the number of associations in cities as well as unifying all African-American YMCAs, he also ventured into another line of work when the Spanish-American War started in 1898. The YMCA had provided for the welfare and relief of soldiers during the Civil War, but it did not establish a permanent committee for work with the military until the Spanish-American War. The YMCA created its Army and Navy Christian Commission in response to concerns that "profanity, gambling, intemperance and impurity" among soldiers would result from "the idle hours of a waiting campaign, the discomforts of enforced camp life in a crowd, the disappointments of inactive service, together with trying climatic and sanitary conditions." The commission proposed to erect tents in which the soldiers could find reading materials and gather for physical, social, and religious activities. On April 30, 1898, the army authorized the YMCA's plan, and in June the navy followed suit.[36]

The Army and Navy Christian Commission made no provision for black troops. Hunton, eager to provide YMCA services to black soldiers, appointed his own subcommittee in June 1898. By the end of the month Hunton and his committee managed to set up twelve tents for the use of the twenty thousand African-American soldiers stationed at Camp Alger, near Washington, D.C. In July they erected a tent for eight hundred African-American soldiers at Camp Corbin, near Richmond, equipped it with an organ, and staffed it with a YMCA secretary, who provided "reading matter, writing material, bibles and hymn-books."[37]

The African-American officers commanding the troops welcomed Hunton's efforts and praised the association's impact on the men's discipline. The YMCA, they claimed, brought to the men the comforts of home and filled "their leisure hours with attractions that helped to allay any spirit of restlessness or discontent." Hunton spend most of the summer of 1898 raising funds to support the work for the troops as well as recruiting secretaries who were willing to serve in the camps without pay.[38] While his work provided many African-American soldiers with YMCA services, it also forced him to neglect temporarily the black college and city associations. By the end of the year the International Committee had come to realize that Hunton could no longer serve the growing field of African-American YMCA work on his own.

Between 1891 and 1898 Hunton had been the only international secretary for African-American work, as well as the sole black representative on the International Committee. During these years Hunton's major source of assistance was his wife, Addie D. Waites Hunton. Addie Waites was born on June 11, 1875, in Norfolk, Virginia, where her father, Jesse Waites, owned a wholesale oyster and shipping business and an amusement park for African-Americans. Her mother died at an early age, and Addie was reared by an aunt in Boston, where she attended the Girls Latin School. After graduating from a business college in Philadelphia, she taught in a vocational school in Normal, Alabama.[39]

Addie Waites met her husband in 1890, when she left Norfolk to visit her sister at Wilberforce University in Ohio. William A. Hunton, then twenty-seven, was on his way to Canada, and he offered to accompany the fifteen-year-old girl as far as Cincinnati. Jesse Waites, who had been a supporter of the Norfolk YMCA, accepted Hunton's offer. During this trip the friendship between Addie and William began, and throughout the next three years they corresponded "almost daily." Addie later recalled that she liked William from the moment she met him. She admitted, however, that she had a feeling of "awe" because William "was so different from the average young man in his general manners and earnestness of purpose." Addie's feelings changed when William took her to a Wild West show. Addie was surprised to see an entirely different side of William: he "yelled, whistled, clapped his knees, and waved his hat with the abandon of all the other 'fans' there. He would recover just long enough to apologize for his over-exuberance and then go off again."

William proposed to Addie in 1893. They were married that year in Norfolk, and Addie effectively became her husband's assistant. She handled most of his correspondence while he was visiting YMCAs throughout the country, and she helped edit the *Messenger*.[40]

Despite his wife's support, William Hunton was overwhelmed by the steadily increasing number of African-American YMCAs, and in 1895 he began to urge the International Committee to employ a second secretary for African-American YMCA work. He explained that the black associations "are scattered over such a large area it is impossible for me to visit any of them oftener than once a year." The International Committee, however, was plagued by a financial crisis, caused by the depression. Instead of expanding its secretarial force, the International Committee cut its staff and reduced the salaries of its secretaries. Nevertheless, Hunton continued to agitate for the employment of an assistant. In 1896 he complained to the International Committee: "I have been making my own plans and programs and carrying them out with but little, if any, criticism from the committee. Of late I have felt this responsibility too much."[41] Although Hunton's complaint illustrated his relative independence, it also reflected the absence of the guidance and support that he apparently expected from the International Committee.

In the following year Hunton appealed to the YMCA convention to support the employment of a second African-American international secretary. He explained that he knew "of a score of large city centers that are ripe for organization . . . but the limited force of the Committee has made it impracticable to render the aid in visitation and counsel." Joseph Hardie, who chaired the convention, pointed out, as he had done earlier, that whites had not only a moral obligation but also self-serving interests in promoting African-American YMCA work. Hardie reminded the delegates: "From this race come our domestics, they prepare your food, they nurse our children, they are with us to stay. . . . are we going to . . . bring these people to God?" The International Committee praised Hunton's work, admitting that it was "progress in the face of many obstacles, but with more encouraging results than the Committee has been able to report to any previous Convention."[42] Nevertheless, the YMCA's financial crisis prevented the appointment of an additional African American to the International Committee that year.

Meanwhile, members of the black YMCAs tried to show their support and raised money for the employment of an assistant for Hunton. In November 1896 at the conference of African-American YMCAs in Hampton, Virginia, the delegates appointed a special committee to raise five hundred dollars for the extension of association work among African Americans. The International Committee, the delegates explained, "has received so little financial support in the past from our Associations that we are not now warranted in asking them to provide an assistant."[43] The *Messenger* was confident that the existing sixty African-American associations would be able to raise the amount "without trouble or delay." By spring 1898, however, only twelve associations had made contributions amounting to $130. The committee issued another appeal, asking the African-American YMCAs: "Shall we not make a much better showing this year. . . . Let us be men, and bear our share of the burden of the work whose benefits we have been so long enjoying."[44] Available records do not indicate whether this appeal was more successful than the first one.

Nevertheless, in the fall of that year the International Committee recovered from its financial crisis and hired an additional African-American secretary. On October 7, 1898, Jesse E. Moorland became Hunton's assistant.[45] Moorland was born in Coldwater, Ohio, on September 10, 1863. His mother died when he was an infant, and his father died when he was twelve years old. But even while Moorland's parents were alive, he was reared largely by his grandparents, who had been "substantial landowners" in Tennessee, where they had exercised the right to vote. When Tennessee placed restrictions on free blacks during the 1850s, they moved to Ohio, where they became successful farmers.[46]

Moorland's grandparents were proud of the free status of the family, which traced its ancestry back to the eighteenth century, when John Moore, a free African American, had married Nancy Mollie Moorland, an Irish woman. Members of Moorland's family had fought in the Black Hawk War, the American Revolution, and the Civil War. His great-grandfather, a Baptist minister, had served an interracial congregation in North Carolina, one of his uncles had been a physician, and his grandfather had worked as a public school teacher. Other members of Moorland's family had been active in the Underground Railroad, and yet another had settled in Liberia in the 1840s. Moorland later recalled, "I always wanted to reflect honor on my family. . . . I heard their story again and again when a boy."[47]

Moorland's grandparents instilled in their grandson the desire for education. His grandfather read the Bible with him in the evenings, and his grandmother's "daily routine at the end of the day included reading aloud Bunyan's *Pilgrim's Progress* and *My Bondage and My Freedom* by Frederick Douglass." Moorland recalled that he was surrounded by books, some of which his family had inherited from his uncle the physician. As a child, Moorland attended a small county school near his family's farm. Later he went to the Northwestern Normal University in Ada, Ohio, where he met Lucy Corbin Woodson, whom he married in 1886. Both taught briefly in public schools in Urbana, Ohio, and then moved to Washington, D.C., where they attended Howard University.[48]

In 1891 Moorland graduated from Howard University's Theological Department as valedictorian of his class. Following his ordination as a Congregational minister, Moorland organized a church in South Boston, Virginia. In 1893 Moorland became pastor of a church in Nashville, and three years later he moved to Cleveland, where he served as pastor of the Mount Zion Congregational Church. Moorland remained in Cleveland until his appointment to the International Committee in 1898.[49]

Moorland first encountered the YMCA while studying at Northwestern Normal University in 1883.[50] Most likely Henry Edwards Brown had visited the school in his attempt to recruit African-American YMCA leaders. Moorland continued to take an interest in the YMCA while studying at Howard University, and on April 20, 1892, the African-American association in Washington, D.C., appointed him as secretary. Moorland held the position until 1893, when he moved to Nashville.[51] Although his official ties with the YMCA were severed in 1893, Moorland continued to take an interest in association work and often assisted Hunton in the organization of the regional African-American conferences.[52]

Moorland met Hunton while he worked for the YMCA in Washington, D.C. Immediately a deep friendship developed between the two men. Hunton often praised Moorland, on one occasion writing his wife, Addie: "How I wish I had a man like Moorland on the International staff helping me!"[53] In 1893 Hunton appealed to Richard C. Morse, general secretary of the International Committee, to appoint Moorland to the committee. Morse assured Hunton that as soon as funds were available the International Committee would hire an assistant for him. Lack of funds, however, delayed Moorland's employment until 1898.[54]

When Moorland finally joined Hunton on the International Committee, the two men tried to assist the African-American YMCAs more systematically. They divided the work into two fields. Hunton, who "found the college work more delightful" than the city work, continued to visit black colleges and universities, trying to stimulate the students' interest in the YMCA. Moorland took charge of the YMCAs in cities, assisting them with membership drives and fund-raising campaigns.[55]

Despite deteriorating race relations and the YMCA's pronounced commitment to segregation, the 1890s were crucial years for the growth and centralization of African-American associations. As the country and the YMCA raised the walls of segregation, Hunton, like many other African Americans, began to advocate self-help and racial solidarity. He fostered systematic planning, encouraged community action, and stressed church, gender, and class cooperation. As a result of Hunton's dynamic leadership, a network of seventeen YMCAs in cities and forty-three YMCAs at colleges spanned the country by 1898 (see appendix A).With the assistance of Moorland, who, like Hunton, devoted his life to the YMCA, the number of African-American associations continued to increase throughout the following decades.

4

Recruitment and Training of African-American YMCA Secretaries, 1898-1943

THE steady growth of African-American associations, which had begun in the 1890s, continued throughout the early twentieth century under the leadership of William A. Hunton and Jesse E. Moorland. Between 1900 and 1920 the number of African-American YMCAs in cities grew from 21 to 44 and those in colleges and universities, from 53 to 113.[1] As the number of African-American associations increased, Hunton and Moorland faced a new problem: the dearth of professional black YMCA secretaries. During the 1890s students, teachers, businessmen, physicians, and ministers had established and managed local associations. By the turn of the century, however, black YMCA volunteers felt that increasing membership as well as growth in property ownership required the attention of full-time professionals.

Increasingly, local associations asked Hunton and Moorland for help in locating qualified men willing to work as YMCA secretaries.[2] Robert B. Bruce, cofounder of the YMCA in Charlotte, North Carolina, was one of many who appealed to Moorland in the search for YMCA secretaries. Bruce explained that in Charlotte "the chances are now very good for a prosperous Y.M.C.A.," but he complained that no one looked "after the work, and no one has been responsible for its success or failure. . . . a secretary would do splendid work here. . . . [He] could arrange for weekly meetings, and concerts; and thereby raise a great deal of money." Many other African-American YMCAs sent out similar appeals. In 1901 Moorland noted, "We are having constant calls for well equipped men."[3]

The YMCA secretaryship represented a relatively new profession. It had emerged in the years following the Civil War, when some of the white associations acquired buildings to serve their members.[4] In 1871 only fourteen white associations had full-time employees.

Within two years the number of professional YMCA secretaries rose to 53, and by 1895 the YMCA employed 1,159 secretaries in the United States. The first African-American association to hire a full-time secretary was the YMCA in Norfolk, Virginia, where Hunton began his career in 1888. A year later only the associations in Norfolk, Richmond, Baltimore, and New Haven employed secretaries. Moorland claimed, however, that five associations were ready to hire secretaries, and he estimated that ten more would need professional workers in the near future. Hunton was concerned about the growing demand for secretaries and admitted: "My heart is depressed with the burden of the need of a few good men for our work. We must find them."[5]

Hunton and Moorland's task was not an easy one. The men they were looking for had to represent a unique blend of Christian social worker and business manager. YMCA secretaries had to appeal to all members of the community, to "*touch* their *hearts* and at the same time *touch* their *pockets*." They had to be willing to work as janitors, librarians, teachers, preachers, counselors, accountants, fund-raisers, athletic instructors, and song leaders. They also had to assist men in finding housing and employment. In addition, African-American YMCA secretaries had to be prepared to work for little money and no assurance of job security. Given the circumstances, Hunton admitted that "it is going to be difficult to secure ideal men, if not quite impossible." Moorland was also skeptical, claiming that "it is easier to get a standard building than it is to make sure of a man with the all-round training to manage the work in such a building."[6]

Despite these seemingly insurmountable obstacles, Hunton and Moorland recruited young men into the secretaryship and actively tried to create a professional class of YMCA secretaries. They sought recruits largely among the African-American college students who had provided the "secretarial timber" since the late nineteenth century. Whenever possible, Hunton and Moorland personally interviewed potential candidates during their frequent visits to campuses. Those men who appeared to be promising were asked to complete a two-page application containing questions about their personal and educational background, employment history, religious affiliation, and previous work in the YMCA. Reflecting the wide-ranging duties of YMCA secretaries, the application also asked men about their ability to teach physical exercise and Bible classes, to lead in singing, to play instruments, and to handle business accounts.[7] Finally, the men had to provide four character references.

Although the YMCA had no requirement concerning a secretary's marital status, Hunton and Moorland favored the employment of single men. Both men were married and drew much strength from their wives, yet based on their own experiences, they concluded that "a single man can endure much that a married man cannot." Hunton, who frequently traveled with his wife, suffered greatly when both of them were subjected to racism. He once wrote his wife: "You and I will travel together as little as possible in the far South. I can endure many things myself for the work's sake; and I can even suffer your enduring them when it is necessary. But I am sure it would go infinitely harder if we together were subjected to indignities." Hunton and Moorland may have also preferred single men because they were aware of the hardships their spouses endured during frequent, long periods of physical separation. Moorland's wife, for example, often complained about loneliness, on one occasion writing: "I do wish that Jesse could be at home more. . . . I rent out most of the house to a young married couple, so I am not alone at nights."[8] Despite their preference for unmarried men, Hunton and Moorland recruited both married and single men for the secretaryship.

The only prerequisite for employment as a YMCA secretary was membership in a Protestant church. While Hunton and Moorland recruited men from all Protestant denominations, some African-American associations preferred certain religious affiliations. Charles C. Dogan, secretary of the association in Norfolk, Virginia, for example, asked Hunton and Moorland for help in finding an assistant secretary. When Moorland suggested a candidate, Dogan rejected him, insisting that "my assistant should be a baptist—not a methodist by any means." Dogan's reasons for rejecting a Methodist secretary are not clear. His request, however, could have been a reflection of the YMCA's policy of avoiding identification with a specific church in order to maintain the association's interdenominational character. Hunton and Moorland knew that the YMCA's ability to gain communitywide support and funding depended on its interdenominational appeal. Thus, they were careful not to alienate African-American ministers and tried to avoid affiliation with any particular church. When they discovered that the secretary of the YMCA in Columbus, Georgia, "was also pastoring the local Episcopal church," they removed him from his position.[9]

Moreover, Hunton and Moorland frequently assured ministers that the YMCA did not compete with the work of the churches but complemented it.[10] Associations did not offer Bible study classes that coincided with those provided by local churches, and Hunton and Moorland were careful not to recruit secretaries who thought of themselves as substitute preachers. The secretaries, they insisted, had to have "sterling character" rather than too much Christian devotion.[11] George F. Robinson, secretary of the YMCA in Nashville, frankly admitted that he was "conducting the association on business principles, having not too much religion but some honesty." Some African Americans were puzzled by the absence of Christianity in the YMCA. A resident of Nashville complained to Moorland that the work of the city's YMCA was "not as *intensely spiritual* as I wish" and reminded him that "*C* stands for *Christian*. There is not enough of Christ in it." A YMCA secretary in Ohio complained about the opposite. Probably fearing the wrath of local ministers, he criticized the work of W.T. Maxwell, secretary of the association in Springfield, claiming that it "savored too much of church work." Maxwell defended himself, insisting, "We need more religion in our associations." W. Edward Williams, secretary of the association in Baltimore, apparently agreed. He resigned because the YMCA did not offer him the opportunity to do "the spiritual work for which I believe I am better fitted." Williams explained that he leaned "too much toward the ministry or at least the Evangelistic work to be satisfied with the details of a local Secretary's work."[12]

Although the YMCA required church membership of its secretaries, religious passion was less important for success than diplomatic skills. A YMCA secretary had to have the ability to work with a diverse group of people, to be a "leader . . . who understands men and knows how to manage them. . . . A man too sensitive would not suit; nor a man too rash or without scruples."[13] Many African-American YMCAs were torn by internal power struggles, and often the fight for control of an association proved as destructive as the lack of money.

Class differences frequently caused internal friction. The work of the African-American YMCA in Columbia, South Carolina, was threatened by such factionalism. In September 1899 W.E. Green, president of the association, informed Moorland that he had replaced some of the YMCA officers because, he claimed, they had "selfish motives." Shortly thereafter, Hunton visited Columbia and apparently found that Green himself was the problem. Hunton suggested that C.L. Walton, a local physician, replace Green as president. Green acknowledged "in good nature" that he did not have the ability to manage the YMCA but complained that Walton was unacceptable because he was "too big for us poor people." Green explained that "big men don't make associations they all seam to have some selfish pursus." He admitted that "Dr. Walton has helped as much as any other man but I don't think it will ad much by makening him President we want men that stand between all classes of men." Despite Green's complaint, Walton became president of the YMCA in Columbia, only to resign the following spring over another dispute with

Green. Upon his resignation Walton suggested his successor, but Green opposed the choice. This time Green objected because he claimed that the man "is sanctifide he claims to be pure and holy and because others cannot see and believe as he do he cannot asoate with us in the YMCA work he belive in faith cure and all salch noncence he has left his church and journed a band of crazie people believing lots of things."[14]

Similar conflicts developed in other communities. L.A. Brown, a member of the YMCA in Petersburg, Virginia, charged that the city's association work was hampered because "two of the most unpopular men in the town, I mean with the masses, are at the head, which thing cannot be remedied." Brown claimed that unless "men who are prominent in the church, and popular among their people" took charge of the work, the Petersburg YMCA was doomed to fail.[15] In Springfield, Ohio, the Board of Directors appointed a secretary without the consent of Thomas W. Burton, chairman of the board. Burton, a physician, opposed the new secretary because he claimed the man "can't read nor write." Unable to resolve the problem, Burton resigned, claiming that the "board is as rotten as a dead rat. . . . My time is too precious to be fooling it away with a set of dummies."[16]

A successful secretary certainly needed tact and diplomacy, yet equally important were business skills. YMCA secretaries had to organize fund-raising campaigns, supervise the collection of membership dues, pay the bills, and keep the books. A man like John Russell Harvey, who applied to become secretary of the association in Petersburg, Virginia, had little chance of employment. In his letter of application, Harvey explained that he was not interested in the secretaryship "for the money that [I] may get out of it but for the good I hope to do my race here." While Harvey assured Moorland of his sincerity, a letter from one of his character references portrayed him in a different light. T.S. Inborden, principal of the Joseph K. Brick Agricultural, Industrial and Normal School in Enfield, North Carolina, advised Moorland not to employ Harvey. Inborden explained that "Harvey is not going to do anything that requires *work*. He is in search of a fat thing where he can be big and not have to work. He has good ability but is too lazy to study. . . . He wants to preach badly. And it is bad. He is not a good pay master and your best advice to him is to tell him to go to school."[17]

Other essential characteristics of a YMCA secretary were integrity and honesty. A man who was unable to gain the trust and confidence of the community could not expect to raise any funds for association work. Most African-American YMCAs apparently did not experience problems resulting from dishonesty, although some did. The YMCA in Charlotte, North Carolina, was particularly hard hit. The founders of the association raised some funds toward a building and gave it to "one of their most prominent members," only to learn that he spent it "for personal purposes." Despite this devastating revelation, the young men of Charlotte were not disillusioned. The culprit confessed and promised to pay back the amount he had taken, and the men launched a new fund-raising campaign. After they raised more money, they appointed another young man as treasurer, only to discover that he "jumped the town." One of the founders of the YMCA in Charlotte expressed his concern, noting that the "young men have been somewhat discouraged."[18]

While Hunton and Moorland searched for men able to handle a multitude of responsibilities and problems, they had little to offer financially. The work of local associations continued to be hampered by lack of money, and secretaries often did not get paid on a regular basis. Some left for better employment opportunities, while others tried to raise their own salaries.[19] The secretary of the YMCA in Springfield, Ohio, complained that he had "to beg from the public" for his salary. John H. Whaley, secretary of the association in Petersburg, Virginia, was not willing to do that and resigned from his post, informing Moorland that "under the present circumstances a living in this field is a matter of impossibility."[20]

The experience of John W. Evans, secretary of the association in Indianapolis, illustrates the risk many men took when they became professional YMCA workers. In April 1902 Evans arrived in Indianapolis to assist the members of an ambitious Young Men's Prayer Band in the organization of a YMCA. During the first two months Evans received no salary. In June a local church offered to raise half of his salary if the YMCA provided the other half. Evans tried to raise the money but was unsuccessful. In July he reported to Moorland that he was "behind some $25" in rent.[21] In some cases financial support from white associations allowed for the employment of black secretaries, but African Americans usually had to rely on their own funds. Lack of reliable income as well as long working hours continued to deter young men from becoming YMCA secretaries. Approximately 25 percent of all new recruits resigned from their posts within a year.[22]

While Hunton and Moorland had no means of alleviating the financial difficulties the secretaries encountered, they tried to assist the men in other ways. In 1902 Moorland launched the publication of the *Secretarial Letter*, a mimeographed compilation of correspondence from African-American YMCA secretaries.[23] Published occasionally between 1902 and 1937, the cost of the *Secretarial Letter* was defrayed by the office of the International Committee.[24]

Similar to the more elaborate but short-lived *Messenger*, the newsletter was a clearinghouse for information, a medium of communication, and a source of inspiration for African-American secretaries. The secretaries exchanged information about the programs and activities of their associations as well as ideas for fund-raising and membership campaigns. Given the lack of financial resources, fund-raising efforts were among the most popular items discussed in the newsletter. The secretaries offered each other advice on how to obtain the necessary funds to purchase a building, to eliminate debts, and to pay for maintenance.[25]

The secretaries also exchanged ideas on how to expand membership.[26] Most of the secretaries were interested in increasing attendance at their associations, although some were troubled by visitors who used the facilities without paying membership fees. D.R. Wallace, secretary of the YMCA in Chattanooga, for example, asked his colleagues for advice when he noticed that "20 to 30 boys of the rougher kind" used the association's rooms regularly. Wallace explained that no municipal, social, or religious agency provided recreational facilities for the boys, and he feared that they would "get into trouble outside." Yet he also pointed out that the boys were not eligible to join the YMCA, "since they are not church members nor are they of good character." Their presence in the YMCA, he noted, was bound to "keep members away."[27] Wallace's eventual course of action remains unclear. His appeal, however, illustrates the importance of the *Secretarial Letter* as a medium of communication for African-American secretaries.

Moorland also used the newsletter to provide the men with guidelines for proper personal and professional conduct. He frequently reminded the secretaries that they were role models and implored them to "pay close attention to details of personal habits" as well as personal appearance. "A leader," he explained, "is always dressed just about right—not over or under." He asked the secretaries to display proper leadership and urged them not to wear "the latest cut clothes nor to show undue economy by wearing threadbare clothes . . . to go with unpolished shoes, with frazzled coat cuffs or any of those things which mark a man as sloven." Moreover, he reminded the men to shave daily and to visit a barber regularly.[28]

Personal appearance seems to have been a consideration in the selection of some secretaries. In at least one case, a candidate for the secretaryship was rejected because of "facial physical deformities." In another case a secretary complained that Moorland slighted him because he was too black. Moorland denied the allegation, insisting that it "is not color that counts but character my brother, some of my dearest friends are blacker than you." Physical appearance may have been a consideration for Hunton and Moorland, but it was certainly not the determining factor, as the case of George R. Arthur illustrates. Arthur, "a dwarfed, hunchback" man who, as a result of a childhood accident, never grew taller "than about four feet," became secretary of the Chicago association.[29]

Moorland used the *Secretarial Letter* to set guidelines not only for personal appearance but also for proper professional conduct. A secretary, he explained, had to be an efficient manager who "transacts his business in his office, answers his mail promptly, says yes or no to questions, files his letters and shows that system is indelibly marked on his very character." Moorland also reminded the secretaries of the importance of proper maintenance of the rooms and buildings the YMCAs occupied. "Good housekeeping," Moorland insisted, "cannot be overestimated. There is no excuse for dirt in an Association building." He urged each secretary to "be on the lookout for cob-webs, dust or anything which may give his building an untidy, uncleanly appearance."[30]

Moorland's editorials in the *Secretarial Letter* illustrate his attempt to establish professional standards for YMCA secretaries. In the absence of training facilities, the newsletter served as an instruction manual and reference guide. As more associations acquired rooms, however, the duties and responsibilities of YMCA secretaries increased, and Hunton and Moorland became concerned about offering the men proper professional training. Aside from their personal experience as YMCA members, the African-American men who became association secretaries at the turn of the century had no special training to prepare them for their tasks.

Whites in the YMCA had started to discuss the necessity of professional secretarial training in the 1870s. During the 1880s the International Committee began to publish instruction manuals for secretaries, which were regularly updated and distributed among new recruits. In the same decade several white associations started to offer internship or apprenticeship programs and summer study sessions for those training for the secretaryship. In 1885 the School for Christian Workers at Springfield, Massachusetts, began to offer classes in association work, and five years later it became officially known as the Springfield YMCA Training School. In the same year the white YMCA of Chicago established a school for the training of secretaries.[31] The Chicago school also became an official YMCA training agency by the end of the century.

Springfield and Chicago did not exclude African Americans, but the YMCA did not encourage black secretaries to enroll. YMCA officials feared that the presence of African Americans would alienate white students from the South. When Edwin D. Ingersoll recruited Hunton in 1886, he explained to the International Committee that it would be impossible for Hunton to attend the Springfield school, because it "had recently commenced operations and the very first student had come from the South." Ingersoll predicated that if "a colored man were sent to that School the one or more Southern students would probably pack their trunks and take the first train for home." Despite the YMCA's concern, few white southerners ever attended the school.[32]

Although fears of racial unrest initially prevented African Americans from attending the Springfield YMCA Training School, the International Committee tried to pave the way for the admission of black students. In the early 1890s the International Committee asked Hunton to present a lecture on "association work among colored young men" to the white students. Apparently Hunton encountered no resentment, but it took another decade before the school began to open its doors to black students. In the fall of 1901 three African Americans, David Wilder, Elmer E. Thompson, and Robert P. Hamlin, enrolled at Springfield.[33]

Despite these admissions, only a few black secretaries attended the school in subsequent years. Apparently this was not the result of racial discrimination or hostility. Hamlin reported that when Wilder became sick, a white "class mate gave up his room, which was more comfortable than Wilder's, for his use during his illness." The low attendance of African-American students at Springfield was largely caused by their lack of financial resources. The school operated like a college, which left little time for outside employment. Not many African Americans had the means to finance a two- or three-year training program. Thompson explained that he had "nothing to wish for except a little work on the outside so as to cut down some expenses." Hamlin reported that he worked part-time during his first semester but realized that he "could not keep apace with the class."[34]

Officials of the YMCA training school in Chicago also began to consider the admission of African Americans at the turn of the century. In 1900 the school's general secretary, John W. Hansel, asked Moorland to recruit black students and even offered to pay for their tuition and to help them secure employment. Hansel, however, encountered opposition from the members of the white YMCA in Chicago, which housed the school. Hansel "was surprised to find that the colored question existed in so acute a form in the membership of the

Chicago Association." He advised Moorland of the problem and explained: "With conditions as they are, it would undoubtedly bring great disappointment to any colored men who might enter the school."[35]

Nevertheless, the Chicago YMCA Training School did not exclude African Americans. In 1902 the school admitted Benjamin J. Fisher, a black student from New York. Hansel informed Fisher that his admission would bring about a host of problems. He explained that "a portion of the school work is identical with the membership privileges of the Central Department. . . . As conditions are today, no discreet colored man would think of joining the Association. . . . Our teachers will welcome you to the classes, but, in connection with the practical work of the school your privileges will necessarily be limited."[36] Moorland advised Fisher to withdraw his application. He insisted that "there is a great Christian principle at stake here" and informed Hansel that the school's racial policy "will damage the ardor of our young men." Although the Springfield and Chicago training schools did not officially exclude African Americans, black secretaries did not attend them in large numbers, either because of financial restraints or in anticipation of racial discrimination and hostility.[37]

In response to the absence of professional training facilities for African-American secretaries, Hunton and Moorland began to discuss the formation of a separate school. Black YMCA representatives had expressed continued interest in such a facility since the 1890s. In 1897, when the delegates of the African-American associations gathered in Raleigh, North Carolina, they recommended the creation of a centrally located "summer training school for colored men."[38] Hunton, however, took no action. He was still the only African-American secretary on the International Committee, and his regular duties left little time for the development of new programs.

The admission of African Americans to the Chicago and Springfield training schools may have further delayed the creation of a school for black YMCA secretaries. By 1904, however, it was apparent that financial problems and racial discrimination prevented most black secretaries from attending Springfield or Chicago. Thus, black association representatives once more demanded the establishment of a separate training agency.[39] Hunton and Moorland were aware of the need for trained secretaries, but the supervision of the growing number of African-American YMCAs took up much of their time.

Only after Hunton and Moorland secured the employment of a third black international secretary, George Edmund Haynes, in 1905 did they consider the creation of a secretarial training agency.[40] In

1907 Hunton, Moorland, and Haynes launched the organization of a YMCA training school for African-American secretaries. They met with the secretaries of the black associations of Richmond, Norfolk, and New Haven at Hampton Institute "to consider the need for a training agency." During their two-day meeting the men decided to establish the Summer Secretarial Institute.[41]

Beginning in 1908 African-American secretaries and new recruits gathered annually for summer training sessions at the Eagle Street YMCA in Asheville, North Carolina. Some of the men from the North, however, resented the jim crow practices of the southern railroads and demanded a location further north.[42] In 1911 the Summer Secretarial Institute moved to a camp site near Arundel-on-the-Chesapeake Bay, Maryland, and the institute was renamed Chesapeake Summer School. In 1915, when a fire destroyed the camp, the school relocated to Storer College in Harpers Ferry, West Virginia, where it remained until 1923. From 1924 throughout World War II the Chesapeake Summer School used the facilities of the Manual Training and Industrial School in Bordentown, New Jersey.[43]

The Chesapeake Summer School was financed largely through contributions from African-American YMCAs and a "small registration fee" that the secretaries or their associations paid.[44] Limited by the lack of financial resources, the African-American YMCAs struggled to raise adequate funds to support the school. Thus, throughout its existence the school lived largely "from hand to mouth" and often incurred debts.[45] Without a reliable source of income, the school was unable to purchase property, so it utilized the facilities and equipment of black colleges and universities.[46]

During the first years of operation, the Chesapeake Summer School had no formal curriculum. Instead, those experienced in YMCA work presented lectures to the students. Initially the school invited black and white secretaries to instruct the men, but by 1929 the Chesapeake Summer School boasted an all-black faculty. Some white secretaries questioned the necessity of a separate secretarial training facility for African Americans, fearing that the "negro leaders continue to think in negro terms instead of Association terms." Yet those who protested did not argue in favor of desegregation but rather insisted that black secretaries should be taught by "the best white leadership, instead of exclusive negro leadership."[47]

At first the YMCA's International Committee did not intervene in the creation of the school or its activities. This changed when a growing number of white YMCAs also established secretarial summer training schools. By 1919 white associations operated seven regional summer schools.[48] In response, the YMCA appointed a

Certification Committee to regulate secretarial training and urged the adoption of standardized courses as well as a uniform credit-hour system.[49] White YMCA officials, concerned about the Chesapeake Summer School's financial problems and its ability to attract qualified teachers, began to encourage African Americans to attend the summer schools operated by whites.[50]

Although most of the white summer schools admitted African Americans, only a few black secretaries attended them.[51] Most African-American secretaries continued to enroll in the Chesapeake Summer School, despite its constant monetary difficulties.[52] African-American secretaries explained that their decision was based on financial considerations. They claimed that the registration fees at white training schools were too high. Tuition at the Chesapeake Summer School was cheaper because the school used the facilities of black colleges and did not have to raise money for equipment, housing, or a building. Moreover, the school did not pay any honorarium to its faculty "other than railroad fare . . . and their expenses at the school."[53]

African-American secretaries admitted, however, that "even if all regional schools were open to colored secretaries, there would still be need of such a school as Chesapeake." The men insisted that a separate school for the training of African Americans was necessary "in maintaining a sense of unity and solidarity."[54] There were "group problems," they argued, "that could only be discussed in such a school." Moreover, they explained that "the regional schools . . . did not give opportunity for the exercise of leadership on the part of colored secretaries in sufficient numbers." White YMCA officials conceded that "there is need of a group 'get-together' such as would not be possible in regional schools except by what would appear [as] self-segregation."[55] Thus, they did not pressure African Americans to attend the summer schools operated by whites.

The main objective of the Chesapeake Summer School was the professional training of new secretaries. The annual gatherings, however, also helped to create a sense of community, as they tightened the bonds of those African Americans already engaged in YMCA work.[56] The summer school sessions provided the black secretaries with a forum to discuss racial issues, and in the 1920s they gradually began to replace the annual conventions of African-American YMCAs.[57] Moreover, as many of the men attended the classes during their summer vacations, the school assumed the character of a summer camp. One observer noted: "There is a congenial colony of teachers and wives and children of secretaries each year." Addie W. Hunton recalled that the summer school session "was a glorious period for our son . . . who had a chance there to be near his father and pal with him for a longer period than at any other time during the entire year. There was freedom and touch with men of the finest type."[58] Despite the relaxed atmosphere, the Chesapeake Summer School was "not a good time trip, but one for hard work." This was particularly true for Moorland, who raised the funds for the school and managed it until his retirement from the YMCA in 1923.[59]

While Moorland took great interest in providing the black YMCAs with "well-trained expert leadership," he was equally concerned about securing competent African-American men for the International Committee.[60] Moorland screened candidates for the International Committee based on criteria similar to those used for the recruitment of local association secretaries. Moorland was particularly selective, since the international secretaries represented the vanguard of African Americans in the YMCA.

The ideal international secretary, Moorland explained, has "all the marks of a well-trained, refined, yet vigorous and forceful gentleman." Moorland realized that the success as well as the reputation of African-American YMCA work often depended on the image and performance of the black international secretaries. The secretary, he explained, "is a man away from home and is constantly compelled to live in other people's homes . . . and it is very necessary that he constantly keep in mind the estimate which is being placed upon the cause he represents based on his personal acts. . . . An International Secretary must be more particular as to his clothing than if he were in a local field inasmuch as he is a stranger everywhere he goes and strangers are oftentimes measured by their clothing." Moorland's prime considerations for the recruitment of an international secretary were a candidate's educational background, personal conduct and appearance, and, since the work required frequent traveling, physical fitness. Nevertheless, Moorland believed that some men, no matter how qualified, were not "made" to be international secretaries. He explained that "there are men who cannot fill such a position, there are men who ought not try, they would commit a sin, they were never made for such a place."[61]

Most important, Moorland was concerned about the men's ability to cope with racism. "A man with the spirit of John Brown," he explained, "could not very well be an International Secretary." Advocating accommodationism rather than confrontation, Moorland stressed "the importance of keeping in as good humor as possible under the discriminations we meet." He likened the role of the international secretary to that of a diplomat, saying that "just as the diplomat is a representative of one government to another and must take care of all interests concerned and keep on friendly terms and bring about beneficent results, so must the International Secretary keep his machinery running smoothly." Despite Moorland's advocacy of accommodationism, he insisted that the international secretaries do not "wink at wrong and oppression" but skillfully display "wrong with right."[62]

Hunton and Moorland accommodated to the YMCA's policy of segregation, but they did not surrender to it. Faced with jim crowism, they avoided "controversial subjects for the sake of harmony," hoping to gain the support of "fair minded unprejudiced men."[63] Since Blacks were excluded from white YMCAs, Hunton and Moorland asked the black YMCA secretaries to do the seemingly impossible, to draw strength from segregation. They urged the secretaries to rely on self-help and racial solidarity in the interest of the race.

The YMCA secretaries came to play important roles in the African-American community. They assumed a position "equal in importance to that of the Public or High School teacher," and letters of recommendation they wrote were held in high esteem by those seeking employment.[64] Yet more important, they were role models who inspired young men. J.A. Green, secretary of the association in Dayton, Ohio, recalled that he joined the YMCA because of his admiration for Hunton and Moorland. "I felt that an organization which could command such a high type of manhood must necessarily be a high type organization itself." African-American YMCA secretaries were equally respected by many white Americans, who regarded them as "the religious leaders of American Negroes." The black secretaries had such a high reputation that even criminals tried to profit from it. In 1932 a gang of racketeers used Moorland's name in a scam to sell tickets for a nonexistent charity.[65]

Ironically, jim crowism not only excluded African Americans from white YMCAs but also provided for the emergence of black-controlled community agencies and the development of African-American leadership. By 1925 the efforts of Hunton and Moorland had resulted in the creation of a nationwide network of black-funded and black-controlled YMCAs, staffed with professionally trained black secretaries. That year 132 African-American YMCAs employed black secretaries, and eight African Americans served on the International Committee. The black international secretaries maintained control over the recruitment and training of African-American secretaries until the YMCA's Personnel Services took charge of all employment records in 1943.[66]

5

Philanthropists and the Construction of YMCA Buildings, 1901-1933

BY the early twentieth century William A. Hunton and Jesse E. Moorland had established a network of associations funded and controlled by African Americans, they had launched annual conferences of black YMCA delegates, and they had institutionalized the training of professional association secretaries. What African-American YMCAs still lacked were adequate buildings for their activities. In 1900 African-American communities in twenty-one cities boasted YMCAs, but only the associations in Norfolk, Richmond, Baltimore, New Haven, and Springfield, Ohio, owned buildings. As Moorland observed, "There is barely room in any of them now for our group work."[1] Lacking the financial resources to purchase buildings, most African-American associations operated in rented apartments or private residences, ill suited for the YMCA's programs.[2]

As the membership of black associations grew and community support stabilized, African-American YMCA leaders increasingly launched fund-raising campaigns to purchase or erect buildings. Their efforts received a boost when philanthropists began to contribute money. Contributions from George Foster Peabody, John D. Rockefeller, Sr., and Julius Rosenwald triggered nationwide fund-raising campaigns and eventually provided twenty-six African-American communities with YMCA buildings.[3]

George Foster Peabody was born in 1852 in Columbus, Georgia, where his parents owned a general store. In 1866, after the Civil War had devastated the Peabody business, the family moved to Brooklyn, where George began work in a wholesale dry goods firm as an errand boy. Shortly after Peabody started work, he "began to look around for some opportunity to read and study." He joined the Brooklyn YMCA and spent many evenings reading at the branch's library. Later Peabody referred to the association as his alma mater. In the following years Peabody became a successful banker, amassing a fortune and donating much of it to philanthropic causes.[4]

Peabody's philanthropy focused largely on the improvement of southern black education.[5] He began to take an interest in African-American education when General S.C. Armstrong, founder of Hampton Institute, appealed to Peabody's Brooklyn church for financial assistance. Peabody, who chaired the committee that handled the church's Sunday school funds, was "deeply moved" and "suggested that the committee vote part of its funds to help the struggling project."[6] Peabody's membership in the YMCA as well as his interest in black education led him to support African-American association work in his hometown.

In the summer of 1901 approximately 250 African Americans organized a YMCA in Brooklyn. They appealed to Peabody for financial assistance, and he supported the group with a two-hundred-dollar contribution. The following spring the men found a suitable three-story building on Carlton Avenue. When Peabody learned that it was not for rent, he purchased it for the black YMCA. In addition, he furnished the building and pledged three thousand dollars to cover the association's expenses for the first three years of its operation.[7]

At the same time Peabody also began to support the efforts of African Americans in his birthplace, Columbus, Georgia. In the spring of 1901 eighty-six African Americans had organized a YMCA in Columbus. Peabody offered to erect an association building for the city's black population, on the condition that African Americans raise one thousand dollars for the furniture and local whites contribute five thousand dollars as a maintenance fund for the first five years of the YMCA's existence.[8]

William Hunton was enthusiastic about Peabody's contribution to the black YMCA in Columbus. He had urged the International Committee to seek financial assistance from northern philanthropists as early as 1893. Hunton was particularly pleased with the conditional nature of the gift. He hoped that this "most important experiment" would stimulate white support for African-American associations in other southern communities.[9]

By 1905 blacks in Columbus had collected sufficient funds to meet Peabody's requirement, but the city's white population had raised only three thousand dollars. Nevertheless, Peabody was impressed by the achievement of the African Americans. He felt "it was safe to put up the building" and authorized its construction. In an effort to ensure the successful start of the association, Peabody asked the African-American secretary to remain in Columbus during the initial five years and "agreed to raise his salary." In 1907 the African-

American association of Columbus opened its building, providing its more than two hundred members with rooms for Bible study and social meetings as well as facilities for physical exercise and educational programs. Other African-American YMCAs asked Peabody for assistance, but he made no further contributions to any association.[10]

While Peabody had assisted the African-American YMCAs of Brooklyn and Columbus out of a sense of personal obligation to his hometown and his birthplace, John D. Rockefeller, Sr., had a different motivation. Rockefeller contributed to the African-American association in Washington, D.C., with the intention of stimulating white support for black YMCAs throughout the United States. Rockefeller's financial support of the YMCA started in the 1870s, when he began to make regular contributions to the International Committee as well as the New York state and New York City YMCAs.[11]

Rockefeller assisted the YMCA because the association's commitment to "character building" appealed to his philosophy of success. Rockefeller, who had risen from a modest background to become one of the richest men in America, believed that success resulted from personal determination. He explained that "the failures which a man makes in his life are due almost always to some defect in his personality, some weakness of body, or mind, or character, will, or temperament. The only way to overcome these failings is to build up his personality from within, so that he, by virtue of what is within him, may overcome the weakness which was the cause for the failure."[12] The YMCA's programs, designed to improve body, mind, and spirit, provided individuals with the opportunity to strengthen their personalities, overcome their weaknesses, and achieve success.

Rockefeller, like Peabody, also took an interest in African Americans and supported black education in the South through contributions to the General Education Board.[13] In 1906, when the white YMCA of Washington, D.C., asked Rockefeller for financial support of a black association building, he promised his assistance.[14] In 1904 a group of nearly three hundred African Americans had established a YMCA in the capital. They immediately made plans to "canvass for a building fund of $20,000." The men appealed to the city's white association for financial assistance, and its members offered to contribute $450 toward the salary of an African-American secretary. Within a year membership in the black association almost doubled, but the group still lacked the financial resources to purchase or erect a YMCA building.[15]

In 1906 S.W. Woodward, president of the white association, asked John D. Rockefeller, Jr., for a conditional gift of $25,000 from his father, for the construction of a $50,000 YMCA building for African Americans. Woodward explained that Washington was in particular need of a black YMCA building because of the lack of "wholesome" recreational facilities for the city's large African-American population. He explained that the capital was "a Mecca for the young men of this race . . . because of its mid-way position between the North and the South." He noted that the city offered them no recreational facilities besides "saloons, dance halls, gambling dens, and the open allurements of sin [that] distract these young men on every side." Woodward assured Rockefeller that the white YMCA was willing to assist African Americans, but it had recently erected a $350,000 association building and the city's white population had "been taxed to its limit."[16] An offer of matching funds, Woodward hoped, would provide the necessary incentive to stimulate local white support for the construction of a black YMCA.

The idea of an offer of matching funds probably appealed to Rockefeller, Jr., because it reflected his father's basic belief that the "only thing which is of lasting benefit to a man is that which he does for himself. Money which comes to him without effort on his part is seldom a benefit and often a curse." While Rockefeller, Sr., favored conditional gifts as a means to stimulate self-help, he opposed contributions that aided "institutions or enterprises that are purely local." Since Washington was the nation's capital, however, Rockefeller, Jr., hoped that an African-American YMCA building would serve as a national "model to other localities."[17]

Rockefeller, Jr., was willing to support the African-American building fund, but he was concerned about its relatively small budget. He doubted whether a $50,000 structure could accommodate six hundred young men, considering that the white association had spent $350,000 on its building. Thus, before Rockefeller, Jr., pledged his father's money, he asked the YMCA to submit an itemized estimate of expenses as well as a statement assessing support from local contributors.[18]

Edward W. Hearne, general secretary of the white association, explained that African Americans in Washington could be expected to raise much of the money because many held "Government positions at fair salaries." Moreover, Hearne predicted that white businessmen who profited from African-American patronage would contribute to the fund-raising campaign. Concerning the size of the black association building, Hearne assured Rockefeller's office that a $50,000 structure was sufficient for African Americans. "Colored men," he explained, "could be cared for in relatively greater numbers, as they have no similar attractions and are accustomed to working and finding enjoyment with fewer facilities than white men." Rockefeller, Jr., did not challenge Hearne's argument in favor of a small and less well-equipped association building for African-American men. On September 7, 1906, he pledged $25,000 on behalf of his father, under the condition that Washington's local population raise an equal amount on or before July 1, 1907.[19]

Rockefeller's matching funds offer was considerably larger than Peabody's conditional gift. The funds for the black YMCA in Columbus were raised mainly among association members. The campaign in Washington, however, encompassed the city's entire African-American population. Rockefeller's contribution resulted in the "first united fund raising effort of its kind for any black community in the United States" and later served as a model for campaigns in other cities.[20]

African Americans enthusiastically greeted Rockefeller's offer and immediately organized a fund-raising committee. Spearheading the building campaign were prominent African Americans such as Professor Kelly Miller of Howard University and Calvin Chase, editor of the *Washington Bee*, as well as the white president of Howard University, Wilbur P. Thirkield. Support for the YMCA building, however, came not only from the ranks of "the very best people." The *Bee* proclaimed that the city was "aflame with enthusiasm" and noted that the fund-raising campaign transcended class lines. "There is not a class of men in the city not represented in this movement . . . educators and professional men working along side of the ordinary day laborer." Some employers allowed their black employees to start work early in the morning, enabling them to collect money for the YMCA in the afternoon. Between April 8 and May 7, 1907, the fund-raising committee, chaired by Thirkield, gathered pledges among African Americans amounting to more than thirty-one thousand dollars. The largest contribution was a five-hundred-dollar pledge made by Henry W. Chase, a former slave then employed in the Government Printing Office.[21]

Although Rockefeller's offer triggered overwhelming enthusiasm and support among Washington's African-American population, the *Bee* nevertheless criticized the YMCA's jim crow policy. The paper insisted that Christians should not "worship separate and apart from each other. If they believe in a God they ought to know there is but one heaven and one hell." Despite this criticism, the *Bee* asked African Americans to close ranks and support the fund-raising campaign, because "the object of the Young Men's Christian Association is a good one and ought to be supported."[22]

Members of the white YMCA had hoped that Rockefeller's gift

would stimulate support among the white population, but the funds for the black association building were raised almost exclusively among African Americans.[23] The lack of white contributions slowed down the fund-raising campaign but had a unifying effect on the city's African-American population. Booker T. Washington, who frequently addressed YMCA fund-raisers, observed that "the generous enthusiasm which united all classes and all denominations . . . has created a spirit of co-operation and a sense of solidarity among the colored population of Washington which will be of lasting good both to them and to the city." The canvass committee not only raised the funds among the black population but also planned to employ African Americans for the construction of the building. The *Bee* reported that the committee hoped to engage "for most if not all the work to be done on the new building . . . colored artisans and workmen."[24] Furthermore, in June 1907 the committee decided to hire a black architect, W. Sidney Pittman, son-in-law of Booker T. Washington, to design the YMCA building.[25] Despite this successful start, the completion of Washington's black YMCA was delayed until 1912.[26]

Many African Americans who had pledged money in support of the association had apparently made promises they were unable to keep. In the spring of 1909, two years after the fund-raising campaign, Calvin Chase complained that only half of the pledges made by African Americans had actually been paid and called it a "disgrace of failure." Chase claimed that Washington's black government employees and public school teachers had a combined annual income of nearly $5.5 million. The failure of African Americans to honor their pledges, he concluded, was not caused by lack of money. Chase was convinced that many African Americans had made pledges to "show off." With little empathy for the plight of the black working class, Chase suggested that those "who subscribed and haven't paid should have their names pasted in a conspicious [*sic*] place in the city, or in every church entrance."[27] Fortunately for those who failed to pay their pledges, the YMCA did not heed Chase's advice.

White YMCA officials, perhaps more realistically, explained that the "subscriptions were mainly among laboring people, whose plans could be easily upset by the loss of a month's wages." Yet they also charged that African Americans "had little or no business experience and lack the traditional understanding of the sacredness and binding force of a business obligation." Washington's white YMCA officials, convinced that African Americans lacked the ability and expertise to administer large amounts of money, assumed control of the funds raised during the campaign.[28]

The completion of the black association building was further delayed when the white association officials decided to erect a building twice as large as originally planned. During the fund-raising campaign, membership in the African-American association grew from six hundred to one thousand, and white YMCA officials believed that the envisioned fifty-thousand-dollar building could not adequately serve the increased number of members. White YMCA officials made plans to construct a building worth a hundred thousand dollars, but they failed to inform Rockefeller of their new plan. Only after the association had collected Rockefeller's donation on July 30, 1909, did YMCA officials inform him of their decision. They then asked him to contribute an additional twenty-five thousand dollars.[29]

Starr J. Murphy, Rockefeller's legal adviser, was outraged. He called the incident "a deliberate and wilful concealment of the facts" and urged Rockefeller, Jr., not only to decline further contributions but also to request a return of the twenty-five thousand already granted. After his initial outburst of anger, however, Murphy had second thoughts. When Rockefeller, Jr., wrote a letter demanding the return of the money, Murphy persuaded him not to send it. Sensitive to the problems involved with such a demand, Murphy cautioned Rockefeller, Jr., against his father's "aversion to controversies." Nevertheless, the incident alienated Rockefeller, who made no further contributions to the capital's black association or to any other African-American YMCA. Members of Washington's black and white associations continued to raise funds for the building, but the Twelfth Street YMCA did not open until May 19, 1912.[30]

Although Rockefeller's support of the African-American YMCA was limited to the association in Washington, his matching funds offer had a much broader impact. As the editor of the *Bee* observed, the capital's fund-raising campaign received national attention and made the public aware of the need for black YMCAs. Encouraged by the Washington campaign, African Americans and whites in other communities cooperated to raise funds, and by 1910 twenty-one of the forty-four African-American associations in cities had acquired some property.[31]

While the number of African-American YMCAs owning property had increased during the first decade of the twentieth century, the association in Columbus, Georgia, still had the only building specifically designed and built for YMCA use. Most black YMCAs still operated in rented facilities, often former saloons or old residences. In 1909 at the annual conference of black YMCA representatives in Louisville, Kentucky, A.G. Clyde Randall, pointed out the continued need for association buildings in cities. "Each American city," Randall claimed, "has buildings in it expensively furnished to destroy young men. The home, state, and church must defend their future saviors from the manifold evils which these vice and shame-inflicting agencies work upon young men. To do it most effectively demands the capitalization of character by a community, demands the establishment of a home of magic-power upon young men."[32]

A year after Randall's call for association buildings, another white philanthropist lent his support to African-American YMCAs. In 1910 Chicago mail-order magnate Julius Rosenwald offered twenty-five thousand dollars in matching funds to all black YMCAs in the United States. According to Jesse Moorland, Rosenwald's offer represented the "outstanding event of the decade." It triggered nationwide fund-raising campaigns and resulted in the construction of twenty-four YMCA buildings for African Americans. Furthermore, the offer stimulated the International Committee to employ three additional African Americans. In 1911 the committee hired Channing H. Tobias, Robert P. Hamlin, and David D. Jones as international secretaries for African-American YMCA work.[33]

Rosenwald was born on August 12, 1862, the second son of German Jewish immigrants. He grew up in Springfield, Illinois, where his parents operated a small retail store.[34] In 1879, without completing high school, he entered the clothing business in New York City as an apprentice to his uncles. Within five years he saved enough money to open a clothing store in New York. After this successful venture, Rosenwald moved to Chicago to produce garments, and in 1895 he bought thirty-five thousand dollars' worth of shares from one of his customers, the Sears Roebuck Company. In 1896 Rosenwald became vice-president of the company and launched a brilliant advertising campaign that firmly established Sears in the mail-order business. By 1909 Rosenwald was president of Sears, and the company recorded annual sales of more than fifty million dollars.[35]

As president of Sears "Rosenwald accumulated a fortune, making more money than he could use." This caused him much concern. Rosenwald was particularly worried about the effect of his wealth on his family. He was afraid that it would become "a millstone about the neck" of his five children. After all, Rosenwald was a self-made man who believed that work was "not a burden but a privilege," and he feared that a large inheritance would deprive his children "of the joy of honest, conscientious labor." Rosenwald claimed that he was also embarrassed about the size of his fortune. As he remarked to a friend: "I really feel ashamed to have so much money."[36]

Rosenwald tried to cope with his "burden of wealth" by adopting Andrew Carnegie's philosophy of civic stewardship.[37] Rosenwald was concerned that the massive urbanization, industrialization, and immigration of the late nineteenth and early twentieth centuries had produced social conditions that were weakening America's democracy. The wealthy, Rosenwald claimed, had an obligation to use their fortunes to seek out and heal "the sore spots of civilization" in order to guarantee that America remained the land of equal opportunity. Accordingly, he argued that the "generation which has contributed to the making of a millionaire should be the one to profit by his generosity." Based on this conviction, Rosenwald supported social improvement and educational activities in Chicago and throughout the nation. He eventually gave away sixty-three million dollars. Nearly half of this money went to African Americans.[38]

Rosenwald's concern for the plight of African Americans was aroused by Dr. Paul J. Sachs, a former partner in Goldman, Sachs and Company, who had taken an interest in the Urban League and tried to enlist Rosenwald's support. In 1910 Sachs presented Rosenwald with the biography of William H. Baldwin, Jr., founder of the Urban League, and Booker T. Washington's *Up from Slavery*. These books influenced Rosenwald more than any other books he ever read.[39]

Rosenwald admired Washington's rise from slavery to the presidency of Tuskegee Institute. Both were self-made men who valued hard work and personal initiative. Moreover, they shared a belief in the civic responsibility of the "better types of citizens" for the less fortunate ones. Rosenwald was particularly impressed with Baldwin's contention that the fate of African Americans in the United States was inseparably linked to the progress of the nation at large. Rosenwald explained that he was interested in African Americans "because I am also interested in the white people. . . . If we promote better citizenship among the Negroes not only are they improved, but our entire citizenship is benefitted."[40]

Rosenwald's concern for African Americans was also influenced by his Jewish heritage, which had made him sensitive to prejudices and discrimination.[41] Addressing an African-American audience in 1911, Rosenwald explained: "I also belong to a race that suffers and has suffered for centuries. . . . You would also probably be surprised to know that there are . . . clubs in the city of Chicago, representing what you might call the best type of citizenship . . . that would not admit a Jew." Rosenwald also believed that, despite these handicaps, America offered Jews and African Americans unparalleled opportunities if they behaved "properly" and displayed "proper citizenship."[42]

Rosenwald's philanthropic efforts on behalf of African Americans began with his support of the YMCA in 1910.[43] He recalled that he was startled when he was first approached by a Christian raising money for missionary work in Africa: "I, a Jew, had no real interest in securing converts for Christianity." Yet, he remembered, "I could not help but think why on earth do people want to spend their time and money on Africans, eight thousand miles away when we have millions of that race who are our citizens, who are anxious to learn, and I have no doubt would be glad to take advantage of any missionary work which might be available . . . and that the time and money would, to my mind, bring far greater results . . . to our own citizens, both black and white." Rosenwald decided to support the YMCA because its institutions provided African Americans with opportunities for self-help and personal improvement and not with charity. By supporting black YMCAs, Rosenwald could assist African Americans, for whom he felt compassion, without compromising his belief in "rugged individualism."[44]

When officials of the white YMCA in Chicago asked Rosenwald for a donation to its building fund in the spring of 1910, he responded: "I won't give a cent to this $350,000 fund unless you will include in it the building of a Colored Men's Y.M.C.A." Rosenwald then offered to give twenty-five thousand dollars, provided that the fund would include a building for the city's black population.[45] The Chicago YMCA accepted Rosenwald's conditions.

In December 1910 the Chicago YMCA asked Moorland to assist in conducting a fund-raising campaign for a black association building. Moorland had investigated the possibility of securing a YMCA building in Chicago three years earlier. In June 1907 he had conducted a survey of Chicago's African-American population but found that, without the support of "some interested friends," African Americans could not raise the funds necessary for the construction of a building. Moorland was convinced, however, that African Americans were able to maintain a building and "make it self-sustaining," so he urged the construction of a black YMCA.[46] Despite this, efforts to raise funds for a black association building did not begin until Rosenwald assured his assistance in 1910.

After Moorland's arrival in Chicago in December 1910, Rosenwald invited him to lunch at his office. During this meeting on December 16, Rosenwald inquired about YMCA work among African Americans throughout the country. Moorland explained that the black international secretaries assisted local groups in the formation of associations and the organization of fund-raising campaigns. To acquire property, however, African-American YMCAs depended on the financial support of the local black population, which often did not have the financial means to contribute to the association fund. As a result, black YMCAs remained ill equipped and provided minimal services.

Perhaps Rosenwald's interest was quickened when Moorland informed him that Peabody had endowed a black association for Columbus, Georgia, and that Rockefeller had contributed twenty-five thousand dollars toward the construction of an African-American YMCA in Washington, D.C. During the lunch Rosenwald offered to contribute twenty-five thousand dollars to every community in the country that raised seventy-five thousand toward the erection of a black YMCA over the next five years. The only other condition of Rosenwald's offer was that he would give the twenty-five thousand only after fifty thousand dollars raised locally were "actually expended for land and building."[47]

Rosenwald's offer reflected his acceptance of Hunton and Moorland's accommodationist philosophy. Instead of challenging the YMCA's jim crow policy, Rosenwald tried to assist African Americans in securing separate facilities. This, he believed, would provide a "needy and worthy group of our citizens" with "a fair chance" to earn the respect of whites. Like Hunton and Moorland, Rosenwald hoped to achieve his goal by fostering cooperation between "the best men of both races" and promoting racial self-help.[48]

Rosenwald was convinced that America's racial problems resulted from a lack of knowledge and understanding between the races. Ignorance, he believed, could only be overcome gradually through cooperation between African Americans and whites, which would eventually help to reduce prejudices.[49] Thus, Rosenwald's proposal was designed to induce both races to cooperate by requiring communities to raise two-thirds of the necessary funds locally.

Moreover, Rosenwald's conditional offer was intended to inspire African Americans to take an active and responsible part in the fund-raising campaigns. Rosenwald, like other philanthropists, endorsed the "ideology of rugged individualism" and rejected "mere" charity. His philanthropy was designed to provide African Americans with "an opportunity, not to be worked *for* but to be worked *with*."[50]

Moorland shared Rosenwald's belief that charity undermined personal initiative and deprived the individual of a sense of pride and achievement that could only be gained through hard work. Moorland criticized Peabody's endowment of the YMCA in Columbus, claiming it had a "weakening and benumbing influence." Perhaps Moorland was right. In 1914 a friend of Booker T. Washington's who had visited the Columbus YMCA said that the association "seems to be 'running down at the heels.' The building . . . is not being kept up either in its physical appearance or ordinary janitor work." Moorland welcomed

Rosenwald's offer because it allowed African Americans to prove their manhood. Moorland explained that "very little would be accomplished by working *for* men or by handing them a ready-made program. This might do very well for children and feeble-minded persons but lasting and effective results could be gotten by working *with* people."[51]

Two weeks after the lunch, Rosenwald confirmed his matching funds offer in a letter to the Chicago YMCA. On January 1, 1911, he announced it at a public meeting of African Americans who had gathered at Chicago's Odd Fellows Hall to launch a fund-raising campaign for a black YMCA.[52] In response to Rosenwald's offer, Norman W. Harris, a prominent Chicago banker, and Cyrus H. McCormick, president of International Harvester, each contributed twenty-five thousand dollars to the building fund.[53] Inspired by these contributions, James H. Tilghman, a retired African-American messenger for the Chesapeake Telephone Company, donated his life's savings of one thousand dollars.[54] Tilghman, who had arrived in Chicago in 1881 "without friends and hardly a dollar," recalled that "he came near going to ruin because there were no places for him to go outside of the saloons [and] gambling dens." Tilghman expressed his hope that a YMCA building would provide travelers and newcomers to the city with "a desirable place where a young man can feel homelike and happy."[55]

After the press publicized Rosenwald's offer, he received enthusiastic responses from all over the country. President William Howard Taft claimed that "nothing could be more useful to the race and to the country."[56] The *Chicago Defender* likened the importance of Rosenwald's offer to the Emancipation Proclamation and compared him to John Brown, Charles Sumner, and Abraham Lincoln. Booker T. Washington called it "one of the wisest and best-paying philanthropic investments of which I have any knowledge." Peabody assured Rosenwald that "no future investments will prove more profitable than those made to further Negro Y.M.C.A. work."[57]

Rosenwald's offer, however, was also criticized for enhancing the YMCA's policy of segregation. W.E.B. Du Bois, editor of the *Crisis*, praised "white philanthropists like Julius Rosenwald" but remained critical of the association's exclusion and segregation. Du Bois charged that "it is an unchristian and unjust and dangerous procedure which segregates colored people in the Y.M.C.A." He cautioned, "We may be glad of the colored Y.M.C.A. movement on the one hand, on the other hand we must never for a single moment fail to recognize the injustice which has made it an unfortunate necessity." Similarly, the *Chicago Broad Ax*, a black newspaper, spoke favorably of Rosenwald's offer but asked: "Why not offer $25,000 to every city in the U.S. which will open its Y.M.C.A. door to their brother in black? . . . We have no faith in any Y.M.C.A. which will not admit a respectable, intelligent young man of color, and we don't believe that God, in his goodness, approves of such develish [*sic*] prejudice, under the guise of a Christian fraternity."[58]

Nevertheless, many African Americans greeted Rosenwald's offer enthusiastically. They were willing to accept segregated facilities rather than forgo the practical benefits they believed a YMCA would offer the community.[59] Moreover, a growing number of white Americans began to support African Americans in their fund-raising efforts, convinced that the YMCA's "wholesome" influence would benefit the community at large. The *Kansas City Journal*, for example, asked: "Would it not be effective economy to build a negro Y.M.C.A. rather than to make a larger appropriation for the police force and the maintenance of the courts and penal institutions?"[60]

White officials of the Chicago YMCA supervised the allocation of Rosenwald funds, while Moorland served as executive officer in the field. Moorland visited communities that considered applying for Rosenwald aid in order to survey the economic situation of African Americans and the state of race relations. When he was convinced that a community was able not only to raise sufficient funds for the construction of a YMCA building but also to maintain it, he sent a positive recommendation to the Chicago YMCA. Moorland then organized and supervised the local fund-raising campaign among African Americans.[61] For a period of ten to fourteen days, teams of local YMCA supporters collected subscriptions or pledges that were to be paid after the completion of the campaign.[62]

During the five-year term of Rosenwald's offer, seven cities conducted successful fund-raising campaigns. African-American YMCA buildings were constructed in Washington, D.C., Chicago, Indianapolis, Philadelphia, Kansas City, Cincinnati, and St. Louis.[63] When the terms of the offer expired at the end of 1915, Rosenwald granted extensions to six other American cities. During the next five years successful campaigns for "Rosenwald YMCAs" were conducted in Brooklyn, Baltimore, Columbus, Harlem, Atlanta, and Pittsburgh.[64]

Rosenwald was pleased with the thirteen YMCA buildings his matching funds policy had helped to create, and he considered renewing the offer in 1920.[65] First, however, Rosenwald asked the YMCA to conduct a survey and evaluate the progress of the existing buildings. He was particularly interested in the services rendered to African Americans and the degree of interracial cooperation his offer had stimulated.

The YMCA asked Moorland as well as a white association official, William J. Parker, to conduct independent studies of the Rosenwald YMCAs. Moorland interviewed the African-American secretaries and reported that the associations served not only their members but also the community at large. The Rosenwald YMCAs had become African-American community centers. A variety of groups from choirs to the NAACP used the buildings for their meetings. Moorland also observed that the fund-raising campaigns had "taught many men how to promote secular business enterprises in the matter of establishing banks, building apartment houses, as well as churches and, in some cases, schools, putting their affairs on a better financial basis."[66] Despite his overall praise, Moorland criticized the fact that the association in Chicago did not have a black chairman, although African Americans served in that capacity in all other Rosenwald YMCAs.

Parker's study was based solely on interviews with white association officials in the thirteen cities with Rosenwald YMCAs. Parker found that the black associations had a "surprisingly large" membership, "fairly competent" secretaries, and the support of "the leading colored professional and business men." In the fields of religion, social events, housing, and recreation, Parker reported satisfactory progress, although neither the physical nor the educational programs compared favorably with work done in the white YMCAs. Moreover, Parker noted that many African Americans had failed to pay the amount they had pledged during the fund-raising campaigns. He explained that African Americans had "pledged in good faith but overestimated their ability to pay" and did not generally have the means to support their associations beyond the payment of membership fees.[67]

Concerning interracial cooperation, Parker observed that the relationship between white and black YMCA officials seemed "to be very intimate and cordial," but he admitted that their contacts were "limited to official occasions." Most important, though, Parker noticed that white associations in cities with Rosenwald YMCAs started to extend financial support to the black associations. White YMCAs often paid the salaries of African-American secretaries through "appropriations from their general funds." The salaries, however, were lower than those of white secretaries. Only one-third of the associations paid African Americans the same salary as whites; the remainder paid them about 25 percent less than whites. Despite these shortcomings, Parker urged Rosenwald to renew his "original offer for a reasonable period."[68]

Although both Moorland and Parker suggested a renewal of

Rosenwald's offer, they proposed different conditions. Parker recommended a continuation of Rosenwald's 1910 offer with new conditions requiring standard-sized buildings equipped with a swimming pool, dormitories, a cafeteria, and physical exercise, recreational, and educational rooms. Parker's proposal reflected his desire to provide African-American communities with YMCA buildings that were equal to those of their white counterparts. Moorland, on the other hand, argued that the matching funds policy worked to the disadvantage of many African Americans, most of whom lived in the rural South.[69] In the South virtually no recreational facilities for African Americans existed, and white southerners were not often willing to make significant contributions in support of black YMCAs. Some cities, such as Nashville, Jacksonville, and New Orleans, had tried to match Rosenwald's offer but failed, apparently because of the lack of white support.[70] Of the first thirteen Rosenwald YMCAs, only three—those in Atlanta, Baltimore, and Washington, D.C.—were in the South, where nearly 90 percent of the African-American population lived. Moorland noted, "The conditions in the South are so different to what they are in . . . the North, that there is no comparison. It would be almost a phenomenon if we discovered a white man in the South would give $25,000.00 to a colored building."[71] Moorland urged Rosenwald to support YMCAs where they were needed, not just where the local black population was willing and able to finance them. He proposed an offer that would allow for smaller and less well-equipped buildings, thereby enabling poorer communities, particularly those in the South, to qualify for Rosenwald aid.[72]

Moorland's efforts to convince Rosenwald to change the conditions of his offer were unsuccessful. After all, Rosenwald's philanthropy was based on the ideology of self-help, and those who could not raise their share, he thought, were certainly not worthy of receiving his share. Rosenwald's renewal offer was much closer to Parker's conditions. On July 6, 1920, Rosenwald announced a two-year renewal of his offer, asking local communities to raise $125,000 in order to qualify for a $25,000 donation. Rosenwald attached several additional conditions to his second offer. He stipulated that YMCA buildings built with his support would have to include the following features: "(1) separate quarters for men and boys; (2) Standard Gymnasium; (3) Swimming Pool; (4) Class and club rooms; (5) Restaurant, and (6) not fewer than fifty (50) dormitory rooms." The increase in the required matching funds and the high cost of building materials following World War I made the offer futile.[73] In the next two years no American city was able to raise sufficient funds, but Rosenwald granted extensions to eleven cities.[74] Between 1924 and 1933 eleven black YMCA buildings were erected in Denver; Detroit; Los Angeles; Buffalo; Dayton; Montclair, New Jersey; Toledo; Dallas; Youngstown, Ohio; Orange, New Jersey; and Harrisburg, Pennsylvania.[75]

The financial assistance of Peabody, Rockefeller, and, particularly, Rosenwald resulted in the construction of twenty-six YMCA buildings, most of which were equipped with a swimming pool, a gymnasium, a cafeteria, reading and class rooms, an employment bureau, and dormitories. The association buildings provided programs and facilities previously unavailable to most African Americans. The pools and gymnasiums offered recreation and exercise, and the reading rooms were stocked with black newspapers and a variety of fiction and nonfiction books, including works by African-American authors. The night schools, designed to enhance the vocational and professional training of association members, enrolled students in courses such as typewriting, architectural and mechanical drawing, stenography, barbering, painting, printing, auto mechanics, and driving. The cafeterias offered affordable and nutritious meals, and for a long time the dormitories were practically the only places where black male travelers could find comfortable and safe sleeping accommodations outside the homes of relatives and friends.[76]

By 1933 the associations that had erected buildings with the support of Rosenwald had a combined membership of nearly twenty thousand men and boys, and many more African Americans who were not YMCA members visited and used the facilities daily.[77] Many associations invited physicians and dentists to conduct health clinics for the local black population.[78] Teachers and students often used the pools and gymnasiums for physical education classes. Businessmen's clubs, merchant associations, ministers, choirs, mutual aid societies, professional, fraternal and civic groups, and NAACP and Urban League chapters convened for their weekly meetings at the YMCA buildings. Aside from churches, YMCA buildings were frequently the only places where large numbers of African Americans could gather comfortably and without white interference. In 1915, when Carter G. Woodson organized the Association for the Study of Negro Life and History, he assembled the charter group at the Wabash Avenue YMCA in Chicago.[79]

The association buildings improved the quality of life for many African-American city residents. The educational programs as well as the recreational and social activities offered black men and boys a meaningful alternative to the city streets. At the YMCA they found male companionship and an environment that provided them with role models and shielded them from racism and discrimination.

James C. Napier, a lawyer and politician from Nashville who came to Washington as a student, had high praise for the YMCA, claiming that "all I am I owe to the Young Men's Christian Association." Similarly, Maxwell Glanville, a member of the association in New York City, called the YMCA "a second home. . . . It is a place where I am sure of friendship and wholesome activity. I have received valuable training in leadership for which I shall always be grateful." Concerned parents could rest assured that a son who spent his afternoon or evening at the YMCA was using his leisure time constructively. The mother of a member of the Washington, D.C., association expressed what many parents must have felt: "Before this building was opened I did not know where my boy was. Now I rest content, knowing that his leisure is being properly directed."[80]

Migrants or visitors who were new to the cities found the association buildings particularly useful. For visitors, the YMCA lounges were ideal places to establish contacts with African-American businessmen, the professional elite, and the religious leaders of the community. For migrants, the dormitories provided affordable, clean, and safe housing, and the employment bureaus helped locate jobs. During the Great Migration, when large numbers of African Americans left the rural South for the urban North, some associations offered the migrants their services free of charge. The Wabash Avenue YMCA in Chicago, for example, provided free night classes, housing, and employment placement in an attempt to help the newcomers adjust to urban life.[81]

The YMCA buildings erected with Rosenwald's support were built largely with money raised among whites. Rosenwald and other whites had provided 86 percent of the funds.[82] African-American YMCA members acknowledged Rosenwald's assistance and established an annual memorial day in his honor. When Rosenwald died on January 6, 1932, the highest-ranking African-American YMCA secretary called him "one of the greatest friends of the Negro race since Abraham Lincoln."[83]

Nevertheless, African Americans considered the association buildings to be products of racial solidarity and self-help. Jesse Moorland, the "Y Building King," had supervised the organization of local fund-raising campaigns, and members of the African-American community had provided the necessary volunteers to collect the pledges. Although African Americans had raised only 14 percent of the building funds, their contributions were considerable given their economic standing in society.[84]

Some African Americans gave relatively large amounts to the YMCA. Henry W. Chase, the former slave who donated $500 to the

Twelfth Street YMCA in Washington, and James H. Tilghman, the retired telephone company messenger who gave $1,000 to the Wabash Avenue YMCA in Chicago, led the way for many other African Americans. Madame C.J. Walker, who made a fortune with beauty aids, contributed $1,000 to the Senate Avenue YMCA in Indianapolis. Thomas W. Troy, a former mail carrier who successfully invested in Los Angeles real estate, donated $1,000 to that city's association. Thomas E. Lassiter, a prosperous businessman who started as a street vendor, gave $1,000 to the YMCA in Atlantic City. Daisy K. Merchant, owner of a lucrative catering business in Cincinnati, contributed $2,300 to the city's Ninth Street YMCA. The Nashville YMCA received a number of large contributions from African-American residents: Dr. R.W. Boyd, secretary of the National Baptist Publishing House, his son Henry A. Boyd, the Reverend Preston Taylor, and the Reverend William Beckam gave $1,000 each, and James C. Napier contributed $500. David T. Howard, a former slave, assisted the Butler Street YMCA in Atlanta with $1,500, and Dr. E.P. Robert, a physician in New York, gave $1,000 to the city's YMCA building fund.[85]

Most African-American pledges, though, were small compared with the donations of some whites. Yet African Americans knew that every contribution, no matter how small, aided in the construction of a YMCA building. The *Southern Workman*, the journal of Hampton Institute, observed that the size of white donations did not intimidate African Americans. The fund-raising campaigns, the journal claimed, "called up latent energies which were heretofore undreamed of [and] established self-confidence among the colored people, who worked earnestly to do their share."[86]

African Americans from all walks of society had closed ranks to support the YMCA fund-raising campaigns. Rosenwald acknowledged the involvement and support of African Americans. At the dedication of Chicago's Wabash Avenue YMCA, Rosenwald reminded his African-American audience: "You now have an enterprise in which you have participated from the start, for you conducted a campaign for raising money to build it. . . . You are organizing the force to operate the plant. You are going to run it, too, what a chance for you to make good! What a grand opportunity to grow strong! What an efficient help to dissipate prejudice!" Proud of their achievements, African Americans regarded the buildings as community centers that served them in their search for cultural self-determination. In 1951, nearly four decades after the opening of the Chicago association, African Americans recalled their role in the city's fund-raising efforts. They proudly proclaimed that the YMCA was not the product of "the familiar 'paternalism' of the patronizing neighbor but the result of aggressive leadership of the people of the community itself."[87]

Some African Americans, however, remained critical of Rosenwald's philanthropy for perpetuating segregation in the YMCA. Rosenwald had stimulated black and white financial collaboration, but his offer failed to induce real interracial cooperation. African Americans and whites worked together for the duration of the fund-raising campaigns, but once the association buildings were completed, interracial cooperation usually came to an end. In 1925 W.E.B. Du Bois observed that "there is gradually rising . . . an independent autonomous colored Y.M.C.A. . . . whose connection with the white Y.M.C.A. is daily growing less and less confined more and more to general policies and the rare personal contacts of a few officials."[88] Moreover, as Moorland had pointed out, Rosenwald's philanthropy favored communities in the North, where a minority of the African-American population lived.

Despite these shortcomings, Rosenwald helped African Americans to build black-controlled community centers, largely in those cities to which subsequent generations of African Americans would migrate.[89] His conditional gifts also stimulated white YMCA officials to support African-American associations financially. White associations frequently paid the salaries of black secretaries long after the buildings were completed. This helped to alleviate some of the financial problems of African-American secretaries and allowed them to devote more of their time to YMCA work rather than raising their own salaries. Despite white financial assistance, however, African-American YMCAs retained their independence from white supervision.

6

Serving African-American Soldiers in World War I

AFRICAN-AMERICAN YMCA work further expanded when the United States entered World War I. During the war black secretaries accompanied the nearly four hundred thousand African-American troops to military camps in the United States and France.[1] The secretaries organized social gatherings, athletic and entertainment activities, and a variety of educational classes in so-called Y-huts. Moreover, the secretaries operated two holiday resorts for black troops serving in France. Nearly twenty thousand African-American soldiers spent their seven-day military leaves at government expense in Chambéry and Challes-les-Eaux.[2] For the first time in its history the YMCA also recruited black women as secretaries to serve with the troops in France.

The army particularly welcomed the YMCA's educational programs as a tool of social control. Government officials feared that the large number of foreign-born and illiterate soldiers as well as the poor education among all draftees would hamper military efficiency and pose a threat to the nation's security. More than 16 percent of the men who had registered were foreign born and had little or no command of the English language. In addition, the draft examinations indicated that 25 percent of the men tested "could not read a newspaper or write an intelligent letter" and that a large portion of functionally literate men had deficient schooling.[3]

Illiteracy rates among the African-American troops were even higher, since 80 percent of the men were draftees from the South who had been systematically deprived of educational opportunities. Illiteracy rates among these men ranged from 35 percent at some camps to 75 percent at others. In addition, some African-American soldiers were ignorant of their own age, while others did not "know right from left." A newspaper charged that the high illiteracy rate among African-American troops constituted an embarrassment to the nation at large. The *Independent* insisted: "Neither pride nor considerations of safety can tolerate in a nation that is trying to make the world safe for democracy a state of affairs which puts us, among the backwards people of the world in respect of elementary education." The African-American *New York Age* was quick to point out that more than America's pride was at stake. According to the *Age*, the alarming lack of education revealed by the mass mobilization made the African-American soldier "a menace to the welfare of the whole nation." Philander P. Claxton, commissioner of education, agreed that illiterate men "do not make good soldiers," because "modern warfare requires many things impossible for soldiers who can not be depended on to make accurate reports. They can not read signs, orders, or the manual of arms."[4]

The army hoped that the YMCA's programs would help improve the fighting efficiency of the troops and maintain "contentment, camp spirit, and camp morale."[5] Military officials were concerned that the mass mobilization would have a detrimental impact on the morals and morale of the drafted men. Newton D. Baker, secretary of war, expressed these concerns, explaining that "our military camps are each to have a population of from thirty to forty-five thousand young men. They are, in other words, cities. The simplicity of their purpose, the singleness of occupation and their uniformity of age and condition make a comparatively simple problem. . . . Here we have 30,000 young men, the greater part of whose days are given to strenuous and exhilarating physical discipline. Their hours of relaxation are to be provided for, in order that idleness, weariness, and homesickness, and monotony may not prejudicially affect their spirit and their lives."[6] The army feared that soldiers loitering in communities adjacent to military camps would resort to alcohol abuse or fall prey to prostitutes and contract venereal disease.[7] The YMCA's presence in the camps, army officials hoped, would help to "surround the men in service with an environment which is not only clean and wholesome but positively inspiring." This, they believed, would prevent the military camps as well as the adjacent communities from becoming "places of peril and temptation." Military officials were also convinced that the YMCA programs would "render a great service in reducing and even averting race friction."[8]

In accordance with its jim crow policy, the YMCA maintained segregation in its work among American soldiers throughout the war and the period of demobilization. YMCA services for African-American troops "were in almost every case inferior" and suffered from a shortage of personnel.[9] During the war the YMCA recruited 12,971 white secretaries but only 300 African Americans to work in Y-huts in the United States.[10] In Europe the situation was even worse: of the

12,955 secretaries who served with the American Expeditionary Force, only 84 were African Americans, and most of them did not arrive until after the Armistice.[11]

During the hostilities, education in the Y-huts served "strictly military purposes." African-American secretaries offered English classes for illiterate soldiers, providing them with skills necessary to understand, give, and execute military orders. They instructed better-educated soldiers in French, preparing them for their service overseas, and they gave lectures in "social hygiene" and civics to maintain health and morale. Although attendance at the classes offered at the Y-huts was voluntary before the Armistice, some camp commanders "cooperated with the [YMCA] by requiring illiterates to attend."[12]

The kind of education as well as the facilities and equipment available to the African-American troops varied from camp to camp. At Camp Shelby, Mississippi, for example, four African-American secretaries without a Y-hut conducted classes for illiterates "in one of the Mess Halls."[13] In contrast, Thomas F. Blue, a Hampton graduate and secretary at Camp Taylor, Kentucky, reported: "We have a splendid, well-equipped building with six secretaries in the service. There are two thousand colored soldiers here and five hundred will come April 26, with more to follow. I have two hundred men in my educational classes. Most of these cannot read and write. The work here is an interesting experience and an opportunity worth while for real, helpful service." Another Hampton graduate organized a school at Camp Pike, Arkansas, and with the help of four African-American teachers instructed two hundred illiterate soldiers. At Camp Alexander, Virginia, the secretary divided the black soldiers into two groups "according to their educational needs and desires. . . . one [group] was taught the elementary English subjects, the other receiving instruction in algebra, agriculture, civics, and other subjects." At Camp Meade, Maryland, where approximately six thousand African Americans were stationed, one corporal remarked that "these men who have come here are trying to learn. Many of them could not read or write. They are fast learning both."[14]

Classes for illiterates not only emphasized reading and writing but also included "a certain amount of instruction in civics and elementary history." Since black and white soldiers used the same textbooks, ironically African Americans also received instruction on the importance of voting in a democracy. For example, a writing exercise in the *Camp Reader for American Soldiers* asked the men to copy the following text: "In the United States the people have a voice in the government. The President of the US is the choice of the people. The people choose the President by their votes."[15]

Writing exercises were often coupled with instructions in "social hygiene." *Soldier's First Book*, especially designed to teach illiterates, informed the troops that many men had been rejected as "physically unfit" because of their "lack of frequent bathing, failure to brush the teeth after each meal, the use of other people's towel or comb or drinking cup, sleeping in a room with windows closed, drinking intoxicating liquor, smoking cigarettes and indulging in vices."[16]

The YMCA's educational work also served as a means to control the spread of sexually transmitted diseases. The War Department did not systematically record the number of men infected with venereal disease, although infection rates seem to have run about seven times higher for African-American soldiers than for whites.[17] Army officials attributed this phenomenon largely to the diseases' greater incidence among the African-American civilian population because of poverty, lack of education, illiteracy and "general ignorance on all matters relating to sex hygiene."[18]

Until the draft, the federal government had been largely indifferent to the health of African Americans. The large number of black soldiers infected with venereal disease, however, made the health of African Americans an issue of national concern. The army appointed Arthur B. Spingarn, a white NAACP official and a commissioned officer, to investigate venereal disease among black troops. Spingarn found that the soldiers' "opportunities for clean and decent recreation" were severely limited. Most of the training camps were in the South, located near small cities that usually excluded African Americans from "public places, baths, theatres, and libraries."[19]

Spingarn also claimed that less desirable forms of leisure activities were more readily available for African-American soldiers. He charged that it was "the policy of southern cities to leave the colored part of the town 'wide open,' and . . . to center in the colored portion much of the vice of the white portion." Walter Howard Loving, an African-American military intelligence officer, confirmed Spingarn's findings. Loving reported that "white sporting districts have been cleared," but he complained "that no steps have been taken to clear out the bad districts inhabited by colored folks." He concluded that African-American soldiers had "free access to . . . houses of prostitution."[20]

Spingarn cautioned the government not to ignore the health of African Americans in the interest of white Americans. The races, he explained, "are thrown in the closest physical contact . . . and [blacks] are continually exposing the white man, woman, and child to the danger of infection from their own syphilis." The army recruited the YMCA to help in the fight against venereal disease. The secretaries provided instruction from textbooks and invited African-American physicians from nearby communities to present lectures on sex and personal hygiene at the Y-huts.[21]

The YMCA's educational efforts were enhanced by the work of the American Library Association, which equipped almost every Y-hut with its own library. The ALA, under the guidance of Dr. Herbert Putnam, the librarian of Congress, opened the first camp library late in 1917. By January 1918 the association had distributed 310,000 books to training camps and 34,000 to smaller posts. It was "through these camp libraries [that] many men who lacked all formal education came into contact with books for the first time." Charles E. Arnold, of the all-black 325th Field Signal Battalion, observed his fellow soldiers at the library at Camp Sherman, Ohio: "It is the most pleasing and inspiring sight to see the Negro troops in the library, reading, not only magazines, and works of fiction but technical books on war tactics, engineering, electricity, radio telegraphy and the like." Despite the ALA's efforts, however, some huts had an insufficient supply of books, magazines, and newspapers. At Camp Upton, New York, for example, a force of six African-American secretaries served four thousand soldiers. Thomas A. Bolling, one of the secretaries, explained that the Y-hut attracted "constantly in the afternoon anywhere from fifty to five hundred men." Yet he complained that "one thing we lack is current literature." The actual impact of the camp libraries on African Americans remains unclear, but the fact that some 30,000 books circulated among them each month indicates that many of the soldiers took advantage of this educational opportunity.[22]

African-American YMCA secretaries who worked in the training camps in the United States apparently encountered no vocal or violent white opposition. This is not surprising. Black and white soldiers were stationed in the same camps in the United States, but they served in segregated units, slept in segregated barracks, and ate in segregated mess halls. Thus, most of the white rank and file were probably not even aware of the work done by the black YMCA secretaries.

Whites who supported African-American YMCA work were higher-ranking military officials, either camp commanders or officers, who were keenly aware of the military necessity of the educational programs. At Camp Dodge, Iowa, for example, the labor battalions were composed of African-American draftees from the coal and cotton fields of Alabama. "Fully one-fourth . . . could not write their names." The white camp commander made attendance at elementary English classes mandatory for illiterate soldiers, and at least 2,300 African Americans enrolled. Harrison J. Pinkett, of the all-black 366th Infantry, described how the Alabama conscripts responded to the YMCA's educational program: "We have night schools running after the day's work of military instruction is over, teaching the illiterate men to read and write. And the boys are learning rapidly. . . . On the first payroll more than fifty per cent of the men signed their names with their mark, although we had been working with them for a month, trying to teach them to sign their names. This month, however, in many cases, we cut the number down to something like ten percent. . . . This does not mean they can read and write, but it does mean that they will learn."[23]

Similarly, a white officer at Camp Hill, Virginia, supported the work of two Hampton graduates who conducted classes for nearly five thousand African-American labor troops, many of whom were unable to read or write.[24] The two secretaries operated out of a tent, and the white officer appealed to the army and to Hampton Institute to support the efforts of its graduates, "who served the soldiers every day . . . distributing stationery and writing letters." In the spring of 1918 the army provided barracks for the use of the African-American soldiers at Camp Hill.[25]

The educational work in American training camps was so popular that the army asked the YMCA to offer similar classes to American soldiers stationed in France. On March 5, 1918, the American Expeditionary Force approved two educational plans for its troops in France. The first plan provided for the education of soldiers during the war and was designed "to help the Army win the war." The second plan devised a program for the period of demobilization that was to prepare the men for civilian life by providing them with "an enlarged vision of citizenship."[26]

During both phases, English and civics classes were at the core of the soldiers' education. The YMCA recruited volunteers in the United States but also used American soldiers on duty in France. The AEF stipulated that no soldier was to "return to America without a knowledge of reading and writing English, and of the elements of American history and government."[27] This goal was probably not met, because educational efforts remained subordinate to military necessity.

To African-American YMCA secretaries in France, military necessity presented only one of many obstacles. The secretares had difficulties maintaining regular class sessions for the 140,000 African-American soldiers who served with the AEF.[28]

Most of them were "detailed to manual labor . . . [and] as a rule, moved more often than white troops." Moreover, the YMCA's educational efforts among African-American troops were obstructed by a shortage of personnel, facilities, and equipment, as well as by white opposition. M.W. Bullock, secretary in a camp in southern France, complained about the lack of adequate facilities and requested "a reading room and more room for school purposes." Thomas M. Clayton, another African-American secretary, complained about the lack of teaching material for the 105 black soldiers who had enrolled in his classes. The men, Clayton reported, were "all anxious to learn," but "I have nothing to work with in the line of books." He appealed to Jesse Moorland, asking him to send English and arithmetic books as well as "300 pencils."[29]

The shortage of teaching materials, Clayton believed, was the result not of inadequate supplies but of racial discrimination. He claimed that the white secretaries "retain all supplies and furnishings for their own use." Apparently, unfair distribution of supplies was not unusual. An African-American YMCA secretary at Melun reported a lack of educational supplies, explaining that he was "unable to get any consideration from the other [white] Y." James Garfield Wiley complained that the white district secretary "slighted" the African-American Y-hut in his camp and did not allocate enough equipment and supplies. In April 1918 Wiley urged Moorland to send a black secretary to supervise YMCA work for African-American soldiers in France, claiming that "our work in America did not accomplish much until our own International men were in charge."[30]

White opposition to African-American YMCA work in France most likely resulted from supply shortages as well as the lack of African-American supervision. In the United States, African-American YMCA secretaries solicited the support of churches, colleges, and other institutions of the black community in order to overcome supply shortages. In France, however, black secretaries could not resort to a local support network but had to compete with white secretaries for very limited supplies. Moreover, in the United States, Moorland supervised the work of African-American YMCA secretaries, whereas in France, the highest-ranking white secretary of each camp was in charge of all YMCA work there.

Moorland was aware of the need for African-American supervision and tried to recruit John Hope, the president of Morehouse College and a member of the Board of Managers of the Butler Street YMCA in Atlanta, for the position.[31] In October 1917 Moorland asked

Hope to join the African-American secretarial force in France. Hope accepted, but his responsibilities at Morehouse delayed his departure until September 1918. After his arrival in France, Hope assumed a "general advisory position" and acted as a liaison official between African-American secretaries and the YMCA headquarters in Paris.[32]

Hope corroborated the secretaries' complaints about racial discrimination. Some white secretaries and officers, he reported, obstructed the work done in the African-American Y-huts. He admitted that "there was much . . . in the Y.M.C.A. in France to embarrass, discourage, and even embitter colored secretaries and colored soldiers." In addition to problems arising from racism, Hope also found that the small number of African-American secretaries hampered the YMCA's service to African-American troops in France.[33]

Despite white opposition and the shortage of personnel, equipment, and supplies, the African-American YMCA secretaries tried to provide many of the 140,000 African-American troops serving in France with a variety of educational programs. Tod B. Galloway, a white secretary, described how one African-American secretary instructed illiterate soldiers "somewhere in France": "The other night I was with the colored stevedores and while there saw the wonderful work which the colored Y.M.C.A. secretary is doing with classes of absolute illiterates. Men who have known absolutely nothing he has taught in two weeks time to sign their names to the pay roll and to write 'Dear Mother. I am very well.' It was to be their first letter home. And how proud they all were of it!"[34]

In addition to classes for illiterates, some Y-huts offered instruction in French to enable the better-educated men to communicate with Allied soldiers and the civilian population. Addie W. Hunton, William A. Hunton's wife, was one of three African-American women who served with the YMCA in France during the hostilities. She recalled that "French professors were employed to visit each hut at stipulated hours, where the men would be taught en masse, the rudiments of conversational French."[35] These French lessons, however, were not well structured or well organized, nor did they offer a systematic approach to the subject. Edward B. Robinson, a former Hampton student, recalled that he was disappointed in the French classes: "It appears to me that I learned very little though my teacher said I was doing nicely."[36] In addition to language instruction, teachers presented lectures on French history and culture, astronomy, and geography, and the secretaries organized tours to historical sites near the camps.[37]

The YMCA also assigned three African-American field secretaries to work among the troops not stationed permanently in supply or debarkation camps. J.E. Saddler served in the Chaumont region, where he successfully organized schools with the help of soldiers who volunteered their services as teachers. B.M. Murell worked in the Verdun region, and Moses A. Davis, equipped with "maps, slides [and] text books," visited African-American troops in the trenches and encouraged them to organize their own classes.[38]

The ALA continued to support the YMCA's educational work for American soldiers in France. It distributed books, magazines, and newspapers among the troops and established libraries in many Y-huts. The ALA operated libraries for the use of African-American soldiers at St. Nazaire, Chambéry, Challes-les-Eaux, Verdun, Brest, and Bordeaux.[39] The libraries contained both fiction and nonfiction, as well as magazines and newspapers, although often not in sufficient numbers. A white officer, commanding nearly three thousand African-American labor troops, moved by the lack of information and education among them, requested 750-1,000 books for their use. "Not at any time in my life," he claimed, "have I been so made to realize the meaning of the expression *thirsting for knowledge*. These colored men from the rural South do." Whenever libraries were available, African-American soldiers used them. While books offering elementary-level education were in particular demand, Theodore W. Koch, an ALA representative, noted that "the most consistent Shakespeare reading in one camp was done by a negro labor battalion."[40]

With the signing of the Armistice in November 1918 and the resulting "moderation of activity and a relaxation of discipline," the YMCA's educational programs gained increased importance. Army officials, concerned that demobilization would take up to two years, feared demoralization among the troops. General John J. Pershing, commander of the AEF, urged the YMCA to continue its programs, to keep the soldiers "in a state which breeds contentment." Thus in January 1919 the army made basic education for illiterates compulsory throughout the AEF.[41]

The second phase of the AEF's educational plan called for the preparation of the soldiers for civilian life, in order to enable the men "to take an active and intelligent part in the future progress of our country." The YMCA urged its secretarial force to emphasize subjects like "citizenship, the importance of respect for law and of the orderly adjustment of social controversies, [and] the meaning of democracy." The irony did not escape African Americans. Max Yergan, a black YMCA official, noted that the object of the civics courses was to "interest men in government, especially municipal and state. Great emphasis is being placed upon the right use of the ballot. The officers have these lectures to give by command of a camp and they must be given as outlined. It's almost a turn of fate that those who have so jealously desired to keep such information away from us must now under military law give it." The YMCA tried to meet the new demands by introducing an enlarged lecture program, and the ALA expanded its library services in response to the growth in leisure time. Soldiers anywhere in France were now able to borrow books from the main AEF library in Paris.[42]

African-American YMCA secretaries in France responded enthusiastically to the mandatory education requirement. George W. Jackson, secretary at Is-sur-Tille, which had 15,000 African-American soldiers, claimed to have cut illiteracy among the men by 90 percent. At Camp Ancona, Bordeaux, where approximately 7,000 African-American troops were stationed, Thomas M. Clayton opened a school, where he taught not only 1,378 illiterates but also 1,457 men with four years of schooling or less, 548 who had attended high school, and 137 who had previously been enrolled in college. When the camp closed, 367 illiterates had learned to write their names, and many had attended a special institute designed to teach them about farming techniques. William Nelson, secretary at Brest, instructed 1,000 illiterate African-American soldiers. According to him, at least 372 of them received a "valuable education."[43]

Whenever possible, the YMCA secretaries used the help of soldier-teachers.[44] In the Chaumont region, a secretary organized schools with teachers recruited from among the African-American troops. They conducted spelling bees and offered prizes "to induce the men to learn to write." They reportedly reduced illiteracy by 60 percent. Joseph L. Whiting, former director of education at Tuskegee, was particularly successful in offering elementary education by utilizing soldier-teachers. Whiting, who served as secretary at Montoir, recruited twenty-four African-American soldiers to teach the men stationed in the camp.[45] These volunteer teachers remained in France after their regiments were demobilized. Whiting, realizing the importance of the soldiers' educational work as well as their personal sacrifice, tried to appease their mothers, informing them: "It gives me much happiness to reprot [*sic*] to you the prosperous condition of your son . . . for he has been selected to fill a unique place among his fellow comrades—looking particularly after those less fortunate than himself, those who are willing to employ a few of the leisure moments in pursuit of a better education." By April 1919, 862 illiterate African-American soldiers at Montoir had enrolled in writing, language, and arithmetic classes. One of the commanding officers, impressed with Whiting's success, thanked him and his staff: "I do not know of any thing more important for them, or that will be more helpful to them when they return to civil life than the educational course they have been through. It has gone far to wipe out illiteracy in my company." In addition to teaching classes at the Y-huts, the YMCA also offered African-American soldiers opportunities to enhance their education while on leave.[46]

In November 1917 the AEF had authorized the YMCA to establish holiday resorts for American soldiers on leave.[47] The creation of these leave areas was the result of strategic considerations. Army officials feared that the dispersal of men on leave throughout France would make it impossible to recall them in case of a sudden German offensive. Moreover, while French and British soldiers usually went home during their furloughs, the American servicemen were confined to a foreign country, and they were largely ignorant of the language and customs of its people. This situation, the AEF believed, created "large possibilities of trouble with the civilian population." The soldiers, attracted by the big cities, would flock into Paris or Marseilles, where they would fall easy prey to "deleterious pleasures" and possibly contract venereal disease.[48]

The idea of supervised leave time was "an absolute novelty in the world's military annals," and it caused some confusion. On January 31, 1918, the YMCA appointed Franklin S. Edmonds to organize a leave area in the Haute Savoie region. Edmonds, unsure about his duties, inquired: "What is a leave area?" Officials at the YMCA headquarters in Paris responded frankly: "We don't know. . . . There has never been anything like it before. Go down and start one." Despite the initial confusion, the YMCA eventually catered to five hundred thousand American soldiers on leave, approximately twenty thousand of whom were African Americans.[49]

The YMCA opened the first leave area for American soldiers at Aix-les-Bains in the Haute Savoie region on February 15, 1918. At first the soldiers had to pay for their furloughs in the leave areas, but within a month the YMCA convinced the AEF to assume financial responsibility. Special military trains transported the men to the leave areas, where YMCA secretaries met them and assigned them to hotels in the vicinity. Some soldiers objected to the idea of spending their furloughs in a prescribed area under the auspices of the YMCA and scornfully referred to Aix-les-Bains as "Aches'n'Pains."[50] Their attitude changed, however, once they arrived in the luxurious resorts and realized that they were not subjected to military routine.[51]

During the hostilities, the leave area at Aix-les-Bains catered to both white and black soldiers. The number of African-American soldiers in the leave area was small, though, and only after the Armistice did they arrive "by train-loads." John Hope was pleased that there was "no race line drawn between the American white and black soldiers either by the Army or the Y.M.C.A." But soon some white southern men and white women serving as YMCA secretaries in the leave areas objected to the presence of African Americans.[52] After "some unpleasant occurrences arose," a group of 1,200 African-American soldiers on leave in the Haute Savoie region requested "an area for their distinct use."[53] They presented their proposition to the district secretary at Aix-les-Bains, who forwarded it to the YMCA's headquarters in Paris.

YMCA officials discussed the proposal with John Hope, who at first opposed separate leave areas, "especially as they had begun without any race lines whatever." White YMCA officials, however, explained that "men would be better satisfied among those of kindred feeling and types, and that the privilege of unlimited self-expression would put more into their leave, than could otherwise be gained if associated with white troops."[54] After Hope inquired about the condition of race relations in Aix-les-Bains, he approved the establishment of separate leave areas for African Americans. Hope explained that he changed his mind in consideration of the black soldiers' safety. He claimed that "the attitude of the white soldiers was such that it seemed best not only for the pleasure but even the protection of colored soldiers to give them an area to themselves." Hope, however, successfully opposed the demand of the commanding officer of the Savoie leave area that black and white soldiers be prohibited from visiting each other. Hope believed that separate leave areas for African-American troops were a necessary evil, but he insisted that "white and colored soldiers should be free and encouraged to visit back and forth between neighboring rest camps."[55]

In December 1918 the YMCA set aside Chambéry and Challes-les-Eaux in the Haute Savoie region as leave areas for African-American soldiers. On January 15, 1919, the first black troops arrived at Chambéry, and two days later the first soldiers came to Challes-les-Eaux. Between January and May 1919, 8,732 African-American soldiers spent their seven-day furloughs in Chambéry, and 7,714 in Challes-les-Eaux.[56]

When Chambéry opened, three white men and one black woman, Helen Curtis, served the African-American troops as YMCA secretaries. The arriving black soldiers, however, resented the white secretaries, and the YMCA eventually replaced the three with five African-American men and three women.[57] At Challes-les-Eaux one white secretary and two African-American secretaries, Addie W. Hunton and William Stevenson, greeted the arriving soldiers. Within two weeks the white man was replaced by a black secretary, and during the following months six additional black men and women were added to the secretarial force.[58]

The African-American secretaries at Chambéry and Challes-les-Eaux offered the vacationing soldiers a variety of facilities and activities. In both towns the secretaries operated canteens, libraries, and game and writing rooms and organized indoor and outdoor athletics. The Y-huts also provided daily entertainment. A typical week's program included "violin and piano music daily 4 to 6, and 8 to 9; movies three times a week; two regular 'Y' shows weekly; daily hikes and sight-seeing." Most of the entertainment featured soldiers or French civilians, but twice a week the regional headquarters at Aix-les-Bains sent some sort of entertainment, mostly bands, to perform for the African-American soldiers.[59]

The time the soldiers spent in the leave areas also offered educational opportunities for the men. The YMCA secretaries invited local teachers to present lectures to the soldiers to acquaint them "with the people, customs and events of the past that they could or would have secured in no other way."[60] Moreover, the secretaries offered guided tours to historical sites, and these excursions reportedly instilled in many men "a new zest for education." These trips were the most popular activity among the soldiers, and the secretaries observed that almost all of the men took notes. This created considerable peer pressure for those unable to read and write. An African-American secretary accompanying the soldiers during a visit to Jean-Jacques Rousseau's home observed a soldier who was equipped with a pen and notebook but did not take any notes. The secretary took the man aside and discovered that he was illiterate. He "wanted to see and hear everything that was worth keeping, but was ashamed to go on the trips and seem to be unable to write down what impressed him as the others did."[61] Following the incident the secretary started to teach the soldier the rudiments of reading and writing.

After their departure, many of the men praised the efforts of the African-American secretaries. One soldier from South Carolina who had spent his furlough in Chambéry wrote: "I was ignorant. This is the first letter I write. You showed me the way. Prays God I get my leave at the YMCA." A private in the 813th Infantry proclaimed: "The 'Y' opened the path of life for me." Other soldiers stressed the historical insights they gained from the excursions: "I have stood upon the stage of history. In my mind's eye I have witnessed Roman, Gaul and Celt repeat the dramas of old for my edification. And who shall I thank for such good fortune? Why, none but you good people at the 'Y'."[62]

While some men praised the educational value of their furlough, others were more impressed with the quality of the food served in the leave areas. One soldier, reminiscing about his leave at Chambéry, wrote: "I'm back in camp. Every time I think of one of those meals I used to get at the 'Y' I feel like passing the mess sergeant a hand grenade minus the firing pin; then tootsweeting it till he finishes saying howdy to the angels, some feed, believe me." William Stevenson, a secretary at Challes-les-Eaux, concluded that the opening of the "leave area for colored soldiers was a master stroke." Hope, who had initially opposed the creation of separate leave areas, agreed and proclaimed that the experiment worked "beautifully."[63]

When the army authorized the YMCA to initiate its services to American soldiers, it did so because of military considerations. The fighting efficiency of the troops was hampered by men who were unable to understand written orders and by those who were unable to fight because of venereal disease. Thus, the YMCA's classroom instruction offered under the auspices of the army aimed at reducing illiteracy and the number of those infected with venereal disease. During the hostilities and particularly during the period of demobilization, army officials also hoped that the YMCA's programs would help to maintain morale and to prepare the soldiers for a smooth integration into civilian society.

Regardless of the army's motivation and despite jim crowism, African-American soldiers greeted the YMCA with enthusiasm. Each month approximately eighty thousand black soldiers attended the two hundred lectures, and ninety thousand enrolled in the fifteen hundred classes offered at the Y-huts.[64] Numerous African Americans learned how to read and write, received instruction in social hygiene, health care, and sanitation, and became acquainted with books and libraries.

The impact of the YMCA's educational programs is difficult to assess and certainly defies quantification. As Jesse E. Moorland noted, some "men, after having learned to write their names, have actually shouted for joy over the new found power which at last had released them from the shackles of an oppressing ignorance." The African-American YMCA secretaries were convinced that the educational programs, despite their shortcomings, had helped to liberate the mind of the African-American soldier and had "in some measure removed the fetters from his soul."[65]

While African-American soldiers generally welcomed the work of the YMCA secretaries, their enthusiasm at least in part derived from the fact that there was little else to do in the camps. The men flocked to the Y-huts to attend even the most boring lectures. Dr. George W. Cabaniss, YMCA secretary at Camp Meade, Maryland, recalled one such incident. The Y-hut was "crowded to the very eaves" when "some learned professor was explaining the intricacies of the internationl tariff treaties with reference to the particular offenses of the German kaiser." The speaker apparently put the soldiers to sleep, and Cabaniss had to trick the men into applauding.[66]

Many soldiers went to the Y-hut because it was a place where they could meet without white supervision and discuss issues of common concern with other African Americans. During so-called chat hours, the men got together to talk about "current topics—apart from the war or army." Addie W. Hunton recalled that the men who gathered at the Y-hut had "talks on race leaders, on work after the war—music, art, religion, and every conceivable subject." They discussed educational and economic opportunities as well as the importance of cooperation in order to improve living conditions for African Americans following the war.[67]

Particularly in France, the Y-hut represented a home away from home. Ruby M. English, who served with the AEF in St. Nazaire, had fond memories of the gatherings at the Y-hut. After the war he thanked Addie W. Hunton in a letter for "those wonderful days . . . when you would have the boys at the hut, in 'your own room' as you called it, for a heart-to-heart talk that kept our heart warm with memories of our own firesides and mothers."[68]

The Y-hut also provided a point of contact for African Americans from diverse socioeconomic and geographic backgrounds. Educated and self-conscious men from Howard, Morehouse, Tuskegee, and Hampton encountered inexperienced and often illiterate African Americans from the rural South. The differences between the men did not divide them but stimulated them to cooperate. Often, better-educated African Americans taught fellow soldiers how to read and write, read to them, and helped them write letters home.[69]

Like the YMCAs in American cities, the Y-huts in the military camps were community centers and safe havens for African-American men. The Y-hut offered the men an escape from the daily military routine as well as the racial abuses of white officers and soldiers. For a few hours in the evening the Y-hut provided the men with a place where they could gather freely in a relaxed atmosphere without the presence of whites. At the Y-hut African Americans could be men regardless of their military rank and despite their skin color.

7

Interracial Dialogue and Cooperation in the 1920s

ASSOCIATION work for African Americans remained segregated throughout World War I, but the YMCA's national leadership began to encourage interracial dialogue and cooperation immediately following the Armistice. In the postwar decade the YMCA's interest in interracial work led to the creation of numerous interracial committees in the South and the appointment of several African Americans to previously all-white local and state committees in the North.

Although white YMCA officials increasingly sought dialogue with their black colleagues, they rarely challenged the association's jim crow policy. Similar to the abolitionists of the early nineteenth century who tried to reform slavery out of existence, those who were active in the YMCA's interracial movement of the 1920s tried to reform segregation. They hoped to improve segregation by making "separate but equal" truly equal.

African Americans welcomed the opportunity for interracial dialogue, but as long as the YMCA denied them equality, they were determined to maintain separate associations. Reluctant to give up their autonomy, African-American YMCA officials insisted on their right "for self-expression and self-determination."[1] Despite their persistence in maintaining separate associations, African Americans condemned segregation in the YMCA, explaining that they accepted "this limited Christian Association merely as the best temporary policy, as a sort of modus vivendi, looking to a more perfect day and accord."[2]

The YMCA's postwar interest in interracial dialogue and cooperation was the result of several factors. The Social Gospel and Progressive reform movements of the early twentieth century in part inspired the YMCA's changing racial policy. Many association leaders were concerned about the effects of urbanization, industrialization, and immigration on American society. Following the war they reexamined the association's mission and assumed a more active role in public affairs.

In 1919 at the YMCA's first postwar convention, the delegates adopted the "Social Ideals of the Churches." The document consisted of fifteen articles outlining the association's interest in social justice, including the fairer distribution of wealth, the right to bargain collectively, the abolition of child labor, the reduction of working hours, and the rights of free speech. In article 13 the YMCA also acknowledged its responsibility to work for "justice, opportunity, and equal rights for all; mutual good will and co-operation among racial, economic, and religious groups."[3] This new commitment to social justice helped pave the way for increased interracial dialogue and cooperation.

More important, though, the YMCA's interest in interracial work was sparked by fears of racial unrest. Many whites were afraid that the returning African-American soldiers were no longer willing to accept second-class citizenship. They feared that the demobilization of the troops "would precipitate ill feeling and possible rioting."[4] As one report stated, the country "was seething with interracial distrust and hostility. . . . White people were obsessed with fear of what the returning Negro soldiers might do or demand, as a result of their training in arms and their experience abroad."[5]

Many African Americans returned from their military service with heightened expectations. They had "closed ranks" in the hope of receiving civil rights in the postwar United States. Instead they were greeted by race riots, a powerful new Ku Klux Klan, and a growing number of lynchings. W.E.B. Du Bois captured the mood of African-American servicemen when he proclaimed: "We return from fighting. We return fighting. Make way for Democracy! We saved it in France, and by the Great Jehovah, we will save it in the United States of America."[6]

Some African-American veterans vocally expressed their discontent with segregation and discrimination. Captain Wormley Jones, who had served in France, told an African-American audience at the Twelfth Street YMCA in Washington, D.C., that he was no longer willing to accept jim crowism. He proclaimed that after "fighting and suffering for democracy abroad . . . when I am insulted and my rights denied . . . I am ready to declare war any minute." Jones was apparently well prepared. He explained that he had "brought back a German machine gun" that he kept at "home with plenty of ammunition. I also have an Austrian high powered rifle and the best automatic revolver made."[7]

White YMCA officials responded swiftly to the threats of racial unrest. In 1919 they created the Commission on Interracial Cooperation to check the "fires of antagonism." The commission was the brainchild of Willis Duke Weatherford, a white international secretary from Nashville.[8] Weatherford had taken an interest in race relations after witnessing the "lawless barbarism" of the Atlanta race riot of 1906.[9]

In 1907 Weatherford established a summer training school for white YMCA secretaries at Blue Ridge, North Carolina. He included in the school's curriculum a course in race relations, hoping to increase the awareness of white association secretaries. In April 1908 Weatherford met with a group of whites and African Americans, among them William A. Hunton, Jesse E. Moorland, and John Hope, to discuss the preparation of a textbook for his course. The group supported the idea, and in 1910 Weatherford published *Negro Life in the South* for use in white YMCA training schools.[10]

Many white colleges and universities in the South also adopted the book and started to offer courses "devoted to a study of race relations." Moorland had some reservations about the manuscript, largely because Weatherford "whipped the book in shape" without consulting African Americans. Nevertheless, he had "no doubt" that it "had a considerable effect in creating at least a human interest in the colored people." Moorland did not anticipate an immediate improvement of race relations in response to the publication, but he predicted that "sowing the seed is one thing and the harvest is true to follow from the seed."[11]

Although Weatherford's book and his work at Blue Ridge paved the way for greater white interest in African Americans, it did not result in interracial cooperation. The YMCA training school Weatherford operated at Blue Ridge did not admit African Americans, and only after World War I did the school begin to invite African-American speakers. Those who addressed white secretaries at Blue Ridge included George Washington Carver, James Weldon Johnson, Robert R. Moton, Mordecai W. Johnson, Monroe Work, Bishop Robert E. Jones, and Mary McLeod Bethune.[12]

When the Armistice was announced on November 11, 1918, Weatherford was at Blue Ridge, conducting a training session for white YMCA secretaries. Within two hours he drafted a plan to prepare "the people in the South for receiving back the soldiers, particularly the Colored soldier." Weatherford's plan called for the creation of a school that would bring together leading white and black men "for frank conference and for cooperating in overcoming race prejudice, eliminating racial discrimination, and building better racial understanding." In December 1918 Weatherford presented his idea to the

YMCA's War Work Council, which appropriated seventy-five thousand dollars for the project.[13]

Weatherford then informed the black international secretaries of his plans. They supported the idea but inquired whether African Americans and whites would attend the same classes. Weatherford explained that "it would not be possible to have white men and colored men sit together in classes." The secretaries were outraged and opposed Weatherford's proposal. Although African Americans had operated separate associations for more than six decades, the secretaries insisted that they "would not submit to segregation in classes."[14]

Jim crowism had forced African Americans to establish separate YMCAs. Those associations were safe havens for African-American men, shielding them from racial humiliation and helping them to preserve their dignity. Weatherford's plan, on the other hand, asked African Americans to sacrifice their self-respect and to attend school with whites but sit in segregated classrooms, eat in segregated dining halls, and sleep in segregated dormitories. African Americans were not willing to expose themselves to such a humiliating experience in the name of interracial cooperation. As one black man pointed out: "My geometry teaches me that two parallel lines never meet. If the arrangements at Blue Ridge are to be constructed along parallel lines what hope is there for getting together?"[15] Weatherford, however, was not willing to admit African Americans to Blue Ridge on an equal basis. Unable to reach an agreement, the men parted, and Weatherford continued to pursue the project without further consulting his African-American colleagues in the YMCA.

In January 1919 Weatherford discussed his plan with a group of white YMCA officials and ministers in Atlanta. The group eventually came to be known as the Commission on Interracial Cooperation. Although black YMCA secretaries had provided Weatherford with a list of interested black ministers, the commission invited no African Americans to attend the meetings. Furthermore, the black international secretaries learned that Weatherford had started the construction of separate sleeping quarters at Blue Ridge and was installing a partition "through the dining room . . . to separate the races."[16]

The black secretaries were outraged and called a meeting with the leading African-American ministers of Atlanta to discuss Weatherford's plan. The ministers vehemently opposed the proposed segregation, insisting that "they could not go to Blue Ridge except on terms that would allow them to keep their self-respect." They demanded that Blue Ridge either admit all men on equal terms or that the Commission on Interracial Cooperation establish a school exclusively for African Americans. Whites initially opposed the operation of two separate schools, claiming that it would be too expensive. The ministers, however, insisted that "we do have to keep our self-respect. We are not willing to concede that we are so contaminating as to need a fence between us and our white brethren." Weatherford did not yield to the first demand, and in mid-February 1919 the commission opened a school for African Americans at Gammon Theological Seminary in Atlanta.[17]

W.A. Bell, a black secretary who had conducted YMCA work for African-American soldiers at Camp Jackson, South Carolina, became the school's director, and Will W. Alexander, a white member of the YMCA's War Work Council, served as its administrative official. By the spring of 1919, 509 African Americans had attended the eight-day training sessions at Gammon, and 902 whites had attended the sessions at Blue Ridge. African-American and white speakers addressed those enrolled in both schools, although the schools for interracial cooperation remained segregated.[18]

African-American YMCA leaders welcomed the opening of the separate school at Gammon but expressed their disappointment "that Christian leaders of the two races cannot have a common ground of assembly" because "whites of the South are not yet ready for such an assembly on terms that colored men can accept." Although white southerners displayed a less than wholehearted commitment to interracial cooperation, joining the commission was a daring step for many. Ku Klux Klan chapters repeatedly threatened white members of the commission with "anonymous letters, mysterious telephone calls, and other threats of personal violence."[19]

Despite the commission's acceptance of jim crowism, its work helped pave the way for increased interracial dialogue and cooperation in the postwar years. The commission frequently presented complimentary copies of books on race relations to students "in theological seminaries in America," and it convinced many colleges in the South to offer courses on the subject. The efforts of state committees often resulted in the establishment of "libraries, rest rooms, parks, playgrounds, pools, day nurseries [and] social centers" for African Americans. Moreover, the commission "waged vigorous warfare against lynching," peonage, and chain-gang brutalities, and it worked to improve the image of African-Americans in white newspapers.[20]

During the 1920s the commission established interracial committees in all southern states. These committees provided African Americans and liberal white southerners with a platform to discuss race relations and the opportunity to deal with "threats of interracial friction at their very inception." Moorland claimed that the work of the interracial committees had "actually changed the attitude from one of hostility to respectful consideration in more than one place." Most important, as Gunnar Myrdal pointed out, the activities of the Commission on Interracial Cooperation "rendered interracial work socially respectable in the conservative South."[21]

The YMCA's International Committee provided most of the funds of the Commission on Interracial Cooperation until 1922. That year the Phelps-Stokes Fund, the Carnegie Corporation, John D. Rockefeller, Jr., and the Laura Spelman Rockefeller Memorial became major contributors. The YMCA, however, continued to contribute to the commission's budget until 1930, and association members as well as secretaries remained active on many local and state committees in the South.[22]

The YMCA's postwar interest in interracial dialogue and cooperation was not limited to the South. After World War I white association officials in the North appointed African Americans to previously all-white local and state committees. White northerners like white southerners, were concerned about racial disturbances. Following the demobilization of the United States Army, race riots erupted in many urban centers of the North, where large numbers of African Americans had settled during the Great Migration. The influx of the African-American soldiers exacerbated housing shortages and job competition. The increased racial tensions culminated in the Red Summer of 1919. To avert racial unrest, white association leaders in the North sought dialogue with their African-American colleagues.

In October 1919 the Cincinnati YMCA, in a pathbreaking move, elected W.T. Nelson, a prominent African-American physician and chairman of the city's black association, to the Metropolitan Board of Directors. One southern-born member of the board resigned in protest, but the others supported Nelson's election. The Cincinnati YMCA was the first to elect an African American to serve on a metropolitan board, but soon other cities and states in the North and West followed suit.[23] By 1925 African Americans served on the metropolitan boards of directors in Flint and Detroit, Michigan, and on state committees in Indiana, Ohio, Pennsylvania, Kansas, Michigan, and Colorado.[24]

The appointment of African Americans to previously all-white committees was a sign of progress, although interracial dialogue and cooperation in the North remained limited to official business meetings and had little impact on the membership or activities of local associations. Alfred G. Bookwalter, secretary of Cincinnati's white

YMCA, admitted that despite Nelson's appointment the white secretaries did not invite him or his wife "to social functions," explaining that "several of our secretaries have Southern wives who would be offended."[25]

Although many white YMCA officials began to take an interest in interracial dialogue and cooperation in the postwar years, their commitment to interracial work had its limits. Whites in the YMCA were willing to talk about improving race relations but they were not willing to challenge the association's jim crow policy. Although they professed an interest in interracial cooperation, they often acquiesced in racial discrimination. In 1922, for example, when the African-American delegates to the international convention arrived in Atlantic City, New Jersey, the convention hotels refused to serve them, and they were forced "to lodge in the 'black belt' of the city." Only the white student delegates, "led by a southern member of the staff," protested and "decided that if their Negro colleagues could not be entertained with them, they would take accommodation with their Negro colleagues in a Negro hotel." The convention as a whole did not address the issue. Following the incident, however, local program committees responsible for arranging subsequent international conventions were instructed to make "careful investigation of the readiness of hotels to treat both whites and Negroes on a basis of equality."[26]

While the international convention organizers made at least some effort to secure hotels and restaurants that offered equal services to black and white delegates, other YMCA committees were less considerate. In 1923, when the YMCA Executive Committee made plans to meet in Washington, D.C., the attendance of Robert R. Moton, principal of Tuskegee Institute, caused considerable problems. William Knowles Cooper, secretary of Washington's white association, who arranged the meeting, informed John R. Mott, the YMCA's highest-ranking secretary, that Moton would be "entirely welcome to attend the sessions of the conference." He explained, however, that it would be "impossible to arrange to accommodate him . . . unless in a private dining room. . . . we shall have to use a part of the main dining room screened off from the other diners."[27]

Instead of moving the meeting to a different location, Cooper suggested that Moton stay with personal friends during the conference. Moton, usually known for his willingness to accommodate, declined to attend the meeting. He explained that "for the sake of the work in which we are engaged . . . I have in the past accommodated myself to the inconvenience. . . . But . . . I am moved to the conclusion that the persistence of such a situation can no longer be supported without compromising the Christian principles of all of us who may be a party to it." W.E.B. Du Bois published the entire correspondence between Moton and the various YMCA committees "without Dr. Moton's knowledge or consent" in the *Crisis*, applauding Moton's decision and congratulating him on "his new-found manhood."[28] Despite the postwar talk of interracial dialogue and cooperation, humiliating incidents like these illustrated that white association leaders were not willing to put an end to discrimination and segregation.

As long as the YMCA failed to challenge jim crowism, African Americans cautiously guarded their autonomy. The African-American delegates who attended the YMCA's first postwar convention in 1919 adopted several resolutions designed to strengthen their autonomy in the YMCA. They insisted that black secretaries maintain control of association work for African Americans and that black men continue to direct and supervise the recruitment and training of African-American YMCA secretaries. Moreover, they demanded an increase in the black secretarial force on the International Committee and the appointment of African-American representatives to all committees devoted to the improvement of race relations.[29]

Responding to the resolutions, the international convention appointed a Commission on Colored Work to study "the field, work, supervision and special problems of the Young Men's Christian Association in its work for colored young men and boys." The commission, composed of African Americans and whites, met on March 3, 1920. During the initial meeting, a group of white southerners issued an unprecedented call for the unification of black and white YMCA work. They suggested "that the service of the International Committee both to the white and negro races should be a unified work. . . . A separate approach to race problems serves only to intensify racial differences." The African-American representatives responded to this suggestion with skepticism. Bishop Robert E. Jones, editor of the *Southwestern Christian Advocate*, expressed his fears that such unification would subject African Americans to white supervision and deprive them of leadership positions in the YMCA.[30] Moreover, he emphasized that the prerequisite for interracial cooperation "is confidence of the Southern white men in the leaders of the Colored Work."[31]

The commission eventually tried to find a balance between interracial cooperation and continued black supervision of YMCA work for African Americans. Alexander L. Jackson, secretary of Chicago's Wabash Avenue YMCA, suggested that the commission pass a resolution endorsing interracial work and encouraging local associations to "provide a point of contact for colored and white leaders for working out common problems." Meanwhile, the commission also recommended more assistance to black associations, an increase in the African-American secretarial force on the International Committee, a "nation-wide plan to provide funds essential to develop work among colored men and boys . . . according to *need* rather than according to *local ability to give*," and African-American representation on all "bodies dealing largely with affairs which directly involve the interests of the colored people."[32] Although the commission's report recommended the enhancement of segregated YMCA services, it represented a victory for the African-American delegates who had hoped to maintain and strengthen their autonomy.

African Americans were further concerned about losing their leadership positions to white supervision when a movement to restructure the American YMCA emerged in the postwar years. Inspired by wartime rhetoric, many association secretaries and laymen demanded a more democratic organization of the YMCA and insisted upon absolute local and state autonomy. Other association leaders, however, believed that the tremendous growth of the YMCA in the early twentieth century called for increased centralization and national supervision.[33]

African-American association leaders feared that the controversy would result in a reorganization of the American YMCA and possibly deprive them of their autonomy. Moorland, who had become senior African-American international secretary after Hunton's death in 1916, insisted that "the integrity of our own department must be rigidly maintained if we are to serve the colored group in the most effective way." Similarly, the national convention of African-American associations demanded "that the branches for Colored men be always represented by members of their own race."[34]

The postwar movement to reorganize the YMCA led to the adoption of a new constitution in 1923. Association representatives decided to curtail the power of professional secretaries and increase the influence of YMCA volunteers. The new constitution abolished the International Committee, which had been composed entirely of professional YMCA secretaries, and replaced it with a National Council made up of secretaries as well as association laymen. The National Council served as a general policy-making body but did not have "legislative authority over local Associations." The restructured YMCA continued the association's long-standing jim crow tradition and created a Colored Work Department within the National Council. The former African-American international secretaries became the staff of the Colored Work Department, and an interracial group of laymen, under the chairmanship of Robert R. Moton, served as an advisory committee.[35]

The newly organized Colored Work Department was placed under the leadership of Channing H. Tobias, who became senior African-American secretary after Moorland's retirement in 1923. Born in Augusta, Georgia, on February 1, 1882, Tobias received a bachelor of arts from Paine Institute in 1902 and a bachelor of divinity from Drew University in 1905. Tobias then taught biblical literature at Paine College until he joined the YMCA's International Committee in 1911.[36]

Tobias continued the policy of his predecessors. He applauded the increasing interracial dialogue as an important step toward the development of "a growing number of personal friendships across race lines." Without the prospect of true equality, however, Tobias believed that African Americans needed to maintain control of their own associations. Only separate associations, he argued, offered African Americans the opportunity to "develop leadership in a way and to an extent that would never be possible . . . in branches made up largely of white people." Tobias insisted that "however willing white men may be to serve colored associations, in the last analysis the real work for years to come must be done by colored men."[37]

Despite his support of separate associations, Tobias was "unalterably opposed to segregation" and not inclined to accept jim crowism quietly. When Howard A. Kester, a white YMCA leader among southern students, urged an African-American audience to be patient in the struggle for equality, Tobias countered: "The young man speaks of patience. What does he think we have been practicing but patience for over 300 years."[38]

Tobias's refusal to accommodate reflected the discontent of a growing number of African Americans who were critical of the YMCA's racial policy and the continued absence of real interracial cooperation. Addie W. Hunton, who had assisted her husband's efforts to centralize black associations during the 1890s and who had served as a secretary in France during World War I, turned her back on the YMCA and joined the NAACP as a regional officer. African-American association leaders often stood in the way of progress, she charged, because they "represent the most conservative element of our people." Alexander L. Jackson, secretary of Chicago's black YMCA, noted that African Americans "have been lukewarm in many communities to the Association program because of the narrow-minded attitude shown by many local Associations. In some places this attitude has been decidedly hostile." In Detroit, for example, the leading African-American citizens "protested vigorously" against the establishment of a black association, "on the ground that it was segregation."[39]

Moreover, Jackson pointed out that the YMCA's jim crow policy was beginning to have a detrimental effect on the recruitment of African-American secretaries. He explained that "young well trained colored men have been unwilling to give their lives to an organization that seemed unwilling to take a positive position on questions affecting their people." Jackson also observed that many of the black secretaries were frustrated and were starting to leave the YMCA for more attractive employment opportunities. Jackson himself resigned from his post to become educational secretary of the National Urban League, explaining that he wanted to devote his "time and energy to the problem of racial relationships in a larger way than my present work permits."[40]

By the mid-1920s many African Americans had become increasingly impatient with the YMCA's racial policy. In 1925, when the representatives of the black associations gathered for a national convention in Washington, D.C., they noted that the exclusion of African Americans from white YMCAs had become "a factor making increasingly difficult the task of building an Association constituency and maintaining the loyalty of educated colored men."[41]

African-American students particularly challenged the YMCA to live up to its ideal of Christian brotherhood. Colleges and universities had been the recruiting ground for African-American YMCA secretaries since the 1870s. By 1925 approximately twelve thousand students had joined college associations, making the YMCA "the largest intercollegiate organization" among African-American students. When whites in the YMCA started to display an interest in interracial dialogue following World War I, African-American students responded with enthusiasm.[42] They were more daring than the older members of the Colored Work Department. Instead of talking about improving race relations, the black students tried to merge their work with that of white students.

A group of liberal white students from the South supported their efforts. The progressive attitude of these white students in part resulted from their exposure to the Social Gospel "years before the parent Y.M.C.A.'s became aware of it." The publication of Weatherford's *Negro Life in the South* and the subsequent introduction of courses on race relations also stimulated some of the white students to take an interest in the topic. World War I and the wartime rhetoric of democracy further increased the white students' growing awareness of racial inequalities and discrimination.[43]

Not all white students favored closer cooperation with black college associations, although many displayed considerable interest in racial issues. In 1923 black and white student delegates of the YMCA, the YWCA, and the Student Volunteer Movement, an organization promoting missionary work, gathered for a national conference to discuss "contemporary economic, social, and political problems." During the three-day meeting in Indianapolis, the students attended forty-four discussion groups focusing on race relations. The delegates agreed "that racial discrimination and prejudice were unchristian, and that the Negro should have equal opportunity for education, life, and justice."[44]

Although those attending the meeting voiced their opposition to discrimination, only a few white students dared to challenge racial barriers in the YMCA. Those who did protest segregation targeted in particular the YMCA training school at Blue Ridge, North Carolina. White students from colleges in the Southeast used the facilities at Blue Ridge for their annual summer conference. The school's jim crow policy, however, forced African-American students from the same region to gather at nearby Kings Mountain. Howard A. Kester, who had earlier received a "spiritual spanking" from Tobias, was among the white students who agitated for the integration of Blue Ridge and Kings Mountain. Weatherford, who had founded Blue Ridge, rejected the proposal, although Kester convinced him to permit the exchange of student delegates.[45]

Beginning in 1926 white student delegates visited Kings Mountain, and African-American representatives came to Blue Ridge. The Kings Mountain conference received the white students on a basis of equality, but African Americans visiting Blue Ridge were "segregated and humiliated." In the summer of 1928 the African-American students at Kings Mountain refused to send their delegates to Blue Ridge. Frank T. Wilson and Benjamin E. Mays, Colored Work Department secretaries in charge of African-American students, informed the officials at Blue Ridge that they would not send delegates until African Americans could be received "without limitations." The white association leaders at Blue Ridge insisted upon segregation, and the exchange of student delegates stopped.[46]

Despite discrimination and segregation, many African-American students were willing to leave the Colored Work Department to form an administrative union with white students. In 1927 the National Council had established a separate Student Division in response to student demand. African-American students believed that their interests would be better served if they left the Colored Work Department and joined the Student Division. The African-American college associations in New Jersey, Delaware, Maryland, West Virginia, North Carolina, Georgia, and the District of Columbia passed resolutions in favor of joining the Student Division.[47] They argued that as students they had more in common with white students than with African-American "citizens in general." Moreover, they hoped that the "placing of Negro students within the Student Division would make for a psychological effect that would be most helpful at the present time." African-American students also pointed out that they would be able to share the budget of the Student Division, which meant access to more financial resources.[48]

The Colored Work Department did not share the enthusiasm of the African-American students. The members of the Colored Work Department feared that the students' joining of the Student Division would result in the dismantling of African-American supervision of black YMCA work. The secretaries in charge of college associations would be transferred from the Colored Work Department to the Student Division, reducing the staff from eight to five men. Moreover, the Colored Work Department would lose control over the recruitment of African-American secretaries. Campbell C. Johnson, secretary of Washington's Twelfth Street YMCA, warned that the result would be "the abolishment of the Colored Work Department as such and the transfer of the men in to the particular department in which, because of the nature of their work, they logically fit."[49]

The members of the Colored Work Department were caught in a dilemma. They did not want "to insist upon the recognition of a race line at any point where it is possible to dispense with it." They were, however, also trying to "prevent the termination of the supervision of the Colored Work by colored men."[50] The Colored Work Department decided to preserve the autonomy of African-American associations and opposed the transfer of the students to the Student Division.

Some of the student representatives were troubled by the decision. J.T. Taylor from North Carolina, for example, insisted that he could not go back "and tell the students we want segregation."[51] The members of the Colored Work Department explained that they rejected the students' proposal not merely for the sake of maintaining racial autonomy but also because they were concerned that the African-American students would not receive equal treatment in the Student Division. The basis of their philosophy, they claimed, was best described by Mordecai W. Johnson, president of Howard University and former YMCA secretary, who said that "Negroes must do a contradictory thing; they must work with all their might against segregation, and at the same time strengthen their so-called segregated institutions as if they expected them to last forever. They must insist that the doors of Harvard and Yale be kept open to Negroes and at the same time build up Howard and Lincoln as if there was no Harvard and Yale." Only the financial crisis caused by the Great Depression forced the Colored Work Department to yield to the demand of the students in 1933.[52]

Throughout the 1920s African Americans welcomed the increased opportunity for interracial work. As long as whites made no attempt to end jim crowism, however, they were not willing to give up their supervision of African-American YMCA activities. Instead, black association leaders focused their energy on maintaining and strengthening their autonomy, and they did so successfully. With the financial help of white philanthropists and the support of African-American communities, thirty-six associations owned YMCA buildings at the end of the decade. Membership rose from almost twenty-six thousand in 1920 to nearly thirty-four thousand by 1930, and the number of secretaries employed by African-American YMCAs reached an unprecedented high of 132 in 1925 (see appendixes). When the stock market crash brought an end to the decade's prosperity, African-American association leaders were fighting for their economic survival as well as their racial autonomy.

8

From Depression to Desegregation, 1929-1946

THE 1930s were years of extreme hardship for African-American YMCAs. After the stock market crash, the country plunged into the longest and most severe depression in its history. African Americans, already at the bottom of the economic ladder, were particularly hard hit, since they were usually "the last hired and the first fired."[1] By 1933 most African Americans "could neither find jobs of any kind nor contracts for their crop at any price."[2]

As unemployment skyrocketed, fewer African Americans were capable of paying their YMCA membership fees, and even fewer could afford to contribute to association fund-raisers. Donations from white philanthropists also declined, reducing the budgets of many African-American associations so drastically that their existences were threatened.[3]

Budget reductions were only part of the problem. While African-American YMCAs were struggling to survive the economic crisis, an ever-growing number of unemployed men flocked to the associations. Ralph W. Bullock, a secretary of the Colored Work Department, observed: "Here we are called upon for new and added service with depleted budgets and reduced staffs." Despite budget cuts, African-American association leaders were determined to serve their growing constituency. The depression, they argued, made their work "even more essential," because "forced idleness" demoralized men. The managers of the Christian Street YMCA in Philadelphia, for example, claimed that high unemployment had contributed to a growing crime rate.[4]

African-American YMCA leaders were not only concerned about the alleged increase in crime. They feared that prolonged periods of unemployment would make African Americans more susceptible to communism or fascism. Channing H. Tobias, senior secretary of the Colored Work Department, claimed that YMCA work was an important factor "in safeguarding Negro Youth from subversive radical influences." Leading white YMCA representatives were similarly concerned that the economic crisis would make "anti-religious forces" more appealing to young African Americans. Francis A. Harmon, general secretary of the YMCA, warned that the reduction of African-American association work would increase the "influence of Communism," especially among the educated elite.[5]

The sincerity of white association leaders who professed an interest in maintaining YMCA services for African Americans was called into question when the National Council was forced to reduce its staff in response to the depression.[6] Between 1929 and 1932 the National Council lost less than 10 percent of its total personnel, whereas the staff of the Colored Work Department was cut by 50 percent.[7] Eventually the Colored Work Department was reduced to three secretaries: Channing H. Tobias, Robert B. DeFrantz and Ralph W. Bullock were in charge of all African-American association work throughout the depression and World War II.[8]

When the economic crisis forced the National Council to cut expenditures, African-American association leaders reconsidered the students' request to leave the Colored Work Department in order to join the Student Division. Members of the Colored Work Department had previously opposed the transfer, fearing that the Student Division would not grant the African-American students fair representation and that the move would undermine racial autonomy. The financial crisis, however, did not give them many options but to consider the students' proposal.

The members of the Colored Work Department nevertheless insisted on some form of assurance that the Student Division would "agree immediately to take Negro Student Work into that division on a parity with all other phases of its work." The African-American students were growing impatient and criticized the Colored Work Department for aggravating "a situation already needlessly bad."[9] In 1932 a black student leader warned that "unless something extraordinary is done . . . not a single Colored student secretary will be left on the National Council staff."[10] In the following year the National Council of Student Christian Associations adopted a resolution incorporating the demands of African-American YMCA leaders and assuring them that the council would "respond to requests that may be voiced by the Colored Work Department."[11] In 1934 black and white student associations merged their work and their budgets.

The depression also brought about changes in local African-American associations. As a result of budget, salary, and staff reductions, many YMCAs were "fighting for their lives." During the first three years of the depression, more than 75 percent of the African-

American associations reported average budget reductions of 21 percent. Despite these cuts, however, only one or two YMCAs ceased to operate. Most associations managed to survive by cutting expenditures and using larger numbers of volunteers. Nearly all associations reduced their secretarial and janitorial force, as well as salaries. Approximately half of the African-American associations dismissed at least two secretaries. The Michigan Avenue YMCA in Buffalo, New York, for example, replaced its physical education directors with part-time employees and started to rely more heavily on "experienced volunteer assistance."[12] Those secretaries who kept their jobs had to submit to steep salary cuts, and the Colored Work Department also asked them to make designated "salary contributions."[13]

African-American associations, despite their financial problems, tried to provide a variety of free services for those without work. YMCA leaders distributed food and clothing to needy families, and associations offered employment counseling and educational and vocational training courses, as well as "socials and entertainment programs for the purpose of building up the morale." By 1932 more than 92 percent of the African-American associations had established employment services, 46 percent gave away food and clothing, nearly 77 percent provided temporary lodging, and approximately 65 percent offered free memberships to those unable to pay their dues. The Senate Avenue YMCA in Indianapolis, for example, provided 4,827 nights of free lodging and more than 3,200 free meals to needy men and boys between January and October 1931. The association also offered "free medical services to 2,000" African Americans and distributed "clothing to over 400 needy men."[14] In addition, several associations even arranged for "loans to tide people over a particular period of financial embarrassment."[15]

Some of the free services, such as the use of dormitory, reading, and game rooms and the use of athletic equipment, did not entail any unusual expenses for the associations. The free use of these facilities, however, further decreased the income of African-American YMCAs. Nearly 80 percent of the operating budget of the black associations came from "sales and revenue bearing facilities." The rental of dormitory rooms was the single largest source of income, representing 34 percent of the annual budget. More than 26 percent was generated through cafeteria sales.[16]

Other association services to the unemployed were financed by local charities or community relief agencies cooperating with the YMCA. Nevertheless, most associations incurred debts, and many were looking for new ways of raising funds. Some YMCA leaders considered the introduction of dances and pool tables as a potential source of income, although not all association members supported the idea. An older generation of association men claimed that dancing and billiards were unwholesome forms of recreation and entertainment. A.Q. Martin, for example, a successful Brooklyn undertaker, resigned from the Committee of Management of the Carlton Avenue YMCA because of his opposition to "dancing in the building."[17] His protest, however, found little support. During the 1930s supervised dances and billiards became popular features of many associations, including the Carlton Avenue YMCA. A 1938 pamphlet distributed by the Harlem YMCA proclaimed that billiards was "a man's game under ideal conditions."[18]

As the depression wore on and YMCA budgets continued to decrease, African-American association leaders began to be less generous with their free services to the unemployed. In 1938 one of the secretaries of the Colored Work Department reviewed the financial situation of the Butler Street YMCA in Atlanta. He advised the Committee of Management to "show a sympathetic attitude toward 'hard-pressed' occupants" of the dormitory, but he reminded them that a "person who is two weeks behind with his rent and who does not show very good prospects of paying should be asked to vacate the room."[19]

Despite their financial troubles, African-American associations were capable of maintaining most of their services with the help of the federal government. Several of the New Deal agencies, particularly the Works Progress Administration and the National Youth Administration, worked in close cooperation with African-American YMCAs. Local associations helped to disseminate information about the availability of federal assistance for African Americans and provided space for government-funded programs such as educational classes, recreational activities, health clinics, and work projects. Moreover, the WPA and the NYA assigned several hundred workers to African-American associations to assist in their daily operation. By 1938 eight hundred WPA and NYA workers had been assigned to assist thirty-eight African-American associations.[20] The Harlem YMCA alone had fifty-five NYA workers who served the association's 2,500 daily visitors.[21]

The duties of the NYA and WPA assistants varied, depending on the skills of each individual and the needs of the associations. Most NYA and WPA employees worked as typists, porters, stenographers, receptionists, sewing and cafeteria assistants, mimeograph and switchboard operators, messengers, file clerks, and physical education instructors.[22] Some set up work projects to create employment opportunities for African-American youths. They established workshops for toy and furniture repair, organized sewing and book-binding projects, and employed artists to design maps, signs, posters, programs, and schedules at the YMCAs.[23] Other New Deal workers prepared health exhibits on venereal disease and tuberculosis, gave instruction in first aid, and set up X-ray machines in the YMCAs.[24]

Many of the WPA workers were engaged in educational programs at the YMCAs. At the Senate Avenue YMCA in Indianapolis, for example, the WPA offered free classes in basic subjects as well as shorthand, business arithmetic, consumer economics, typing, and electronics. At the Harlem YMCA, the WPA established vocational and academic classes, including drama, machine drawing, African history, Spanish, radio operation, shorthand, and photography. The WPA classes provided African Americans with a broad spectrum of educational opportunities, and the government-funded programs created employment for many African-American teachers.[25]

Other NYA and WPA workers were busy repairing YMCA buildings and equipment. Some government workers painted the building and planted trees on the grounds of the Hunton YMCA in Camden, New Jersey, and others helped to renovate the Butler Street YMCA in Atlanta.[26] In Trenton, New Jersey, a group of NYA workers built a playground, basketball and volleyball courts, and an outdoor fireplace for the African-American association. At the Paseo Street YMCA in Kansas City, Missouri, an NYA unit constructed a tennis court and recreation center, and in Pontiac, Michigan, NYA workers remodeled an old school building and turned it into the Negro Southwestern Civic YMCA.[27]

African-American association leaders welcomed the support of the federal government.[28] They were aware that the work of the New Deal agencies not only contributed to the survival of African-American associations but also helped them to preserve their autonomy. African Americans continued to insist on separate associations as long as whites denied them complete equality. After more than a decade of interracial dialogue and cooperation, the YMCA had made little progress toward improving race relations or lowering racial barriers in the association. In 1934 the National Council admitted that interracial work was "limited largely to discussion and the exchange of ideas, possibly bearing fruit in greater tolerance." It found "little evidence of an attempt at practical application."[29]

During the depression, race relations further deteriorated when job competition between African Americans and whites increased and racial tensions and violence intensified.[30] This also left its mark on the YMCA. In the summer of 1930 Dr. Errold D. Collymore and Dr.

Arthur M. Williams, members of the Committee of Management of the African-American YMCA in White Plains, New York, purchased homes in a white residential neighborhood. A white "mob" tried to dislodge the two African-American physicians and burned a "huge cross in Dr. Collymore's yard." Local police provided "prompt and efficient" protection and prevented further escalations of violence. White residents, however, continued to harass Collymore and Williams, and white business owners threatened to dismiss their black employees. Despite the threats, the two men did not surrender. Collymore explained that he could not "move without being disloyal to the best interests of his wife, his race and himself."[31]

Unable to remove the men from their homes, the white residents turned to the city's white YMCA and "demanded that the two doctors be dropped from their positions on the Committee of Management." The protesters also requested the dismissal of Samuel R. Morsell, secretary of the African-American YMCA. Morsell, they charged, knew of the two men's intention to move into a white neighborhood and failed to prevent it. Moreover, they claimed that Morsell had "embarrassed the Y.M.C.A. by lodging at Dr. Collymore's house."[32] The Board of Directors of the white association did not support Williams, Collymore, and Morsell. Instead the board members were considering ways to remove the three African-American YMCA leaders from their positions, particularly after whites threatened to withhold donations from the city's white association.

The White Plains incident had considerable repercussions throughout the American YMCA. Many white secretaries criticized the YMCA in White Plains for its failure to denounce the violence and threats directed at Collymore and Williams, charging that such behavior encouraged "the lawless element in the city to go still further in support of their determination to 'keep the Negro in his place.'"[33] In response to the controversy, the National Council, for the first time in its history, passed a resolution condemning lynchings and urging white associations to "stand in unmistakable opposition to threats of force or the use of force as a means of dealing with acute racial situations . . . [and] to protect the right of individuals." Implementation of the resolutions, however, depended on the willingness of individual YMCAs, since the National Council did not exercise authority over local associations.[34]

African-American association leaders were outraged about what had happened in White Plains. They condemned the acquiescence of the city's white association, and William B. West, dean of men of Howard University, suggested "a showdown in all interracial groups pretending Christianity." Channing H. Tobias, however, although he had almost become the victim of a lynch mob while conducting YMCA business in Georgia during World War I, was careful to avoid a direct confrontation. He insisted that as long as African Americans exercised control over their associations, they should try to effect "a change from within" and "bring about changes of policy in local situations as rapidly as those responsible for the conduct of the Associations may embrace."[35]

Tobias, like so many of the African-American association leaders, pursued an accommodationist and gradualist approach, but he was not submissive. Tobias frequently challenged the American YMCA to end its jim crow policy. In 1926, for example, he appealed to the World's Conference of YMCAs in Helsinki, Finland. Addressing the large gathering of international YMCA delegates, Tobias exposed racism in the American YMCA and criticized the American associations for their failure "to live up to the brotherhood ideals of Christ." African Americans, Tobias charged, were "puzzled about a Christian leadership that has for more than 50 years without serious protest witnessed flagrant violations of the 14th and 15th amendments to the constitution."[36]

The delegates to the world's conference responded quickly to Tobias's speech. They acknowledged their responsibility "to work out guiding principles for Christian policy and action in the realm of race relations" and appointed a commission to study intercultural and interracial relations in the YMCA.[37] In subsequent years Tobias continued to appeal to the World's Conference of YMCAs in an attempt to embarrass white delegates from the United States and to shame them into action.

In 1931 the world's conference met for the first time in the United States, and the American YMCA was responsible for arranging the meeting. American association leaders faced a troublesome situation when the convention hotels in Cleveland refused to accord "equal treatment to darker-skinned delegates." The American YMCA, fearing international embarrassment, threatened to withdraw the conference. The hotel managers, apparently concerned about the financial loss, reversed their decision.[38]

The American YMCA resolved the problem before the conference, but the international delegates were aware of the dispute their lodging had caused and in response passed several resolutions addressing racial discrimination and segregation. They urged YMCAs throughout the world to organize association meetings so that "all delegates may be received without discrimination as to accommodation and privileges." Moreover, the 765 delegates unanimously passed a resolution condemning racial discrimination and calling for an end to segregation in the YMCA. Racial and cultural diversity, they explained, offers "an opportunity for enrichment of culture through fellowship across racial and cultural lines." Finally, the delegates urged local associations to take a more active role in improving race relations. They conceded "that society may not be changed in a day and that the Y.M.C.A. must exist in the midst of society." They insisted, however, "that patience without effort towards improvement is unchristian" and recommended that all associations start offering educational programs in order to eliminate racial prejudices.[39]

Although the resolutions of the 1931 world's conference were not legally binding, they represented a moral force with which the American YMCA had to come to terms. In the same year the American YMCA delegates gathered for their national convention and adopted a resolution urging all associations to "move forward in remedying this condition of inter-racial inequality and injustice as rapidly as possible." The resolution did not represent a departure from the YMCA's previous racial policy. Since the end of World War I, white association leaders had tried to overcome racial inequalities through interracial dialogue and cooperation without challenging segregation. Tobias praised the resolutions of the world's conference and the American YMCA but noted that if they "are to mean more than mere expressions of conviction and hope, definite steps will have to be taken locally to have them translated into action."[40]

White associations in the United States were reluctant to implement the resolutions passed in 1931. A YMCA study conducted in 1936 found that white associations continued to exclude African Americans except in "towns having a small non-Caucasian population." Even when they were admitted, high membership fees barred "all but a few of them." White YMCA officials, the study revealed, were afraid that the admission of African Americans would alienate white members. One white secretary explained that the policy of his association was to move "as far toward racial equality as we believe we possibly can without offense to the opinions of considerable groups in our participating constituency." The commission preparing the study, however, charged that many white associations were not moving but drifting and called that policy "compromising or even cowardly." The commission urged white YMCAs to be more daring "in the practice of racial brotherhood" and suggested that every association "examine itself and . . . check its practice against its professed ideals."[41]

While the white associations had made little progress, the study found that the student YMCAs in the North "reveal practically no explicit racial discrimination." Northern student associations, however, frequently failed "to treat non-Caucasians as comrades: they tend either to neglect or to patronize them." In the South, African-American and white students attended segregated schools and, thus, continued to have separate associations. Despite the promising progress of the students in the North, the commission concluded that the American YMCAs "are very far from living up to Christian ideals of racial relations."[42]

Tobias related the findings of the commission to the World's Conference of YMCAs in Mysore, India, in 1937. Tobias, who co-chaired with a South African delegate the World's Conference Commission on Race Relations, reported that "America and South Africa are practically the only countries in the world where racial exclusion is practiced in YMCA's."[43] Tobias urged the World's Conference to formulate a constructive policy to end segregation and "warned that it was useless to go on repeating high-sounding resolutions."[44]

The international delegates, however, could do little but reaffirm the Cleveland resolutions of 1931, stating that "no Association . . . should adopt a racially exclusive membership policy or close any of its activities to any man on the ground of his race or color."[45] The world's conference did not have the power to force associations to implement any resolutions because its authority was limited to the formulation of general recommendations and policy statements. Nevertheless, Tobias's repeated appeals to the world's conference must have embarrassed the white delegates from the United States and exerted at least some moral pressure on the American YMCA.

Another source of pressure forcing the American YMCA to reexamine its racial policy was the political developments in Germany, Italy, and the Soviet Union. Observing the rise of totalitarian regimes abroad and the persistence of the economic depression, American YMCA leaders became increasingly worried about potential repercussions in the United States. The National Council urged local associations to study totalitarianism, to safeguard civil liberties of minorities, and to "use their influence in the life of the community when civil rights are threatened." The National Council warned that the denial of "equal treatment of all citizens regardless of race, creed, or economic status, constitute influences" that tend "to drive aggrieved citizens to the espousal of the violent panaceas of fascism and communism."[46] Although white associations continued their jim crow practices, the concern about totalitarianism paved the way for a reexamination of the YMCA's racial policy during World War II.

The Second World War became a watershed for African Americans in the United States and in the YMCA.[47] The war did not end racism, segregation, or discrimination, but it did accelerate the breakdown of jim crowism and give rise to the civil rights movement of the postwar years. African Americans, disillusioned by their World War I experience, challenged segregation more aggressively and demanded equality and civil rights. Sociologist Alain Locke observed, "Not since the Civil War has the Negro's cause been of greater significance."[48]

Stimulated by the democratic rhetoric of the war years, African Americans launched the Double V campaign, proclaiming that they were fighting for a double victory—for democracy overseas as well as for democracy in the United States.

African-American YMCA leaders joined the ranks of the protesters and rejected further interracial cooperation without the elimination of segregation. For decades they had worked within the YMCA, trying to change the association's racial policy, but they had had little success. The interracial dialogue of the 1920s and the recommendations of the world's conference during the 1930s had resulted in high-sounding resolutions. None of them had been translated into action.

By World War II African-American association leaders had exhausted accommodationism and gradualism as a strategy for racial advancement. They were, the newsletter of the Harlem YMCA claimed, running out of patience: "Even in times of national stress . . . the Negro remains loyal and keeps faith with his country. But we might inquire, how long!!!" Leading African Americans refused to cooperate with the YMCA because of the association's jim crow policy and its lack of interracial progress. Perry B. Jackson, a prominent citizen of Cleveland, declined to serve on the Board of Trustees of the city's African-American YMCA. Jackson explained: "In spite of the numerous interracial conferences at which distinguished citizens . . . have advocated elimination of discrimination on the basis of race alone, I do not know of a single racial barrier that has been even partially lifted during the past 20 years." Many YMCA members shared Jackson's disappointment. African-American association leaders noted that a "growing attitude of disillusionment and skepticism, and often bitterness, is rapidly approaching the point where open rebellion and conflict are imminent possibilities in many localities."[49]

In response to the wartime protest, African-American association leaders renounced accommodationism. Disillusioned with the results of twenty years of interracial dialogue and cooperation, they announced that "the day has passed when education and cooperation can be the goal of any acceptable program dealing with America's race relations." African Americans, association leaders explained, "have arrived at a state of mind which no longer permits them to accept the inferior and discriminatory status assigned them within the framework of American society in general, and in the Young Men's Christian Association in particular." Thus association leaders demanded that the YMCA "remove all bars to membership based upon race and color alone. The reason is obvious: it is simply unchristian to refuse the privileges of membership to a man or boy because of color or national origin."[50]

African-American association leaders realized that if their demand for desegregation was met they would also have to give up their control of separate associations. In the past they had carefully guarded their autonomy in the YMCA, but the wartime protest against segregation made it impossible for them to continue to insist upon racial separation. Tobias explained that "the trend of the Y.M.C.A. Movement now is in the direction of integration . . . rather than toward the strengthening and multiplication of separate racial branches."[51]

African-American YMCA leaders not only renounced accommodationism and racial separatism but also started to question the notion that individual achievement was the key to racial advancement. For nearly a century association leaders had operated under the assumption that the development of Christian character and manhood would provide African-American men with the necessary tools to achieve personal success, which would then lead to racial advancement. During the war, however, African-American YMCA leaders left the relative safety and isolation of their association and started to collaborate with other organizations in the struggle to achieve equality.

African-American association leaders organized joint conferences with representatives of government agencies, the National Urban League, the NAACP, the Brotherhood of Sleeping Car Porters, the Council on African Affairs, the National Negro Congress, and the National Association of Colored Graduate Nurses. Among those who attended the YMCA-sponsored meetings were A. Philip Randolph; Walter White; Roy Wilkins; Lester Granger; Judge William H. Hastie, civilian aide to the secretary of war; Campbell C. Johnson, assistant to the director of the National Selective Service Administration; Emmett J. Scott; Rayford W. Logan; George E. Haynes; Max Yergan; Adam Clayton Powell, Jr.; Paul Robeson; and Mabel Staupers.[52]

The purpose of the conferences was to discuss the role of African Americans in the war effort and to develop a joint strategy to ensure equal participation in the military and in defense industry employment. Association leaders and civil rights representatives demanded the full integration of African Americans "and other minority groups into all defense projects and national service, to the end that the democratic ideal may be kept alive for all peoples."[53] Moreover, African-American YMCA leaders agreed to cooperate with civil rights groups in order to apply "community pressure" to the various departments of the government, to ensure African Americans equal opportunity in the defense of the country.

Many white YMCA officials were equally concerned about the inconsistency between the association's jim crow policy and the nation's defense of democracy. African-American association leaders had challenged their white colleagues to live up to the YMCA's Christian ideals for some time. Not until World War II called into question their moral integrity, however, did white YMCA officials respond. The YMCA's National Council urged local associations to "demonstrate at home that practice of Christian democracy which we commend to the rest of the world." White association leaders were particularly embarrassed by a YMCA study that compared racism in the United States to anti-Semitism in Germany. The white southern author of *Background for Brotherhood* asked his readers: "What essential difference, if any, do you see between Hitler's theory of the master race and the ordinary ideas that white Americans in general hold about persons of darker color?" Many white YMCA officials, aware of the discrepancy between the YMCA's jim crow policy and the nation's democratic ideals, also began to question the feasibility of improving race relations while sustaining segregation. In a 1944 study, entitled *Negro Youth in City YMCAs*, the National Council questioned for the first time "the long established practice of attempting to achieve improvement in race relations by operating equal but separate services." In the same year Eugene E. Barnett, general secretary of the YMCA, urged the members of the National Council to "keep faith with democracy." Barnett charged that racial discrimination was incompatible with the YMCA's Christian ideals, and he insisted that the YMCA must "translate its high purposes into steady and courageous action."[54]

White association officials, however, were slow to respond to Barnett's suggestion. They were afraid that a decision to desegregate during the war was likely to split the YMCA just as the slavery issue had divided the YMCA during the Civil War. Thus, they avoided a showdown until after the war. In 1946, as a result of the wartime debate over the YMCA's role in a democracy, the National Council as well as the YMCA representatives to the national convention passed a resolution urging local associations to "work steadfastly toward the goal of eliminating all racial discriminations." Moreover, the National Council abolished racial designations in all its publications and dissolved the Colored Work Department. Tobias retired that year, and the remaining secretaries of the Colored Work Department, Ralph W. Bullock and Robert B. DeFrantz, were assigned to other departments in the YMCA.[55]

The 1946 resolution represented the beginning of the end of segregation in the YMCA. In subsequent years the national leadership of the YMCA continuously urged white associations to end segregation, although many continued to insist on their autonomy and refused to desegregate. The African-American associations, which had never formally excluded whites from membership, also became a "stumbling block hindering desegregation."[56] Some African-American secretaries and directors of local associations were apparently not willing to give up their autonomy. Most of the opposition to desegregation, however, came from white secretaries. By 1950 more than half of all YMCAs in the United States had open membership policies. All associations in Maine, Massachusetts, and Rhode Island, most YMCAs in the West and Midwest, and nearly all those along the Pacific coast operated on an interracial basis. None of the white YMCAs in the Southeast and Southwest, however, admitted African Americans.[57]

In 1952 Eugene E. Barnett observed that the association had not yet achieved complete desegregation. He noted "considerable progress," however, and reported that the number of associations "practicing non-segregation is increasing, the number unapologetically segregated is decreasing, [and] the associations which are compromising this fundamental principle of brotherhood because of community pressure are increasingly troubled by conscience."[58] The ensuing struggle to desegregate the YMCA, particularly the associations in the South, provides a fascinating story, but it lies beyond the scope of this book.

Although some African Americans criticized black association leaders for accepting jim crowism in the YMCA, the approach did have far-reaching consequences. During the decades of interracial dialogue and cooperation, African-American association leaders planted the seeds for a moral dilemma that white YMCA officials were forced to face during World War II. As a result, the YMCA adopted a policy of desegregation two years before the United States Army did and eight years before the *Brown* decision reversed the "separate-but-equal" ruling of *Plessy v. Ferguson.*

Conclusion

IN 1944 Eugene E. Barnett, general secretary of the YMCA, reminded an audience of association leaders that future historians examining their racial practices would ask "Did they keep faith?" African Americans, looking back at the first century of the YMCA's work in the United States, already knew the answer. The YMCA's racial policy was one of neglect, discrimination, and segregation, and as an African-American association leader observed, it reflected "poor Americanism and worse Christianity."[1] The Christian brotherhood did not lead the way in challenging discrimination or segregation but followed public sentiment in its treatment of African Americans. It moved from benign neglect in the 1850s and 1860s to benevolent paternalism during Reconstruction and finally adopted a jim crow policy when the nation raised the walls of segregation.

The YMCA's position on racial issues is not surprising. The association, like other institutions in the United States, was part of American society, and its members were likely to share contemporary racial beliefs. Thus the YMCA tried to avoid addressing controversial issues, afraid to alienate part of its membership.[2] The attempt to suppress a discussion of slavery before the Civil War illustrates that fear. Moreover, the YMCA was by definition not an organization devoted to changing society. Rather it was trying to assist the individual man in his struggle to remain or become a Christian gentleman.

Despite the YMCA's refusal to accept African Americans on equal terms, members of the black educated elite were often eager to provide association services for African-American men and boys. African Americans who joined the YMCA movement knew that the association's call for a Christian brotherhood was not racially inclusive. They were willing to accommodate, however, in order to provide the men and boys of their race with opportunities otherwise unavailable to them. African-American association leaders insisted that it was better to serve African Americans in separate YMCAs "and hope for a final adjustment . . . that would be fair and Christian than to withhold services from the disadvantaged group until the millennium could come."[3]

African Americans who joined the YMCA were generally conservative men who believed in the promise of the American dream and the Victorian ideal of manhood. They were convinced that despite racism and segregation African-American men could achieve success if they lived up to the Protestant work ethic and displayed personal initiative and rugged individualism. Equally important, however, was that they remained at all times Christian gentlemen who could command the respect of any man. The YMCA's function was to provide African-American men and boys with the proper environment, stimulation, and role models to build their work ethic and their manhood.

The YMCA's role, however, was not limited to aiding young men and boys in their struggle to become gentlemen and to achieve personal success. African-American association leaders also believed that their work was instrumental for racial advancement. They were convinced that once African-American men displayed all the characteristics of refined Christian gentlemen, surely no white gentleman would withhold justice from them. African-American association leaders tried to provide black men and boys with the opportunity to develop their manhood and to exercise their leadership that white society denied them.

In the process, African Americans created a network of black-controlled YMCAs that became safe havens for the men and boys of their race. They shielded their members from racism and humiliation and allowed them to develop their manhood with dignity and without losing their self-esteem. Although African-American associations were the product of racism, Channing H. Tobias insisted that the "Y is our source of refuge." Indeed, associations served as sanctuaries that preserved African-American manhood and prepared men and boys for their leadership in the struggle for equality. "A race that does not provide for its young men and surround them with proper influences for right character building," Jesse E. Moorland explained, "is defeated before the battle begins."[4]

African-American association leaders advocated a unique strategy for racial advancement. The YMCA's manhood and leadership training program not only represented an alternative to the racial advancement strategies of W.E.B. Du Bois and Booker T. Washington but also complemented both. African-American association leaders shared with Du Bois the belief that racial advancement was linked to the ability of a leadership group. While Du Bois merely called on the Talented Tenth to lead the masses in the struggle for equality, association leaders were busy providing these men with the opportunity to test, exercise, and improve their leadership skills. Yet African-American association leaders also shared Washington's belief that personal initiative, hard work, and rugged individualism were essential for racial advancement. Washington urged African Americans to acquire the necessary skills and trades to become successful businessmen and property owners, insisting that "no one will very long object to a man's voting who owns the largest business establishment and is the largest tax-payer in his community."[5] Association leaders likewise believed in the power of individual achievement, and YMCAs offered a variety of programs designed to allow African Americans to improve body, mind, and spirit.

While Du Bois criticized association leaders for their accommodationist and gradualist approach, Washington acknowledged the important work of the YMCA. He insisted, however, that industrial training was, at least for the time being, more important for the advancement of African Americans than association work. He argued: "A race improves in its morals and Christian education, as a rule, after it gets an industrial foundation. It is a hard thing to make a good Christian of a man who is hungry and lives in a rented one-room cabin."[6] Washington's reservations about the value of YMCA work reflected his concern for the plight of the masses of sharecroppers in the South. African-American YMCA leaders, however, had little interest in providing association services in the rural South: their goal was to serve the growing number of African Americans who had moved to the northern cities in search of better working and living conditions.

African-American association leaders worked under adverse circumstances created by racism, but they did not surrender to jim crowism. They maintained their dignity and found strength in racial solidarity and self-help. Insisting on self-determination, they consciously fostered a sense of racial unity among African-American YMCAs and established a network of autonomous associations. Behind the walls of segregation, black YMCAs became symbols of pride and not of racism. African Americans helped to finance associations, they staffed and managed them, and in many cases they provided the work force to construct them.

YMCAs became important community-based organizations for African Americans living in cities. Unlike the churches and fraternal organizations, the association catered to men of all religions and professions. It was a place for social interaction, professional networking, and male bonding for African-American men. Moreover, a variety of clubs, choirs, mutual aid societies, and professional, civic, fraternal and civil rights groups gathered for their meetings at the association building. Although YMCAs were single-gender institutions, African-American women supported them in the interest of racial advancement. Some, like Madame C.J. Walker of Indianapolis and Daisy K. Merchant of Cincinnati, made large financial contributions, while others volunteered their time and raised funds through ladies' auxiliaries.

YMCAs provided many African-American communities with facilities and programs no other urban institutions offered. The association's recreation and physical exercise programs launched the careers of many nationally known athletes, including Jesse Owens, John Woodruff, Dave Albritton, De Hart Hubbard, Eddie Tolan, and Edward Gordon. Gordon was the son of a YMCA secretary, so he grew up in the association. Roy Campanella and Jackie Robinson not only belonged to the YMCA but for some time also coached boys at the Harlem association.[7]

The YMCA's educational programs provided association members with opportunities to enhance their vocational and professional training, while the reading rooms offered access to black newspapers and fiction and nonfiction books at a time when most public libraries did not admit African-American patrons. The YMCA's educational work was of particular importance to the black soldiers in World War I. Many previously illiterate men from the rural South learned to read and write under the guidance of African-American YMCA secretaries.

YMCA dormitories provided affordable, clean, and safe housing for travelers and newcomers to cities. Those migrating from the South to the North were aided by the YMCA's employment and housing bureaus. Visitors found that the associations were ideal places to establish contacts with the businessmen, the professional elite, and the religious leaders of African-American communities.

For many African-American secretaries, the YMCA also served as a stepping-stone to a more prestigious career. Several of the secretaries, for example, went on to become college presidents, including David D. Jones of Bennett College, J.B. Watson of Arkansas State College, John W. Davis of West Virginia State College, Mordecai W. Johnson of Howard University, and Benjamin E. Mays of Morehouse College.[8] Others attained government positions. George E. Haynes became special assistant to the secretary of labor in World War I, Ralph W. Bullock served with the National Youth Administration during the 1930s, Campbell C. Johnson was assistant to the director of the National Selective Service Administration in World

War II, and Channing H. Tobias was appointed to President Truman's Committee on Civil Rights.

The YMCA and its leadership did not reach all African Americans, but the associations certainly touched many more lives than did the writings and philosophical quarrels of Booker T. Washington and W.E.B. Du Bois. Yet men like Hunton, Moorland, and Tobias are virtually unknown today—perhaps because they labored quietly behind the walls of segregation trying to provide African-American men and boys with opportunities that white society denied them. It is difficult to assess and impossible to measure the influence of the YMCA and its leaders on African Americans. But maybe one member of the Cleveland association expressed what many African-American men and boys felt. In a letter to Moorland, he wrote: "I speak this with all truth, I know of no man whose influence has more inspired me than that of your's [*sic*] as one of the leaders of young men. The world will never know the wonderful power resulting from your contact with us as young men until after you will have gone to your reward."[9]

Appendixes

All appendixes have been compiled from *Association Men*; the YMCA *Year Book*; the *Proceedings* of the YMCA conventions; YMCA International Committee, *The Colored Men's Department of the YMCA* (New York: YMCA International Committee, 1894); the Jesse E. Moorland Papers, Moorland-Spingarn Research Center, Howard University; the Julius Rosenwald Papers, University of Chicago; the Records Relating to YMCA Work with Blacks, 1891-1979, and Education Records, 1889-1980, both in the YMCA of the USA Archives, University of Minnesota Libraries, Minnesota; and the Rockefeller Family Archives, Rockefeller Archives Center.

Appendix A. *Number of African-American YMCAs, 1853-1945*

The YMCA *Year Book* discontinued its practice of listing African-American college associations separately in 1932 and those in cities in 1946. The African-American and white student associations merged in 1934.

Year	*City YMCAs*	*College YMCAs*	*Total*
1853	1	0	1
1866	3	0	3
1867	1	0	1
1869	0	2	2
1870	9	0	9
1871	10	0	10
1872	18	0	18
1873	3	0	3
1874	1	0	1
1875	5	1	6
1876	6	0	6
1877	2	1	3
1878	4	0	4
1879	8	2	10
1880	8	3	11
1881	8	4	12
1882	5	6	11
1883	10	19	29
1884	8	16	24

Year	*City YMCAs*	*College YMCAs*	*Total*
1885	9	26	35
1886	10	28	38
1887	10	26	36
1888	14	26	40
1889	14	25	39
1890	12	24	36
1891	15	22	37
1892	12	22	34
1893	12	27	39
1894	16	27	43
1895	18	31	49
1896	21	40	61
1897	17	41	58
1898	17	43	60
1899	17	48	65
1900	21	53	74
1901	23	63	86
1902	29	66	95
1903	34	69	103
1904	37	72	109
1905	35	74	109
1906	36	82	118
1907	38	85	123
1908	37	89	126
1909	39	91	130
1910	42	93	135
1911	41	91	132
1912	44	82	126
1913	44	100	144
1914	46	103	149
1915	45	102	147
1916	46	104	150
1917	36	104	140
1918	43	107	150
1919	44	113	157
1920	44	113	157
1921	55	119	174
1922	55	118	173
1923	43	97	140
1924	46	114	160
1925	51	128	179
1926	45	92	137
1927	53	105	158
1928	53	70	103
1929	51	47	98
1930	60	57	117

Year	*City YMCAs*	*College YMCAs*	*Total*
1931	54	43	97
1932	53		
1933	54		
1934	50		
1935	54		
1936	55		
1937	55		
1938	62		
1939	63		
1940	67		
1941	69		
1942	63		
1943	71		
1944	72		
1945	84		

Appendix B. *International Secretaries for African-American YMCA Work*

African-American international secretaries were members of the International Committee until 1923, when the YMCA established a Colored Work Department. The international secretaries then became known as Colored Work Department secretaries.

Name	*Years of service*
George D. Johnston	1876-78
Henry E. Brown	1879-91
William A. Hunton	1891-1916
Jesse E. Moorland	1898-1923
George E. Haynes	1905-8
John B. Watson	1908-20?
Channing H. Tobias	1911-46
Robert P. Hamlin	1911-28
David D. Jones	1911-14
Alexander L. Jackson	1914-15
Max Yergan	1915-16
Mordecai W. Johnson	1916-17
George W. Moore	1916-17
R.T. Weatherby	1918-19?
Henry K. Craft	1921
William C. Craver	1921-31
Robert B. DeFrantz	1921-46
John H. McGrew	1921-31
L.K. McMillan	1925-26
Ralph W. Bullock	1925-46
Frank T. Wilson	1925-31
John Dillingham	1926-28
Benjamin E. Mays	1928-30
Henry W. Pope	1929-31
J.C. McMorris	1929-31

Appendix C. *African-American YMCA Conventions*

After 1929 African-American YMCA conventions were held in conjunction with the secretarial training sessions of the Chesapeake Summer School.

Year	*Location*	*Year*	*Location*
1890	Nashville, Tenn.	1901	Knoxville, Tenn.
1891	Richmond, Va.		Petersburg, Va.
1892	Lynchburg, Va.		Charleston, S.C.
1893	Norfolk, Va.	1902	Danville, Va.
	Nashville, Tenn.		New Orleans, La.
1894	Atlanta, Ga.	1903	Atlanta, Ga.
	Petersburg, Va.		Montgomery, Ala.
1895	Atlanta, Ga.	1904	Talladega, Ala.
	Richmond, Va.		Portsmouth, Va.
1896	Hampton, Va.	1905	Greensboro, N.C.
1897	Raleigh, N.C.	1906	Asheville, N.C.
1898	Raleigh, N.C.	1908	Columbus, Ga.
	Charlotte, N.C.	1909	Louisville, Ky.
	Asheville, N.C.	1921	Cincinnati, Ohio
1899	Orangeburg S.C.	1925	Washington, D.C.
	Norfolk, Va.	1929	Chicago, Ill.
1900	Salisbury, N.C.		
	Baltimore, Md.		
	Tuskegee, Ala.		
	Tougaloo, Miss.		

Appendix D. *Buildings Owned by African-American YMCAs*

These figures reflect only buildings specifically designed and constructed for YMCA use. Many African-American associations either rented rooms, apartments, or buildings or purchased former residences for their use.

Year	*Number of Buildings*
1900	5
1905	13
1910	21
1915	28
1920	26
1925	31
1930	36

Appendix E. *Membership in African-American YMCAs*

Year	*Members*
1900	5, 100
1905	6, 700
1910	10, 460
1915	13, 096
1920	25, 925
1925	32, 341
1930	33, 924
1935	36, 607
1940	51, 834
1944	81, 209

Appendix F. *Professional African-American YMCA Secretaries*

Year	*Number of Secretaries*
1888	1
1889	3
1890	5
1891	5
1893	5
1895	8
1897	8
1898	6
1899	5
1900	6
1905	17
1910	36
1915	35
1920	54
1925	132
1930	108
1935	103
1940	115
1944	149

Appendix G. *Location of Rosenwald YMCAs*

1910 OFFER

City	*Association*	*Date Opened*
Washington, D.C.	Twelfth Street	1912
Chicago, Ill.	Wabash Avenue	1913
Indianapolis, Ind.	Senate Avenue	1913
Philadelphia, Pa.	Christian Street	1914
Kansas City, Mo	Paseo Deparment	1914
Cincinnati, Ohio	Ninth Street	1916
Brooklyn, N.Y.	Carlton Avenue	1918
Baltimore, Md.	Druid Hill Avenue	1919
St.Louis, Mo.	Pine Street	1919
Columbus, Ohio	Spring Street	1919
New York, N.Y.	135th Street	1919
Atlanta, Ga.	Butler Street	1920
Pittsburgh, Pa.	Centre Avenue	1923

1920 OFFER

City	*Association*	*Date Opened*
Denver, Colo.	Glenarm Branch	1924
Detroit, Mich.	St.Antoine	1925
Los Angeles, Calif.	Twenty-eighth Street	1926
Buffalo, N.Y.	Michigan Avenue	1928
Dayton, Ohio	Fifth Street	1928
Montclair, N.J.	Washington Street	1928
Toledo, Ohio	Indiana Avenue	1930
Dallas, Tex.	Moorland	1930
Youngstown, Ohio	West Federal Street	1931
Orange, N.J.	Oakwood Avenue	1932
Harrisburg, Pa.	Forster Street	1933

Notes

Introduction

1. Carl Murphy to Leo B. Marsh, YMCA National Council, March 4, 1949, installment I, box 7, no. 9, Benjamin E. Mays Papers, Moorland-Spingarn Research Center, Howard University, Washington, D.C.; hereinafter cited as Mays Papers.

2. Jesse E. Moorland, "The Young Men's Christian Association: A Potent Agency in the Salvation of Young Men," n.d., box 126-27, no. 563, p. 2, Jesse E. Moorland Papers, Moorland-Spingarn Research Center, Howard University, Washington, D.C.; hereinafter cited as JEM Papers.

3. Jesse E. Moorland, "The Work of the YMCA among Colored Young Men," ca. 1901, p. 5, JEM Papers, box 126-27, no. 554; and Moorland, "The Opportunity and Responsibility of the International Committee in the Progress of the Department," January 1, 1913, pp. 2-3, JEM Papers, box 126-60, no. 1149.

4. Jesse E. Moorland, "The Association Today," n.d., JEM Papers, box 126-23, no. 334.

5. Jesse E. Moorland, "The Work of the YMCA among Colored Young Men," ca. 1901, p. 5, JEM Papers, box 126-27, no. 554.

1. The Origins of Racial Divisions in the YMCA, 1852-1875

1. For a discussion of Williams's background, see J.E. Hodder Williams, *The Father of the Red Triangle: The Life of Sir George Williams, Founder of the Y.M.C.A.* (New York: Hodder and Stoughton, 1918).

2. Terry Donoghue, *An Event on Mercer Street: A Brief History of the YMCA of the City of New York* (New York, [ca. 1952]), 12.

3. C. Howard Hopkins, *History of the YMCA in North America* (New York: Association Press, 1951), 4; Owen E. Pence, *The YMCA and Social Need: A Study of Institutional Adaptation* (New York: Association Press, 1939), 12; Sherwood Eddy, *A Century with Youth: A History of the YMCA from 1844 to 1944* (New York: Association Press, 1944), 2. Since no exact records of the first meeting were kept, wording of the quote differs.

4. Eddy, *Century with Youth*, 2-3; Donoghue, *Event on Mercer Street*, 12; Hopkins, *History of the YMCA*, 5.

5. Donoghue, *Event on Mercer Street*, 14.

6. Hopkins, *History of the YMCA*, 4-6; Donoghue, *Event on Mercer Street*, 13-14.

7. Hopkins, *History of the YMCA*, 16.

8. For a discussion of the YMCA's emergence as an institutional response to the social disruptions of urbanization, see Paul Boyer, *Urban Masses and Moral*

Order in America, 1820-1920 (Cambridge, Mass.: Harvard Univ. Press, 1978), 113, 108-20.

9. Boyer, *Urban Masses*, 111, 113-14; Hopkins, *History of the YMCA*, 6, 239.

10. *Christian Watchman and Reflector*, Oct. 30, 1851, p. 1; Donoghue, *Event on Mercer Street*, 21; Hopkins, *History of the YMCA*, 16-18, 22-23.

11. Donoghue, *Event on Mercer Street*, 9, 12, 22 (quote); Allan Stanley Horlick, *Country Boys and Merchant Princes: The Social Control of Young Men in New York* (London: Associated Univ. Presses, 1975), 228-30, 233.

12. Hopkins, *History of the YMCA*, 15, 22-23. For example, YMCA branches were founded in Worcester and Springfield, Massachusetts; Hartford, Connecticut; Portsmouth, New Hampshire; Detroit; Baltimore; New Orleans; Louisville and Lexington, Kentucky; San Francisco; Chicago; and St. Louis.

13. Hopkins, *History of the YMCA*, 56-57, 61-63.

14. *Journal of Proceedings of the 1st Annual Convention of YMCAs of the US and British Provinces*, Buffalo, New York, June 7-8, 1854, p. 12, YMCA of the USA Archives, University of Minnesota Libraries, Minnesota. Convention papers are hereinafter cited as *Proceedings*.

15. William Chauncey Langdon, *The Early Story of the Confederation of YMCAs*, 1888, p. 23, Biographical Records, "William Chauncey Langdon," no. 2, YMCA Archives. These records will hereinafter be cited as Biographical Records.

16. Donoghue, *Event on Mercer Street*, 27-28; Hopkins, *History of the YMCA*, 58-60; Murray G. Ross, *The YMCA in Canada: The Chronicle of a Century* (Toronto: Ryerson Press, 1951), 45; Langdon, *Early Story*, p.23.

17. Ross, *YMCA in Canada*, 44; Langdon, *Early Story*, 22; Laurence L. Doggett, *History of the Young Men's Christian Association* (New York: Association Press, 1922), 199.

18. Langdon, *Early Story*, 24; Doggett, *History of the YMCA*, 196.

19. Quoted in Hopkins, *History of the YMCA*, 51.

20. Langdon, *Early Story*, 24; William Chauncey Langdon, *Early Autobiography, 1831-1858*, p. 83, Biographical Records, "William Chauncey Langdon," no. 3.

21. Langdon, *Early Story*, 24.

22. Ibid., 31.

23. Quoted in Ross, *YMCA in Canada*, 45.

24. Ross, *YMCA in Canada*, 46; Hopkins, *History of the YMCA*, 75, 78; Doggett, *History of the YMCA*, 175-76; Timothy L. Smith, *Revivalism and Social Reform: American Protestantism on the Eve of the Civil War* (New York: Harper and Row, 1957), 193.

25. Ross, *YMCA in Canada*, 46; Langdon, *Early Story*, 31; Doggett, *History of the YMCA*, 199.

26. "Circular 5," July 10, 1855, quoted in Langdon, *Early Story*, 32; Doggett, *History of the YMCA*, 197.

27. Doggett, *History of the YMCA*, 193-95 (board quoted on 194).

28. Ibid., 201.

29. Hopkins, *History of the YMCA*, 52; Donoghue, *Event on Mercer Street*, 29; Harold C. Harlow, Jr., "Racial Integration in the YMCA: A Study of the Closing of Certain Negro YMCAs with Special Reference to the Role of Religious Factors," Ph.D. diss., Hartford Seminary, 1961, 6; Laurence L. Doggett, *Life of Robert R. McBurney* (Cleveland: F.M. Barton, 1902), 40.

30. Hopkins, *History of the YMCA*, 51, 30; Donoghue, *Event on Mercer Street*, 29-30; Doggett, *Life of Robert R. McBurney*, 40-42; idem, *History of the YMCA*, 195-96.

31. Quoted in Ross, *YMCA in Canada*, 47.

32. Hopkins, *History of the YMCA*, 51-52.

33. New York City YMCA, *The War Correspondence between the Young Men's Christian Associations of Richmond, Virginia, and of the City of New York* (New York: G.P. Putnam, 1861), 4, 6; Hopkins, *History of the YMCA*, 85-86; Doggett, *History of the YMCA*, 205-6.

34. Quoted in Hopkins, *History of the YMCA*, 87.

35. Robert T. Handy, *A Christian America: Protestant Hopes and Historical Realities* (New York: Oxford Univ. Press, 1984), 54-55; Mark A. Noll, *One Nation under God? Christian Faith and Political Action in America* (San Francisco: Harper and Row, 1988), 105-27; Donoghue, *Event on Mercer Street*, 42; Hopkins, *History of the YMCA*, 94.

36. Harlow, "Racial Integration," 4; Hopkins, *History of the YMCA*, 94. In the South only the Richmond and Charleston associations organized relief work for soldiers of the Confederacy. See Richard C. Lancaster, *Serving the U.S. Armed Forces, 1861-1986: The Story of the YMCA's Ministry to Military Personnel for 125 Years* (Schaumburg, Ill.: Armed Services YMCA of the USA, 1987), 10.

37. Lancaster, *Serving*, 2, 8; M. Hamlin Cannon, "The United States Christian Commission," *Mississippi Valley Historical Review* 38 (1951-52): 61-80; Hopkins, *History of the YMCA*, 92.

38. *Proceedings*, Boston, June 1-5, 1864, p. 9; Hopkins, *History of the YMCA*, 111.

39. "Address of Acting President Joseph A. Pond," *Proceedings*, 1864, p. 23.

40. Hondon B. Hargrove, *Black Union Soldiers in the Civil War* (Jefferson, N.C.: McFarland and Co., 1988), 181; Lemuel Moss, *Annals of the US Christian Commission* (Philadelphia: J.B. Lippincott, Co., 1868), 437-38, 442, 452-54. For a general discussion of the education of black soldiers during the Civil War, see James McPherson, *The Negro's Civil War: How American Negroes Felt and Acted during the War for the Union* (Urbana: Univ. of Illinois Press, 1982), 211-14; John W. Blassingame, "The Union Army as an Educational Institution for Negroes, 1862-1865," *Journal of Negro Education* 34 (1965): 152-59; and Robert Stanley Bahney, "Generals and Negroes: Education of Negroes by the Union Army, 1861-1865," Ph.D. diss., Univ. of Michigan, 1965.

41. *Proceedings*, Montreal, June 19-23, 1867, p. 79; Jesse E. Moorland, "The Colored Men's Department," ca. 1920, JEM Papers, box 126-59, no. 1132; Trevor Bowen, *Divine White Right: A Study of Race Segregation and Interracial Cooperation in Religious Organizations and Institutions in the United States* (New York: Harper and Brothers, 1934), 159.

42. Willis Duke Weatherford, *Present Forces in Negro Progress* (New York: Association Press, 1912), 169-70; *Proceedings*, Indianapolis, June 22-26, 1870, p. 67.

43. *Proceedings*, Washington, D.C., May 24-28, 1871, p. 112; Moorland, "Colored Men's Department," JEM Papers, box 126-59, no. 1132; *Proceedings*, Portland, Maine, July 14-18, 1869, p. 59; Harlow, "Racial Integration," 7.

44. Hopkins, *History of the YMCA*, 37; L.K. McMillan, Jr., "Anthony Bowen and the YMCA," *Negro History Bulletin* 21 (April 1958): 159-60. For a history of black Washingtonians, see Constance McLaughlin Green, *The Secret City: A History of Race Relations in the Nation's Capital* (Princeton, N.J.: Princeton Univ. Press, 1967).

45. Thomas B. Hargrave, Jr., *Private Differences—General Good: A History of the YMCA of Metropolitan Washington* (Washington, D.C.: YMCA of Metropolitan Washington, 1985), 17-21; McMillan, "Anthony Bowen," 159-60; Ella

Payne Moran (great-granddaughter of Anthony Bowen), "Founder and 1st President YMCA for Colored Men and Boys, 1853," Biographical Records, "Anthony Bowen—1976-1977."

46. Hopkins, *History of the YMCA*, 37; Hargrave, *Private Differences*, 19; Moorland, "Colored Men's Department," JEM Papers, box 126-59, no. 1132. Although these three claim that Langdon assisted Bowen in the establishment of a black YMCA, Langdon's autobiography does not indicate whether the two actually met. See Langdon, *Early Autobiography*.

47. Hargrave, *Private Differences*, 19; Green, *Secret City*, 48.

48. Hargrave, *Private Differences*, 37. Following his involvement with the YMCA, Bowen continued to take an interest in improving educational opportunities for blacks. In 1865 Bowen led a group of blacks who petitioned Washington's mayor to provide free public schools for blacks. In 1867 Congress appropriated funds for the first school, built on land Bowen had donated. When Bowen died in 1871, the school was named in his honor. See Moran, "Founder and 1st President," Biographical Records, "Anthony Bowen—1976-1977."

49. Weatherford, *Present Forces*, 169; Hopkins, *History of the YMCA*, 211-13; *Constitution of the Colored Young Men's Christian Association, Washington, D.C., organized December 26, 1866* (Washington, D.C.: R.O. Polkinhorn, 1879), p. 2, in the possession of Thomas B. Hargrave, Jr., president of the YMCA of Metropolitan Washington, D.C.

50. White YMCA officials claimed that the brief existence of the black branch resulted from the "lack of interdenominational tolerance and comity among the colored churches of the period." See Richard C. Morse, *My Life with Young Men: Fifty Years in the YMCA* (New York: Association Press, 1918), 400. The actual relationship between the white and black branches remains obscure.

51. Hopkins, *History of the YMCA*, 211; *New York Age*, Jan. 22, 1914, p. 1. Eato, who worked as an insurance agent, was also president of the African Society for Mutual Relief, a member of the board of trustees and superintendent of the Sunday school of Mother Zion Church, and a member of several Masonic organizations.

52. Jesse E. Moorland, "Historical Statement concerning the Work of the YMCA, among Colored Young Men and Boys," Jan. 1919, p. 2, Records Relating to YMCA Work with Blacks, 1891-1979, box 1, History and Organization Reports, 1919-38, YMCA Archives. These records are hereinafter cited as Black YMCA Records.

53. *Proceedings*, 1867, p. 78.

54. Ibid., 79.

55. *Minutes of the Convention of the Colored Young Men's Christian Associations of the State of South Carolina*, Columbia, Aug. 22-24, 1870; *Minutes of the Convention of the YMCA*, Charleston, Aug. 24, 1871; *Proceedings of the 3rd Annual Convention of the YMCA of South Carolina*, Winnsboro, Aug. 28-30, 1872; *Minutes of the 5th Annual Convention of the YMCA of South Carolina*, Newberry, Aug. 26-29, 1875, Black YMCA Records, box 4, Miscellaneous Conference Materials, 1920s-50s.

56. For a discussion of the black struggle for education during the Civil War and Reconstruction, see James D. Anderson, *The Education of Blacks in the South, 1860-1935* (Chapel Hill: Univ. of North Carolina Press, 1988), 4-32; Joel Williamson, *After Slavery: The Negro in South Carolina during Reconstruction, 1861-1877* (Chapel Hill: Univ. of North Carolina Press, 1965), 209-39; Eric Foner, *Reconstruction: America's Unfinished Revolution, 1863-1877* (New York: Harper and Row, 1988), 96-100; Howard N. Rabinowitz, *Race Relations in the Urban*

South, 1865-1890 (Urbana: Univ. of Illinois Press, 1980), 152-81; W.E.B. Du Bois, *Black Reconstruction in America: An Essay toward a History of the Part which Black Folk Played in the Attempt to Reconstruct Democracy in America, 1860-1880* (1935; New York: Atheneum, 1985), 637-69; Luther P. Jackson, "The Educational Efforts of the Freedmen's Bureau and Freedmen's Aid Societies in South Carolina, 1862-1872," *Journal of Negro History* 8 (Jan. 1923): 1-40; and Blassingame, "The Union Army as an Educational Institution," 152-59.

57. Anderson, *Education of Blacks*, 3; Du Bois, *Black Reconstruction*, 642, 648; Foner, *Reconstruction*, 96.

58. Williamson, *After Slavery*, 223-33; Du Bois, *Black Reconstruction*, 381-430.

59. Blacks represented a majority at the constitutional convention attended by 124 delegates. See Du Bois, *Black Reconstruction*, 389, 649, 663; John Hope Franklin, *From Slavery to Freedom: A History of Negro Americans* (New York: Knopf, 1988), 315; and Kenneth M. Stampp, *The Era of Reconstruction, 1865-1877* (New York: Vintage Books, 1965), 169, 172.

60. Du Bois, *Black Reconstruction*, 649, 650; Williamson, *After Slavery*, 209-39. In 1869, 10 percent of South Carolina's children attended school; by 1876 the proportion had risen to 50 percent. Among black children the increase was even more dramatic. While in 1869 only 4 percent of the state's black children attended school, 44 percent were attending by 1876.

61. Williamson, *After Slavery*, 219; Du Bois, *Black Reconstruction*, 649.

62. Jackson, "Educational Efforts," 4; Stampp, *Era of Reconstruction*, 135; Williamson, *After Slavery*, 226, 229-33, 236, 215.

63. *Minutes of the Convention of the Colored Young Men's Christian Associations of the State of South Carolina*, Columbia, Aug. 22-24, 1870, p. 9, Black YMCA Records, box 4, Misc. Conference Materials, 1920s-50s; hereinafter cited as *Columbia Convention.* The YMCA delegates represented black branches in Charleston, Columbia, Abbeville, Winnsboro, Beaufort, Orangeburg, Georgetown, and Camden, South Carolina, and Jacksonville, Florida.

64. *Minutes of the Convention of the YMCA*, Charleston, Aug. 24, 1871, p. 8, Black YMCA Records, box 4, Misc. Conference Materials, 1920s-50s; hereinafter cited as *Charleston Convention.*

65. *Columbia Convention,* pp. 7-9; *Charleston Convention,* p. 8; and *Proceedings of the 3rd Annual Convention of the YMCA of South Carolina*, Winnsboro, Aug. 28-30, 1872, pp. 10-17, Black YMCA Records, box 4, Misc. Conference Materials, 1920s-50s; hereinafter cited as *Winnsboro Convention.*

66. *Columbia Convention,* pp. 3; *Winnsboro Convention,* p. 17, 6.

67. *Columbia Convention*, p. 8; *Winnsboro Convention*, pp. 13-15.

68. *Winnsboro Convention*, p. 20.

69. Williamson, *After Slavery*, 206-7; *Columbia Convention*, p. 3; *Charleston Convention,* p. 7; Peggy Lamson, "Cain, Richard Harvey," *in Dictionary of American Negro Biography*, ed. Rayford W. Logan and Michael R. Winston (New York: Norton, 1982), 84-85; *New York Times*, June 15, 1874, p. 1, and July 3, 1874, p. 1.

70. *Minutes of the 5th Annual Convention of the YMCA of South Carolina*, Newberry, Aug. 26-29, 1875, p. 6, Black YMCA Records, box 4, no. Misc. Conference Materials, 1920s-50s; hereinafter cited as *Newberry Convention*; Morse, *My Life*, 400; YMCA International Committee, *The Colored Men's Department of the YMCA* (New York: YMCA International Committee, 1894), 10, Black YMCA Records, box 3, Colored Work Department—Pamphlets—1894-1904.

71. Stampp, *Era of Reconstruction*, 156, 161; Williamson, *After Slavery*, 260, 266-67.

72. Stampp, *Era of Reconstruction*, 156.

73. The only exception was the New Orleans branch, which proclaimed that it "admitted colored men equally to membership with white men" during the 1868 convention at Detroit. See Willis Duke Weatherford, "The Colored YMCA, the Interracial Committee and Related Subjects," June 13, 1949, p. 3, Black YMCA Records, box 1, History and Organization Reports, 1919-38.

74. Hopkins, *History of the YMCA*, 112.

2. White Supervision of African-American YMCA Work, 1875-1891

1. Until 1873 the term *agent* or *missionary* was used to identify YMCA workers. When the first full-time YMCA worker was hired, the term *secretary* became the official title. Owen E. Pence, *The YMCA and Social Need: A Study of Institutional Adaptation* (New York: Association Press, 1939), 95, 98. See appendix B.

2. C. Howard Hopkins, *History of the YMCA in North America* (New York: Association Press, 1951), 208, and 211.

3. For a discussion of YMCA work with American ethnic groups, see Hopkins, *History of the YMCA*, 179-244.

4. On the YMCA's missionary efforts abroad, see Hopkins, *History of the YMCA*, 309-60. YMCA secretaries went to Sudan in 1890, to Brazil and Mexico in 1891, and to China in 1895. For a discussion of YMCA work in Africa, see Kenneth James King, *Panafricanism and Education: A Study of Race Philanthropy and Education in the Southern States of America and East Africa* (Oxford: Clarendon Press, 1971). On black Americans as missionaries in Africa, see Walter L. Williams, *Black Americans and the Evangelization of Africa, 1877-1900* (Madison: Univ. of Wisconsin Press, 1982).

5. *Proceedings*, Baltimore, May 21-25, 1879, pp. 31-32; *Proceedings*, Milwaukee, May 16-20, 1883, pp. 103-4; YMCA International Committee, *Report of the International Committee, 1883-84*, pp. 56-57, YMCA Archives; *Proceedings*, Atlanta, May 13-17, 1885, p. 92; YMCA, *Year Book, 1884-85*, 83; hereinafter cited as *Year Book*.

6. Hopkins, *History of the YMCA*, 144, 141-47. The alteration of the committee's role was largely the result of the YMCA's new interest in physical education. Many associations acquired buildings to offer physical exercise programs to their members. The maintenance and administrative work connected with the buildings required more time than volunteers could provide and led to the emergence of the professional YMCA worker.

7. George M. Fredrickson, *The Black Image in the White Mind: The Debate on Afro-American Character and Destiny, 1817-1914* (Middletown, Conn.: Wesleyan Univ. Press, 1971), 199, 204, 209, 214-15. For a discussion of the continuity of paternalism following the war, see Joel Williamson, *The Crucible of Race: Black-White Relations in the American South since Emancipation* (New York: Oxford Univ. Press, 1984), 85-88.

8. *Los Angeles Tribune*, May 17, 1915; Hopkins, *History of the YMCA*, 133, 214-15, 218; Thomas M. Owen, *History of Alabama and Dictionary of Alabama Biography* (1920; Spartanburg, S.C.: Reprint Co., 1978), 744.

9. Fredrickson, *Black Image*, 199; Owen, *Dictionary of Alabama Biography*, 744; *Proceedings*, 1883, p. 104. Hardie was also a major supporter of Tuskegee

Institute. Booker T. Washington reportedly claimed that "despite the fact that much of the money necessary for the establishment of the school came from the north, had it not been for Major Hardie's support the school would not have been the success that it is today." *Los Angeles Tribune*, May 17, 1915.

10. Fredrickson, *Black Image*, 210.

11. Richard C. Morse, *My Life with Young Men: Fifty Years in the YMCA* (New York: Association Press, 1918), 401; Charles H. Welsey, "A Historical Study of the Y.M.C.A. Services to Colored Youth," address delivered at the National Conference of Laymen and Secretaries, Bordentown, New Jersey, July 14, [1949?], p. 6, Black YMCA Records, box 4, Surveys and Studies, 1926-47. The records do not indicate who supported or opposed Wheeler's admission.

12. Beginning in 1922 the YMCA held its conferences only in hotels willing to give equal accommodation to black delegates. Galen M. Fisher, *Public Affairs and the Y.M.C.A.: 1844-1944, With Special Reference to the United States* (New York: Association Press, 1948), 88.

13. William A. Hunton, "The Growth and Prospects of Association Work among Colored Young Men," in *Proceedings*, Indianapolis, May 10-14, 1893, p. 49; *Proceedings*, Richmond, May 26-30, 1875, p. 106; Hopkins, *History of the YMCA*, 214, 218; "Beginnings of Colored Work," Jan. 25, 1876, typewritten extracts from the minutes of the meetings of the International Committee, Black YMCA Records, box 2, Miscellaneous Articles, Reports, and Historical Statements, 1910-50.

14. *Proceedings*, Toronto, July 12-16, 1876, pp. 89-90; Hopkins, *History of the YMCA*, 214.

15. *Proceedings*, 1876, pp. 86-90; Morse, *My Life*, 402; Willis Duke Weatherford, *Present Forces in Negro Progress* (New York: Association Press, 1912), 171; Hopkins, *History of the YMCA*, 214-15; Jesse E. Moorland, "The Colored Men's Department," ca. 1920, p. 8, JEM Papers, box 126-59, no. 1132. Apparently this was the only contribution Williams ever made to any American association.

16. "Beginnings of Colored Work," Aug. 10, 1876, and Oct. 12, 1876; [Jesse E. Moorland?], "Essential Portions of a Memorial Address on William A. Hunton, St. Mark's Church, January 7, 1917," p. 5, JEM Papers, box 126-62, no. 1188; Cephas Brainerd to Jesse E. Moorland, June 4, 1908, JEM Papers, box 126-59, no. 1136; "Beginnings of Colored Work," Oct. 12, 1876.

17. Owen, *Dictionary of Alabama Biography*, 916-17; Clement A. Evans, *Confederate Military History* (Secaucus, N.J.: Blue and Grey Press, 197?), 419-20; Albert Burton Moore, *History of Alabama and Her People*, vol. 2 (New York: American Historical Society, 1927), 314-15. Following his work with the YMCA, Johnston became superintendent of South Carolina's military academy in Charleston, a post he held from 1885 to 1890. In 1892 Johnston became a member of the United States Civil Service Commission, and in 1893 he began a seven-year term in the Alabama state senate.

18. Weatherford, *Present Forces*, 171; *Proceedings*, Louisville, June 6-10, 1877, pp. xv-xvi; Hopkins, *History of the YMCA*, 215; *Proceedings*, 1877, p. xvi; "Beginnings of Colored Work," Dec. 14, 1876, Jan. 10, 1877, and Feb. 8, 1877.

19. Moorland, "Colored Men's Department," pp. 8, 9; Weatherford, *Present Forces*, 171; Jesse E. Moorland, "Historical Statement concerning the Work of the YMCA among Colored Young Men and Boys," Jan. 1919, p. 7, Black YMCA Records, box 1, History and Organization Reports, 1919-38; [Moorland?], "Essential Portions of a Memorial Address on William A. Hunton"; Brainerd to Moorland, June 4, 1908, JEM Papers, box 126-59, no. 1136.

20. "Beginnings of Colored Work," Feb. 19, 1879; YMCA International Committee, *Report of the International Committee, 1883-84*, p. 52, YMCA Archives; *Proceedings*, 1883, p. 101.

21. Morse, *My Life*, 402; Joe M. Richardson, *Christian Reconstruction: The American Missionary Association and Southern Blacks, 1861-1890* (Athens: Univ. of Georgia Press, 1986), 129; Mary C. Venn, Oberlin College Library, to Cleo Mitchell Espy, Nov. 16, 1949, Biographical Records, "Henry E. Brown," no. 1; Margaret H. Scott, Talladega College Library, to Cleo Mitchell Espy, Nov. 12, 1949, Biographical Records, "Henry E. Brown," no. 2; "Beginnings of Colored Work," Feb. 19, 1879.

22. *Proceedings*, 1883, p. 103; YMCA International Committee, *Report of the International Committee, 1883-84*, 56-57; *Year Book, 1884-85*, 83; *Proceedings*, Atlanta, May 13-17, 1885, p. 92.

23. YMCA International Committee, *Report of the International Committee, 1883-84*, pp. 53, 55, 54; *Proceedings*, 1883, pp. 103, 102.

24. YMCA International Committee, *Report of the International Committee, 1883-84*, pp. 55, 53-54; *Year Book, 1889*, p. 28.

25. "Beginnings of Colored Work," Jan. 21, 1879; *Proceedings*, 1879, pp. xxii, 32.

26. "Brainerd, Cephas," in *The Twentieth Century Biographical Dictionary of Notable Amerians*, vol. 1 (Boston: Biographical Society, 1904).

27. Ira Hutchinson Brainerd, "Memoir," p. 196, Biographical Records, "Cephas Brainerd," box 4, no. 12. This memoir, written by Cephas Brainerd's son, was left unfinished at his death in 1935. Eveline Warner Brainerd edited the document in 1947.

28. Hopkins, *History of the YMCA*, 117, 118, 142; Brainerd, "Memoir," 196.

29. Hopkins, *History of the YMCA*, 52; Brainerd, "Memoir," p.7, Biographical Records, "Cephas Brainerd," box 4, no. 12; William V. Rowe, "Memorial of Cephas Brainerd," in *Year Book of the Association of the Bar of the City of New York*, 1912, p. 4, Biographical Records, "Cephas Brainerd," box 4, no. 1.

30. Brainerd to Brown, Feb. 5, 1891, Jan. 14, 1890, Feb. 5, 1891, and Jan. 21, 1890, all in Biographical Records, "Cephas Brainerd," no. 5.

31. Brainerd to Brown, Feb. 22, 1890, June 23, 1879, July 5, 1879, June 23, 1879, Feb. 1, 1880, and March 17, 1880, all in Biographical Records, "Cephas Brainerd," nos. 5 (Feb. 1890 only) and 3.

32. Brainerd to Brown, April 25, 1881, March 20, 1881, April 25, 1881, and March 20, 1881, both in Biographical Records, "Cephas Brainerd," no. 3; *Proceedings*, 1879, pp. xxi, 32.

33. *Proceedings*, Cleveland, May 25-29, 1881, p. 98; "Report of Henry E. Brown," in *Year Book, 1880-81*, 31-32; *Year Book, 1881-82*, xxxix.

34. *Year Book, 1882-83*, 30; *1881-82*, xxxviii-xxxix; *1882-83*, 30.

35. *Year Book, 1882-83*, 32; *1884-85*, 82; *1882-83*, 30-31.

36. *Proceedings*, 1883, pp. 102-3. See appendix A.

37. *Year Book, 1885*, 55.

38. YMCA International Committee, *Report of the International Committee, 1883-84*, 56; *Year Book, 1884-85*, 81.

39. *Year Book, 1886*, 56-58. See appendix A.

40. *Proceedings*, San Francisco, May 11-15, 1887, pp. xlv, p. 51.

41. Hopkins, *History of the YMCA*, 217; Addie W. Hunton, *William Alphaeus Hunton: A Pioneer Prophet of Young Men* (New York: Association Press, 1938), 14, 19. Smithson had been active in the first prayer group established by George

Williams in London. His relationship with the American YMCA, however, is unclear.

42. Moorland, "Colored Men's Department"; Hopkins, *History of the YMCA*, 217; Hunton, *William Alphaeus Hunton*, 14.

43. Moorland, "Colored Men's Department"; Hunton, *William Alphaeus Hunton*, 13; Morse, *My Life*, 402; "Statement by Edwin D. Ingersoll of the International Committee from 1877 to 1887 Inclusive," Biographical Records, "William A. Hunton, 1888-1978."

44. Stanton Hunton was apparently active in the Underground Railroad and aided John Brown in the preparation of his raid on Harper's Ferry. See Hunton, *William Alphaeus Hunton*, 3.

45. Hunton, *William Alphaeus Hunton*, 7.

46. Rayford W. Logan, "Hunton, William A.," in *Dictionary of American Negro Biography*, ed. Rayford W. Logan and Michael R. Winston (New York: Norton, 1982), 338; Hunton, *William Alphaeus Hunton*, 9, 11.

47. Hunton, *William Alphaeus Hunton*, 14 (Morse quote), 16; Hopkins, *History of the YMCA*, 218 (Brown quote).

48. Hunton, *William Alphaeus Hunton*, 9, 17; YMCA International Committee, *The Colored Men's Department of the YMCA* (New York: YMCA International Committee, 1894), 4-5, JEM Papers, box 126-59, no. 1147.

49. Hunton, *William Alphaeus Hunton*, 21-22; "Annual Report of Henry E. Brown," in *Year Book, 1889*, 28; "Annual Statement of Henry E. Brown," in *Year Book, 1888*, 70.

50. *Proceedings*, Philadelphia, May 8-12, 1889, pp. 49, 24.

51. Brainerd to Brown, Dec. 25, 1889, Biographical Records, "Cephas Brainerd," no. 4.

52. Hunton, *William Alphaeus Hunton*, 23; Brainerd to Brown, Jan. 21, 1890, Feb. 22, 1890, Feb. 8, 1890, and Feb. 22, 1890, all in Biographical Records, "Cephas Brainerd," no. 5.

53. Hunton, *William Alphaeus Hunton*, 23, 24, 25, 26. Brown continued as a member of the International Committee until 1893. He advised Hunton but was no longer responsible for black association work. Both men remained friends after Brown left the YMCA to become head of the Church Envelope Company in Ohio. See Oberlin University Alumni Association, *Oberlin Alumni Catalogue, 1936* (Oberlin, Ohio: Oberlin Alumni Association, 1936).

3. Growth and Centralization under African-American Leadership, 1891-1898

1. For a more detailed discussion of the deterioration of race relations in the South, see Rayford W. Logan, *The Negro in American Life and Thought: The Nadir, 1877-1901* (New York: Dial Press, 1954), 79-96; C. Vann Woodward, *The Strange Career of Jim Crow* (Oxford: Oxford Univ. Press, 1955), 43, 67-109; idem, *Origins of the New South, 1877-1913* (Baton Rouge: Louisiana State Univ. Press, 1951), 321-95; August Meier, *Negro Thought in America, 1880-1915: Racial Ideologies in the Age of Booker T. Washington* (Ann Arbor: Univ. of Michigan Press, 1963); Thomas F. Gossett, *Race: The History of an Idea in America* (New York: Schocken Books, 1965), 144-75, 253-96; and Joel Williamson, *The Crucible of Race: Black-White Relations in the American South since Emancipation* (New York: Oxford Univ. Press, 1984).

2. Meier, *Negro Thought*, 42, 121-57.

3. For a discussion of Booker T. Washington's racial ideology, see Samuel R.

Spencer, Jr., *Booker T. Washington and the Negro's Place in American Life* (Boston: Little, Brown and Co., 1955); Meier, *Negro Thought*, 83-118; Louis R. Harlan, *Booker T. Washington: The Making of a Black Leader, 1856-1901* (New York: Oxford Univ. Press, 1972); idem, *Booker T. Washington: The Wizard of Tuskegee, 1901-1915* (New York: Oxford Univ. Press, 1983); idem, "The Secret Life of Booker T. Washington," *Journal of Southern History* 37 (Aug. 1971): 393-416; idem, "Booker T. Washington and the *Voice of the Negro*, 1904-1907," *Journal of Southern History* 45 (Feb. 1979): 45-62; and idem, "Booker T. Washington and the Politics of Accommodation," in *Black Leaders of the Twentieth Century*, ed. John Hope Franklin and August Meier (Urbana: Univ. of Illinois Press, 1982), 1-18.

4. The *Messenger* was published by the black YMCA in Richmond. Several issues are located in Black YMCA Records, box 3, Colored Work Department—Periodicals—The *Messenger*, 1896-97.

5. C. Howard Hopkins, *History of the YMCA in North America* (New York: Association Press, 1951), 219; Cephas Brainerd to Henry E. Brown, Jan. 30, 1891, Biographical Records, "Cephas Brainerd," no. 5.

6. Addie W. Hunton, *William Alphaeus Hunton: A Pioneer Prophet of Young Men* (New York: Association Press, 1938), 35-36, 34; William B. Whiteside, *The Boston Y.M.C.A. and Community Need: A Century's Evolution, 1851-1951* (New York: Association Press, 1951), 157; John Daniels, *In Freedom's Birthplace: A Study of the Boston Negroes* (New York: Negro Universities Press, 1914), 170-71, 186-87, 292, 380; Channing H. Tobias, "Memorandum," May 8, 1945, p. 2, Black YMCA Records, box 6, Colored Work Department—Reports, 1940-49.

7. Hunton, *William Alphaeus Hunton*, 36; *Association Men*, July 1902, p. 455.

8. *Proceedings*, Kansas City, Missouri, May 6-11, 1891, p. 103; Hunton, *William Alphaeus Hunton*, 35-36; *Proceedings*, Indianapolis, May 10-14, 1893, p. 50.

9. Hunton, *William Alphaeus Hunton*, 35-36; *Proceedings*, 1893, p. 50.

10. William A. Hunton, "The Association among Colored Men," *Men*, Dec. 18, 1897, p. 249.

11. YMCA International Committee, *The Colored Men's Department of the YMCA* (New York: YMCA International Committee, 1894), 20, Black YMCA Records, box 3, Colored Work Department—Pamphlets—1894-1904. For a discussion of the African-American elite's sense of noblesse oblige, see Willard B. Gatewood, *Aristocrats of Color: The Black Elite, 1880-1920* (Bloomington: Indiana Univ. Press, 1990).

12. "Booker T. Washington on the Negro in the American City and His Needs," *Association Men*, Jan. 1911, p. 149; YMCA International Committee, *Colored Men's Department*, 1.

13. *Proceedings*, 1891, p. 112; Jesse E. Moorland, "The Young Men's Christian Association among Colored Men," ca. 1902, p. 3, JEM Papers, box 126-27, no. 559; William A. Hunton, "Colored Men's Department of the Young Men's Christian Association," *Voice of the Negro*, June 1905, p. 394.

14. Hopkins, *History of the YMCA*, 129-30 (*Era* quoted on 129).

15. Hunton, *William Alphaeus Hunton*, 32.

16. Hunton, *William Alphaeus Hunton*, 33.

17. YMCA International Committee, *Colored Men's Department*, 15; B.J. Watkins to Jesse E. Moorland, April 24, 1902, JEM Papers, box 126-22, no. 317; W.E. Williams to Moorland, March 4, 1899, JEM Papers, box 126-22, no. 326; Benjamin E. Johnson to Moorland, July 8, 1902, JEM Papers, box 126-19, no. 252.

18. Moorland, "Young Men's Christian Association among Colored Men," p.

7; D. Williams to Moorland, June 4, 1902, JEM Papers, box 126-22, no. 324; W.H. Singleton to Moorland, Dec. 29, 1902, JEM Papers, box 126-21, no. 303.

19. *Year Book, 1892*, 36; *Proceedings*, 1893, p. 50.

20. *Proceedings*, 1893, p. 50; "The Association Work among Colored Young Men: Its Present Peculiar Need," paper read by William A. Hunton, in *Proceedings*, Springfield, Mass., May 8-12, 1895, pp. 81-82.

21. Hunton, *William Alphaeus Hunton*, 36, 37; newspaper clipping, Nov. 25, 1892, JEM Papers, box 126-47, no. 946.

22. *Year Book, 1894*, 12.

23. YMCA International Committee, *Colored Men's Department*, 10. See appendix C.

24. Hunton, *William Alphaeus Hunton*, 34; YMCA International Committee, *Colored Men's Department*, 10-12, 14, 25; "The Conference of Colored Associations," *Men*, Dec. 18, 1897, p. 255.

25. William A. Hunton, *Colored Young Men: History, Methods and Relationships of Association Work among Them* (New York: YMCA International Committee, [ca. 1900]), 28; YMCA International Committee, *Colored Men's Department*, 11, 19, 14.

26. S.G. Atkins, "The Mental Improvement of Colored Men," *Men*, Dec. 18, 1897, pp. 252, 253.

27. *Proceedings*, 1891, p. 112; YMCA International Committee, *Colored Men's Department*, 20, 22.

28. *The Monthly Bulletin of the Colored Young Men's Christian Association*, Baltimore, July 1899, JEM Papers, box 126-22, no. 326; Hopkins, *History of the YMCA*, 6; Jesse E. Moorland, "The Young Men's Christian Association: A Potent Agency in the Salvation of Young Men," n.d., p. 1, JEM Papers, box 126-27, no. 563.

29. YMCA International Committee, *Colored Men's Department*, 17-19, 20. For a discussion of women in the YMCA, see Jodi Vandenberg-Daves, "The Manly Pursuit of a Partnership between the Sexes: The Debate over YMCA Programs for Women and Girls, 1914-1933," *Journal of American History* 78 (March 1992): 1324-46.

30. YMCA International Committee, *Colored Men's Department*, 21, 24.

31. W.E. Green to Moorland, March 31, 1899, JEM Papers, box 126-18, no. 236; John W. Evans to Moorland, April 30, 1902, and May 9, 1902, JEM Papers, box 126-17, no. 225; W.H. Singleton to Moorland, Dec. 29, 1902, JEM Papers, box 126-21, no. 303.

32. "Literary Committee YMCA," [Columbia, S.C.?], April 3-5, 1899, JEM Papers, box 126-18, no. 236; John W. Evans to Moorland, May 9, 1902, and April 30, 1902, JEM Papers, box 126-17, no. 225; Hunton to Moorland, Oct. 14, 1901, JEM Papers, box 126-63, no. 1207; *Monthly Bulletin of the Colored Young Men's Christian Association*, Baltimore, July 1899, p. 1; W.E. Williams to Moorland, March 14, 1902, JEM Papers, box 126-22, no. 326.

33. Hunton, *William Alphaeus Hunton*, 39; *Messenger* Jan. 1897, p. 2, and March 1897, p. 2. The editors were D. Webster Davis and R.T. Hill of Richmond, P.L. Barber of Norfolk, J.M. Colson of Petersburg, Walter P. Hall of Philadelphia, James H. Meriwether of Washington, D.C., and N.C. Bruce of Raleigh, North Carolina.

34. *Messenger*, Nov. 1896, p. 2; Jan. 1897, p. 2; Dec. 1896, p. 4; April 1897, p. 3; Dec. 1896, p. 4; and April 1897, p. 3.

35. *Messenger* Jan. 1897, p. 2.

36. "Report of the Army and Navy Department of the International Commit-

tee," in *Year Book, 1899*, ii, i, iv; Richard C. Lancaster, *Serving the U.S. Armed Forces, 1861-1986: The Story of the YMCA's Ministry to Military Personnel for 125 Years* (Schaumburg, Ill.: Armed Services YMCA of the USA, 1987), 21; Hopkins, *History of the YMCA*, 452-54.

37. Hunton, *William Alphaeus Hunton*, 45-46; circular by William A. Hunton, Aug. 1, 1898, JEM Papers, box 126-58, no. 1115.

38. "Report of the Army and Navy Department," viii; Hunton, *William Alphaeus Hunton*, 46.

39. Jean Blackwell Hutson, "Hunton, Addie D. Waites," in *Dictionary of American Negro Biography*, ed. Rayford W. Logan and Michael R. Winston (New York: Norton, 1982), 337.

40. Hunton, *William Alphaeus Hunton*, 37, 38-39. In 1907, as a result of Addie's early involvement with the YMCA, the National Board of the YWCA appointed her as a secretary for work among black students. During World War I Addie returned to the YMCA to serve as one of three black women with black troops in France.

41. *Year Book, 1895*, 30; Hunton to Moorland, Aug. 16, 1897, JEM Papers, box 126-63, no. 1196; Hunton, *William Alphaeus Hunton*, 40.

42. *Year Book, 1897*, 35; *Proceedings*, Mobile, Ala., April 21-25, 1897, pp. 47, 21.

43. "Editorial Notes," ca. 1896, JEM Papers, box 126-62, no. 1194; *Messenger*, Jan. 1897, pp. 2, 3. The committee consisted of Charles C. Dogan of Norfolk, S.C. Burrell of Richmond, and Robert R. Moton of Hampton. In 1898 J.H. Johnston, president of the Virginia Normal and Collegiate Institute, replaced Burrell.

44. *Messenger*, March 1897, p. 2; "Circular Letter," March 10, 1898, JEM Papers, box 126-58, no. 1115.

45. "Employment Agreement," Oct. 7, 1898, JEM Papers, box 126-20, no. 276. For biographical information about Moorland, see Biographical Records, "Jesse E. Moorland—1940"; "Short Sketch of Life of Jesse E. Moorland," March 16, 1925, JEM Papers, box 126-7, no. 123; Michael R. Winston, "Moorland, Jesse Edward," in *Dictionary of American Negro Biography*, ed. Rayford W. Logan and Michael R. Winston (New York: Norton, 1982), 448-52; *New York Times*, May 2, 1940, p. 24; *Journal of Negro History* 25 (July 1940): 401-3; and "Biographical Statement," n.d., JEM Papers, box 126-7, no. 123.

46. "Short Sketch of Life of Jesse E. Moorland."

47. Ibid.

48. Ibid.

49. Winston, "Moorland," 448-52; *New York Times*, May 2, 1940, p. 24; *Journal of Negro History* 25 (July 1940): 401-3; "Biographical Statement"; "Short Sketch of Life of Jesse E. Moorland."

50. "Biographical Outline," n.d., Biographical Records, "Jesse E. Moorland—1940."

51. Hunton, *William Alphaeus Hunton*, 30; Winston, "Moorland," 448-52; *New York Times*, May 2, 1940, p. 24; *Journal of Negro History* 25 (July 1940): 401-3; "Biographical Statement"; "Short Sketch of Life of Jesse E. Moorland."

52. Hunton, *William Alphaeus Hunton*, 50.

53. Ibid., 30, 50, 51; Hunton to Moorland, Oct. 3, 1896, JEM Papers, box 126-63, no. 1196.

54. Hunton, *William Alphaeus Hunton*, 88; Hunton to Moorland, Aug. 16, 1897, JEM Papers, box 126-63, no. 1196.

55. Hunton, *William Alphaeus Hunton*, 49; Jesse E. Moorland, "The Colored Men's Department," ca. 1920, pp. 11-12, JEM Papers, box 126-59, no. 1132.

4. Recruitment and Training of African-American YMCA Secretaries, 1898-1943

1. See appendix A.

2. Jesse E. Moorland, handwritten report, ca. 1904, p. 2, JEM Papers, box 126-60, no. 1161; [Jesse E. Moorland?], "The Colored Men's Department of the YMCA of North America," n.d., p. 3, Black YMCA Records, box 1, History and Organization Reports, 1919-38.

3. Robert B. Bruce to Moorland, Dec. 22, 1901, JEM Papers, box 126-16, no. 204; Moorland to W.R. Coles, Jr., Sept. 11, 1901, JEM Papers, box 126-17, no. 213.

4. Some white branches had paid executives before the Civil War, but usually these men did not make YMCA work a career. See C. Howard Hopkins, *History of the YMCA in North American* (Nw York: Association Press, 1951), 161.

5. Hopkins, *History of the YMCA*, 162, 168: Colored Men's Department, "September Conference, 1899, City Work," p. 1, JEM Papers, box 126-58, no. 1116; Hunton to Moorland, Feb. 6, 1900, JEM Papers, box 126-63, no. 1202.

6. H.W. Porter to Moorland, Dec. 2, 1901, JEMPapers, box 126-21, no. 289; Hopkins, *History of the YMCA*, 166; Hunton to Moorland, Aug. 8, 1899, JEM Papers, box 126-63, no. 1200; "The Jesse E. Moorland Y.M.C.A. Training Fund: To Train Colored Men for the Y.M.C.A. Secretaryship," ca. 1923-24, JEM Papers, box 126-21, no. 283.

7. "Minutes Staff Conference, Colored Men's Department," Jan. 18-20, 1921, p. 5, JEM Papers, box 126-60, no. 1155; "Secretaryship Application," JEM Papers, box 126-18, no. 240.

8. Hunton to Moorland, Oct. 14, 1901, JEM Papers, box 126-63, no. 1207; Addie W. Hunton, *William Alphaeus Hunton: A Pioneer Prophet of Young Men* (New York: Association Press, 1938), 74, 39; Lucy C. Moorland to Aunt Nicy[?], March 13, 1904, JEM Papers, box 126-2, no. 32.

9. Charles C. Dogan to Moorland, Nov. 5, 1901, JEM Papers, box 126-17, no. 219; John B. Watson, "Report of Service at Conference of Secretaries, Colored Men's Department," Jan. 1, 1913, pp. 2-3, Black YMCA Records, box 3, Colored Work Department—Secretaries' Reports—1910-24.

10. Jesse E. Moorland, "The Young Men's Christian Association: A Potent Agency in the Salvation of Young Men," n.d., JEM Papers, box 126-27, no. 563; idem, "Y.M.C.A. Work among Colored Young Men," n.d., JEM Papers, box 126-27, no. 559.

11. Robert J. Macbeth to Moorland, Sept. 17, 1902, JEM Papers, box 126-20, no. 264; Jesse E. Moorland, "The Work of the Young Men's Christian Association among Colored Young Men," ca. 1901, p. 5, JEM Papers, box 126-27, no. 554; Hunton to Moorland, Feb. 6, 1900, JEM Papers, box 126-63, no. 1202; Hunton to Moorland, Aug. 8, 1899, JEM Papers, box 126-63, no. 1200.

12. George F. Robinson to Moorland, Aug. 1899[?], JEM Papers, box 126-21, no. 294; Joanna P. Moore to Moorland, Oct. 2, 1906, and Oct. 23, 1906, JEM Papers, box 126-20, no. 274; W.A. Kling to Moorland, Jan. 10, 1900, JEM Papers, box 126-19, no. 259; W.T. Maxwell to Moorland, July 23, 1900, JEM Papers, box 126-20, no. 268; W. Edward Williams to Moorland, Nov. 3, 1900, JEM Papers, box 126-22, no. 326.

13. E.W. Newsome to Moorland, Dec. 28, 1902, JEM Papers, box 126-21, no. 280.

14. W.E. Green to Moorland, Sept. 28, 1899, Oct. 28, 1899, and April 18, 1900, all in JEM Papers, box 126-18, no. 236.

15. L.A. Brown to Moorland, June 25, 1902, JEM Papers, box 126-16, no. 203.

16. Thomas W. Burton to Moorland, Oct. 10, 1900, and Sept. 8, 1900, both in JEM Papers, box 126-16, no. 209. For a brief discussion of the black YMCA in Springfield, see T.C. McMillen, *The Springfield, Ohio, YMCA, 1854-1954* (Springfield, Ohio: Springfield Tribune Printing Co., 1954), 115-19.

17. John Russell Harvey to Moorland, Sept. 4, 1902; T.S. Inborden to Moorland, Sept. 13, 1901, both in JEM Papers, box 126-18, no. 240.

18. J.R. Kirkpatrick to Moorland, May 19, 1899, JEM Papers, box 126-19, no. 259.

19. W.J. Trent, secretary, Butler Street YMCA, Atlanta, to Moorland, April 8, 1922; Moorland to John Hope, April 11, 1922; and W.A. Bell to Hope, Oct. 20, 1926, all in Papers of John and Lugenia Burns Hope, Robert A. Woodruff Library, Atlanta University Center, Atlanta, Georgia, microfilm, University Publications of America, reel 12; hereinafter cited as Hope Papers.

20. W.T. Maxwell to Moorland, July 23, 1900, JEM Papers, box 126-20, no. 268; John H. Whaley to Moorland, Feb. 5, 1902, JEM Papers, box 126-22, no. 320.

21. S.A. Furniss and H.L. Hummins to Moorland, April 11, 1902; John W. Evans to Moorland, June 9, 1902, and July 18, 1902, all in JEM Papers, box 126-17, no. 225.

22. Jesse E. Moorland, handwritten report, ca. 1904, p. 5, JEM Papers, box 126-60, no. 1161; "Minutes Staff Conference, Colored Men's Department," Jan. 12-14, 1922, p. 3, JEM Papers, box 126-60, no. 1155.

23. The *Secretarial Letter* varied in length from one to fifteen pages. Copies of the *Secretarial Letter* are located in JEM Papers, box 126-60, no. 1169, and box 126-61, nos. 1170, 1171, 1172, and 1176; and Black YMCA Records, box 2, Miscellaneous Articles, Reports, and Historical Statements, 1910-50, and box 3, Colored Work Department—Periodicals—*Secretarial News Letter*, 1910-15.

24. "Letter Number One," probably Nov. 1902, Black YMCA Records, box 2, no. Misc. Articles, Reports, and Historical Statements, 1910-50; *Secretarial Letter*, Jan. 1937, JEM Papers, box 126-61, no. 1176.

25. *Secretarial Letter*, April 1908, p. 3, JEM Papers, box 126-61, no. 1170; *Secretarial Letter*, Sept. 1907, p. 1, JEM Papers, box 126-60, no. 1169; *Secretarial Letter*, April 1908, p. 4, and Jan. 1909, p. 6, JEM Papers, box 126-61, no. 1170; *Secretarial Letter*, Dec. 1910, p. 3, JEM Papers, box 126-61, no. 1171.

26. *Secretarial Letter*, Jan. 1910, p. 3, JEM Papers, box 126-61, no. 1171.

27. *Secretarial Letter*, June 1909, p. 4, JEM Papers, box 126-61, no. 1170.

28. *Secretarial Letter*, Nov. 1912, p. 2, Black YMCA Records, box 3, Colored Work Department—Periodicals—*Secretarial News Letter*, 1910-15.

29. Watson, "Report of Service at Conference of Secretaries," 2; Moorland to George F. Robinson, May 19, 1900, JEM Papers, box 126-21, no. 294; William Anderson, "George Robert Arthur," n.d., YMCA of Metropolitan Chicago Records, box 2, no. 22, Chicago Historical Society, Chicago.

30. Watson, "Report of Service at Conference of Secretaries," 3; *Secretarial Letter*, Dec. 1912, p. 1, JEM Papers, box 126-61, no. 1172.

31. Hopkins, *History of the YMCA*, 172, 175-176; J. Quincy Ames, *The Advance in Professional Standards of the Secretaryship of the Young Men's Christian Associations* (Chicago: YMCA College, 1929), 4-6; International YMCA College, *Catalog, 1927-29*, 14-17, Laura Spelman Rockefeller Memorial, Rockefeller Archive Center, Pocantico Hills, North Tarrytown, New York, ser. 3, subser. 4, box 20, no. 213. For a discussion of the Chicago YMCA Training School, see Frederick Roger Dunn, "The Central Y.M.C.A. Schools of Chicago: A Study in Urban History," Ph.D. diss., Univ. of Chicago, 1940.

32. "Statement by Edwin D. Ingersoll of the International Committee from

1877 to 1887 Inclusive," p. 2, Biographical Records, "William A. Hunton, 1888-1978"; George P. Antone, "The YMCA Graduate School, Nashville, 1919-1936," *Tennessee Historical Quarterly* 32, no. 1 (1973): 68.

33. Hunton, *William Alphaeus Hunton,* 75; Hunton to Moorland, Sept. 24, 1901, JEM Papers, box 126-63, no. 1207; Robert P. Hamlin to Moorland, Dec. 14, 1901, JEM Papers, box 126-18, no. 238; Sarah A. Allen, "A New Profession: The First Colored Graduate of the Y.M.C.A. Training School, Springfield, Massachusetts," *Colored American Magazine,* Sept. 1903, pp. 661-63.

34. Robert P. Hamlin to Moorland, Dec. 14, 1901, JEM Papers, box 126-18, no. 238; Elmer E. Thompson to Moorland, Oct. 1, 1901, JEM Papers, box 126-22, no. 308.

35. John W. Hansel to Moorland, Aug. 7, 1900, May 13, 1901, and Oct. 20, 1902, all in JEM Papers, box 126-18, no. 239.

36. John W. Hansel to Benjamin J. Fisher, Nov. 10, 1902, JEM Papers, box 126-18, no. 239. The sources do not indicate whether Fisher ever attended the YMCA training school in Chicago.

37. Moorland to John W. Hansel, Oct. 24, 1902, JEM Papers, box 126-19, no. 247; "Annual Statement of the Work of the Colored Work Department of the National Council," Sept. 1, 1926-Aug. 31, 1927, p. 3, JEM Papers, box 126-60, no. 1156; "Report of the Proceedings of the National Conference on the Work of the Young Men's Christian Association among Colored Men and Boys," p. 7, JEM Papers, box 126-61, no. 1176.

38. Newspaper clippings, n.d., JEM Papers, box 126-58, no. 1115.

39. "The 15th Annual Conference of the Colored Men's Department of the YMCA, Talladega College, Talladega, Alabama, November 10-13, 1904," p. 7, Black YMCA Records, box 2, Staff and Lay Conferences—Minutes and Reports, 1899-1945.

40. In 1908 Haynes left the International Committee to study social work at Columbia University. He was replaced by John B. Watson. See Inabel Burns Lindsay, "Haynes, George Edmund," in *Dictionary of American Negro Biography* ed. Rayford W. Logan and Michael R. Winston (New York: Norton, 1982), 298-300; Hunton, *William Alphaeus Hunton,* 57-58; Daniel Perlman, "Stirring the White Conscience: The Life of George Edmund Haynes," Ph.D. diss., New York Univ., 1972, pp. 26-49; Samuel K. Roberts, "George Edmund Haynes: Advocate for Interracial Cooperation," in *Black Apostles: Afro-American Clergy Confront the Twentieth Century,* ed. Randall K. Burkett and Richard Newman (Boston: G.K. Hall, 1978), 97-127. See appendix B.

41. "Chesapeake Association Summer School Twentieth Anniversary Session Held at Manual Training and Industrial School, Bordentown, New Jersey," July 7-21, 1927, JEM Papers, box 126-38, no. 792.

42. William O. Easton to Frank K. Sanders, July 19, 1923, Education Records, E 10, Various Summer Schools—Correspondence Reports, 1922-25, YMCA Archives. These records are hereinafter cited as Education Records.

43. In 1945 the Chesapeake Summer School moved to Wilberforce University in Ohio, where it remained until its last session in 1948. See Ralph W. Bullock, "Brief Report of Activities and Services Rendered between September 1 and December 31, 1945," Biographical Records, "Ralph Waldo Bullock, 1927-50"; Education Records, E 9, Chesapeake Summer School—Conference Pamphlets, 1912-48, Chesapeake Summer School, 1941, and Various Training Schools; E 10, Various Summer Schools—Correspondence, Reports—1922-25, and Various Summer Schools—Announcements—Guides—Manuals, 1916-38; E 11, Reports; JEM Papers, box 126-38, no. 792.

44. Until 1920 the YMCA's International Committee contributed to the school's budget. See *Year Book, 1919*, 578; *Year Book, 1921*, 16; Jesse E. Moorland, "Circular Letter," May 15, 1911, Black YMCA Records, box 4, Miscellaneous Conference Materials 1920s-50s; R.B. DeFrantz to John Hope, Oct. 23, 1920, Hope Papers, reel 12; and Campbell C. Johnson, "Report to the Permanent Committee on the Association Vocation Regarding the Chesapeake Summer School Association, Summer School, Harpers Ferry, West Virginia, July 9-23," p. 4, Education Records, E 10, Various Summer Schools—Correspondence, Reports—1922-25.

45. "Report on the Association Summer Schools during 1923, February 1, 1924," p. 2, Education Records, E 10, Various Summer Schools—Correspondence, Reports—1922-25; "Report of the Proceedings of the National Conference on the Work of the Young Men's Christian Association among Colored Men and Boys," Chicago, Oct. 18-20, 1929, p. 7, JEM Papers, box 126-61, no. 1176.

46. William Knowles Cooper to Frank K. Sanders, Sept. 16, 1924; and William O. Easton, "Report on the Association Summer Schools during 1923, February 1, 1924," p. 2, both in Education Records, E 10, Various Summer Schools—Correspondence, Reports—1922-25.

47. "Quotation from the Report of the Permanent Committee on Vocational Training; Presented to and Unanimously Approved by the 41st International Convention of the YMCA of North America, Atlantic City, New Jersey, November 15, 1922," p. 1, Education Records, E 10, Various Summer Schools—Correspondence Reports—1922-25; Channing H. Tobias to Moorland, July 16, 1929, JEM Papers, box 126-39, no. 828; "Summary of Report on the Work for Colored Men and Boys," Jan. 18, 1916, pp. 5, 6, Black YMCA Records, box 1, Addresses, 1893-1935.

48. White YMCAs established regional summer schools at Silver Bay, New York (1900), Hot Springs, Arkansas (1908), Hollister, Missouri (1911), Lake Forest, Illinois (1911), Blue Ridge, North Carolina (1912), Asilomar, California (1914), and Seabeck, Washington (1919). Hopkins, *History of the YMCA*, 614-18.

49. "21st Session Chesapeake Association Summer School, Manual Training and Industrial School, Bordentown, New Jersey, July 6-20, 1928," p. 6, Education Records, E 9, Chesapeake Summer School—Conference, Pamphlets—1912-48; Frank V. Slack, "The Work of the Summer Schools of the YMCAs for 1925: A Summary of the Reports Made to the Permanent Committee on the Association Vocation," p. 16, Education Records, E 10, Various Summer Schools—Announcements—Guides—Manuals, 1916-38; "Report of Committee on Summer Schools, March 23-24, 1915," Education Records, E 10, Various Summer Schools—Correspondence, Reports—1922-25; and "Training Program of the YMCA," n.d., Laura Spelman Rockefeller Memorial, Rockefeller Archive Center, ser. 3, subser. 4, box 23, no. 241.

50. J. Edward Sproul, "The Summer Schools of the YMCAs in 1926: A Study of Their Educational Problems and Opportunities," p. 29, Education Records, E 10, Various Summer Schools—Announcements—Guides—Manuals, 1916-38.

51. Only the schools at Blue Ridge, North Carolina, and Hollister, Missouri, denied admission to blacks. "Annual Statement of the Work of the Colored Work Department of the National Council," Sept. 1, 1926-Aug. 31, 1927, p. 3, Black YMCA Records, box 3, Colored Work Department—Secretary Reports, 1927; "Report of the Proceedings of the National Conference on the Work of the Young Men's Christian Association among Colored Men and Boys," Chicago, Oct. 18-20, 1929, p. 7, JEM Papers, box 126-61, no. 1176.

52. By 1926, 245 black men had attended the school's summer sessions. "Chesapeake Association Summer School Twentieth Anniversary Session Held

at Manual Training and Industrial School, Bordentown, New Jersey," July 7-21, 1927, JEM Papers, box 126-38, no. 792; Sproul, "Summer Schools of the YMCAs in 1926," 29.

53. "Annual Statement of the Work of the Colored Work Department of the National Council," Sept. 1, 1926-Aug. 31, 1927, p. 3; Campbell C. Johnson to Moorland, Jan. 19, 1925, JEM Papers, box 126-38, no. 792.

54. "Annual Statement of the Work of the Colored Work Department of the National Council," Sept. 1, 1926-Aug. 31, 1927, p. 3; Sproul, "Summer Schools of the YMCAs in 1926," 29.

55. "Annual Statement of the Work of the Colored Work Department of the National Council," Sept. 1, 1926-Aug. 31, 1927, p. 3; Sproul, "Summer Schools of the YMCAs in 1926," 29; Slack, "Work of the Summer Schools of the YMCAs for 1925," 17.

56. Johnson, "Report to the Permanent Committee on the Association Vocation Regarding the Chesapeake Summer School Association," 3; "16th Session Chesapeake Summer School, Storer College, Harper's Ferry, West Virginia, July 11-25, 1923," JEM Papers, box 126-38, no. 792.

57. William O. Eaton to Frank K. Sanders, July 19, 1923, p. 3, Education Records, E 10, Various Summer Schools—Correspondence, Reports, 1922-25; "Report of the 12th Session of the Chesapeake Summer School, Harper's Ferry, July 2-16, 1919," p. 2, Education Records, E 9, Chesapeake Summer School—Conference Pamphlets—1912-48; "National Y.M.C.A. Conference of Laymen and Secretaries, Chesapeake Summer School Association, August 5-8, 1948," Education Records, E 9, Chesapeake Summer School—Conference Pamphlets—1912-48; Moorland to John Hope, April 4, 1921, Hope Papers, reel 12; and appendix C.

58. Moorland, "Circular Letter," May 15, 1911; "21st Session Chesapeake Association Summer School, Manual Training and Industrial School, Bordentown, New Jersey, July 6-20, 1928," 5; Hunton, *William Alphaeus Hunton*, 85.

59. Moorland, "Circular Letter," May 15, 1911. Following Moorland's retirement, local black secretaries elected officers and trustees who were responsible for the school's annual program. Johnson, "Report to the Permanent Committee on the Association Vocation Regarding the Chesapeake Summer School Association"; Jesse E. Moorland, "The Pioneering Work of the Y.M.C.A.," ca. 1922, p. 2, Black YMCA Records, box 1, History and Organization Reports, 1919-38.

60. Moorland, "Circular Letter," May 15, 1911.

61. Jesse E. Moorland, "The Opportunity and Responsibility of the International Committee in the Progress of the Department," Jan. 1, 1913, pp. 3, 2, JEM Papers, box 126-60, no. 1149.

62. Ibid., 2, 3, 4.

63. Moorland Notebook, July 21, 1924, JEM Papers, box 126-73, no. 1388.

64. J.H. McGrew to P.M. Flock, June 13, 1928, JEM Papers, box 126-38, no. 792; *Secreterial Letter*, Oct. 1912, p. 1, JEM Papers, box 126-61, no. 1172; George R. Arthur, *Life on the Negro Frontier: A Study of the Objectives and the Success of the Activities Promoted in the Young Men's Christian Associations Operating in "Rosenwald" Buildings* (New York: Association Press, 1934), 92.

65. J.A. Green to Moorland, Dec. 21, 1929, JEM Papers, box 126-18, no. 236; Will W. Alexander to Arthur W. Packard, Dec. 11, 1931, Rockefeller Family Archives, RG 2, JDR, Jr.—Welfare Interests—Youth, box 33, National Council—YMCA—Colored Work, Rockefeller Archive Center; Clipping, Oct. 12, 1932, JEM Papers, box 126-7, no. 125.

66. "Memorandum," Jan. 18, 1943, Black YMCA Records, box 1, Policy—Correspondence and Statements, 1913-41. See appendixes B and F.

5. Philanthropists and the Construction of YMCA Buildings, 1901-1933

1. Jesse E. Moorland, "Notes," ca. 1903, JEM Papers, box 126-61, no. 1177; *Year Book, 1903,* 226; William A. Hunton, "Colored Men's Department of the Young Men's Christian Association," *Voice of the Negro,* June 1905, p. 394; William A. Hunton, *Colored Young Men: History, Methods and Relationships of Association Work among Them* (New York: YMCA International Committee, [ca. 1900]), 25-26. See appendixes A and D.

2. Moorland and Hunton, "Circular Letter," Oct. 15, 1900, JEM Papers, box 126-58, no. 1116.

3. For a discussion of philanthropy during the early twentieth century, see Robert H. Bremner, *American Philanthropy* (Chicago: Univ. of Chicago Press, 1970), 105-42. The black YMCAs in Brooklyn and Columbus, Georgia, were acquired with the help of Peabody, and the Twelfth Street branch in Washington, D.C., was built with the support of Rockefeller and Rosenwald. For a complete listing of black YMCA buildings constructed with Rosenwald's financial support, see appendix G.

4. Louise Ware, *George Foster Peabody: Banker, Philanthropist, Publicist* (Athens: Univ. of Georgia Press, 1951), 12; Louise Ware, "Peabody, George Foster," in *Dictionary of American Biography*, suppl. 2, p. 520.

5. Peabody was a member of the board of trustees of the American Church Institute for Negroes, Penn Normal and Industrial and Agricultural School in South Carolina, Hampton Institute, and Tuskegee Institute. He also served as treasurer of the Southern Education Board, the General Education Board and the Negro Rural School Fund. Ware, "Peabody," 520.

6. Ware, *George Foster Peabody*, 13.

7. Richard C. Morse [?] to Peabody, Jan. 16, 1905, George Foster Peabody Papers, box 73, YMCA (ca. 1901-8), Library of Congress, Washington, D.C. hereinafter cited as GFP Papers; N. Barnett Dodson, "Carlton Avenue Branch of the Brooklyn, N.Y., Young Men's Christian Association," *Colored American Magazine*, Feb. 1904, p. 117; Jesse E. Moorland, "Report to International Committee and Secretaries Conference," 1902, p. 3, Black YMCA Records, box 3, Colored Work Department—Secretary Reports—1901-9; E. Clark Worman, *History of the Brooklyn and Queens Young Men's Christian Association, 1853-1949* (New York: Association Press, 1952), 98; Editorial, *Association Men,* July 1902, p. 456; *New York Age*, May 11, 1905, p. 3; untitled manuscript, n.d., p. 3, JEM Papers, box 126-60, no. 1160.

8. P.H. Foster to president, officers, and members of the Colored YMCA, Columbus, Jan. 24, 1902, GFP Papers, box 73, YMCA (ca. 1901-8); Moorland to L.G. Myers, Washington, D.C., July 13, 1908, GFP Papers, box 73, YMCA, Columbus, Georgia (Negro), (ca. 1905-9); Ware, *George Foster Peabody*, 91.

9. Addie W. Hunton, *William Alphaeus Hunton: A Pioneer Prophet of Young Men* (New York: Association Press, 1938), 37; Hunton to Peabody, Feb. 8, 1905, GFP Papers, box 73, YMCA (ca. 1901-8).

10. Moorland to L.G. Myers, Washington, D.C., July 13, 1908, GFP Papers, box 73, YMCA, Columbus, Georgia (Negro), (ca. 1905-9); Ware, *George Foster Peabody*, 91; John W. Evans to Peabody, n.d., GFP Papers, box 73, YMCA (ca. 1901-8).

11. Richard C. Morse to John D. Rockefeller, Jr., Nov. 23, 1905, Rockefeller Family Archives, RG 2, JDR, Jr.—Welfare Interests—Youth, box 30, YMCA—International Committee—Home Work, Rockefeller Archive Center, Pocantico

Hills, North Tarrytown, New York; hereinafter cited as RF Archives. See also the John D. Rockefeller Papers, Financial Materials, Charities Index series, Rockefeller Archive Center.

12. John D. Rockefeller, *Random Reminiscences of Men and Events* (Tarrytown, N.Y.: Sleepy Hollow Press and Rockefeller Archive Center, 1984), 98-100.

13. For a discussion of Rockefeller's philanthropy, see Allan Nevins, *John D. Rockefeller: The Heroic Age of American Enterprise*, vol. 2 (New York: Charles Scribner's Sons, 1940), 614-65; John W. Klein, "The Role and Impact of Rockefeller Philanthropy during the Progressive Era," Ph.D. diss., Fordham Univ., 1980; and John Ensor Harr and Peter J. Johnson, *The Rockefeller Century* (New York: Charles Scribner's Sons, 1988), 66-88, 120-24.

14. Henry B.F. MacFarland to Rockefeller, Jr., Jan. 2, 1906, RF Archives, RG 2, box 36, YMCA—Washington D.C.; Thomas B. Hargrave, Jr., *Private Differences—General Good: A History of the YMCA of Metropolitan Washington* (Washington, D.C.: YMCA of Metropolitan Washington, 1985), 70. Prior to beginning his support of the black branch, Rockefeller had contributed fifty thousand dollars to the building fund of Washington's white YMCA. Starr J. Murphy [?] to Rockefeller, Jr., July 24, 1906, RF Archives, RG 2, box 36, YMCA—Washington, D.C.

15. "Twelfth Street Financial Items Minutes of Board of Directors, Beginning July 11, 1898," p. 1, manuscript in the possession of Thomas B. Hargrave, Jr., president of the YMCA of Metropolitan Washington, D.C.; *Washington Bee*, Dec. 31, 1904, p. 1. For a history of black Washingtonians, see Constance McLaughlin Green, *The Secret City: A History of Race Relations in the Nation's Capital* (Princeton, N.J.: Princeton Univ. Press, 1967).

16. Hargrave, *Private Differences*, 70; S.W. Woodward to Rockefeller, Jr., ca. July 1906, RF Archives, RG 2, box 36, YMCA—Washington, D.C.

17. Rockefeller, *Random Reminiscences*, 98; Rockefeller, Sr., quoted in Barbara Howe, "The Emergence of Scientific Philanthropy, 1900-1920: Origins, Issues, and Outcomes," in *Philanthropy and Cultural Imperialism: The Foundations at Home and Abroad*, ed. Robert F. Arnove (Bloomington: Indiana Univ. Press, 1980), 38; Rockefeller, Jr., to S.W. Woodward, Sept. 7, 1906, RF Archives, RG 2, box 36, YMCA—Washington, D.C.; Howe, "Emergence of Scientific Philanthropy," 38.

18. Rockefeller, Jr., to Starr J. Murphy, n.d., and Starr J. Murphy to S.W. Woodward, July 17, 1906, both in RF Archives, RG 2, box 36, YMCA—Washington, D.C.

19. Edward W. Hearne to Starr J. Murphy, July 20, 1906, and Rockefeller, Jr., to S.W. Woodward, Sept. 7, 1906, both in RF Archives, RG 2, box 36, YMCA—Washington, D.C.

20. Hargrave, *Private Differences*, 70.

21. *Washington Bee*, Oct. 20, 1906, pp. 1, 4; April 27, 1907, p. 1; Dec. 7, 1907, p. 5. Edward W. Hearne to Rockefeller, May 14, 1907, and Hearne to Starr J. Murphy, May 14, 1907, RF Archives, RG 2, box 36, YMCA—Washington, D.C.

22. *Washington Bee*, Feb. 6, 1909, p. 4.

23. Only a few members of the board of directors of the white branch contributed several hundred dollars to the black building fund. Edward W. Hearne to Starr J. Murphy, May 14, 1907, RF Archives, RG 2, box 36, YMCA—Washington, D.C.

24. *Washington Bee*, Dec. 7, 1907, p. 5; May 11, 1907, p. 1. George Otis Smith to Rockefeller, Jr., Aug. 3, 1909, RF Archives, RG 2, box 36, YMCA—Washington, D.C.

25. Hargrave, *Private Differences*, 71; *Washington Bee*, Oct. 12, 1907, p. 1; Louis R. Harlan, *Booker T. Washington: The Wizard of Tuskegee, 1901-1915* (New York: Oxford Univ. Press, 1983), 95, 118-20. Pittman graduated from Tuskegee Institute in 1897 and three years later graduated from Drexel. He returned to Tuskegee, where he taught for five years. During that period he also designed Tuskegee's Collis P. Huntington Memorial building and Rockefeller Hall. In 1905 he established an office in Washington, D.C., where he worked for black and white clients. On October 31, 1907, Pittman married Portia Washington at Tuskegee.

26. Lewis E. Johnson, executive secretary, Twelfth Street branch, Washington, D.C., to Rockefeller, Jr., June 16, 1912, RF Archives, RG 2, box 36, YMCA—Washington, D.C.

27. *Washington Bee*, March 6, 1909, p. 4; May 5, 1909, p. 4; Feb. 6, 1909, p. 4.

28. George Otis Smith to Rockefeller, Jr., Aug. 3, 1909, and Starr J. Murphy to Rockefeller, Jr., Oct. 1, 1909, both in RF Archives, RG 2, box 36, YMCA—Washington, D.C.

29. George Otis Smith to Rockefeller, Jr., Aug. 3, 1909, RF Archives, RG 2, box 36, YMCA—Washington, D.C.

30. Starr J. Murphy to Rockefeller, Jr., Sept. 20, 1909, and Sept. 24, 1909, both in RF Archives, RG 2, box 36, YMCA—Washington, D.C.; *Washington Bee*, April 16, 1910, p. 4; April 30, 1910, p. 4; May 4, 1910, p. 4; May 14, 1910, p. 4; March 4 and 18, 1911, p. 4; May 6, 20, and 27, 1911, pp. 1, 4; Dec. 30, 1911, p. 1; May 18, 1912, p. 1; Lewis E. Johnson to Rockefeller, Jr., June 16, 1912, RF Archives, RG 2, box 36, YMCA—Washington, D.C.

31. *Washington Bee*, May 5, 1909, p. 4; Dec. 7, 1907, p. 5. See appendixes A and D, and C. Howard Hopkins, *History of the YMCA in North America* (New York: Association Press, 1951), 458. Hopkins estimates that nineteen black YMCA buildings existed, while J. Max Bond lists twenty-five associations in "Manuscript on the Historical Development of the YMCA among Negroes, 1931," p. 9., Julius Rosenwald Fund Archives, Fisk University, Nashville, Tennessee, box 371, folder 5. The YMCA *Year Book, 1910-11* gives two different numbers: nineteen and sixteen buildings (pp. 21, 264). For accounts of black and white cooperation during fund-raising campaigns, see *Secretarial Letter,* June 1906 and March 1907, JEM Papers, box 126-61, no. 1169; *Secretarial Letter,* Jan. 1908 and Jan. and June 1909, JEM Papers, box 126-61, no. 1170; and *Secretarial Letter,* Jan. and Dec. 1910, JEM Papers, box 126-61, no. 1171.

32. A.G. Clyde Randall, "Settled Principles of Association Work," conference of black YMCAs, Louisville, Kentucky, 1909, p. 9, JEM Papers, box 126-47, no. 950.

33. "Leadership Environment and Fellowship for the Colored Men and Boys of North America," ca. 1915, p. 8, JEM Papers, box 126-59, no. 1147; International Committee to Rockefeller, Jr., Jan. 19, 1911, RF Archives, RG 2, box 30, YMCA—International Committee—Home Work. See appendixes B and G.

34. For biographical information about Rosenwald, see Pauline K. Angell, "Julius Rosenwald," *American Jewish Yearbook* 34 (Oct. 1, 1932-Sept. 20, 1933): 141-76; Morris Robert Werner, *Julius Rosenwald: The Life of a Practical Humanitarian* (New York: Harper and Brothers, 1939); Edwin R. Embree and Julia Waxman, *Investment in People: The Story of the Julius Rosenwald Fund* (New York: Harper and Brothers, 1949); Kathleen Williams Boom, "The Julius Rosenwald Fund's Aid to Education in the South," Ph.D. diss., Univ. of Chicago, 1949; A. Gilbert Belles, "The Julius Rosenwald Fund: Efforts in Race Relations, 1928-1948," Ph.D. diss., Vanderbilt Univ., 1972; and Lawrence P. Bachmann, "Julius Rosenwald," *American Jewish History Quarterly* 66, no. 1 (1976): 89-105.

35. Werner, *Julius Rosenwald,* 13; *New York Times,* Jan. 7, 1932, p. 18; Embree and Waxman, *Investment in People,* 8.

36. Belles, "Julius Rosenwald Fund," 3; Julius Rosenwald, "The Burden of Wealth," *Saturday Evening Post,* Jan. 5, 1929, p. 136; Embree and Waxman, *Investment in People,* 13; Rosenwald quoted in Werner, *Julius Rosenwald,* 81.

37. Andrew Carnegie, "Wealth," June 1889, in *Great Issues in American History: From Reconstruction to the Present Day, 1864-1981,* ed. Richard Hofstadter and Beatrice K. Hofstadter (New York: Vintage Books, 1982), 79-84. For a discussion of Rosenwald's philanthropic philosophy, see Rosenwald, "Burden of Wealth," 12-13, 136; idem, "Principles of Public Giving," *Atlantic Monthly,* May 1929, pp. 599-606; and idem, "A New Chapter in Philanthropy," *Whitman College Quarterly,* Jan. 1931, pp. 3-19. Additional information can be obtained from Edwin R. Embree, "The Business of Giving Away Money," *Harper's Magazine,* Aug. 1930, pp. 320-29; J. Scott McCormick, "The Julius Rosenwald Fund," *Journal of Negro Education* 3 (Oct. 1934): 605-26; Embree and Waxman, *Investment in People*; Boom, "Julius Rosenwald Fund's Aid to Education in the South"; Daniel J. Boorstin, "Transforming the Charitable Spirit," in *The Julius Rosenwald Centennial* (Chicago: Univ. of Chicago, 1962), 5-33; A. Gilbert Belles, "The College Faculty, the Negro Scholar, and the Julius Rosenwald Fund," *Journal of Negro History* 54, no. 4 (1969): 383-92; John H. Stanfield, *Philanthropy and Jim Crow in American Social Science* (Westport, Conn.: Greenwood Press, 1985), 97-118; and Belles, "Julius Rosenwald Fund."

38. Rosenwald, "Burden of Wealth," 12; *New York Times,* Jan. 7, 1932, p. 18; Werner, *Julius Rosenwald,* 86-92, ix; Embree and Waxman, *Investment in People,* 15, 25; *New York Times,* Jan. 7, 1932, p. 18.

39. *New York Times,* Feb. 19, 1965, p. 35; Bachmann, "Julius Rosenwald," 95; John G. Brooks, *An American Citizen: The Life of William H. Baldwin, Jr.* (New York: Houghton Mifflin Co., 1910); Booker T. Washington, *Up from Slavery* (New York: Sun Dial Press, 1917); Werner, *Julius Rosenwald,* 107; Embree and Waxman, *Investment in People,* 25; McCormick, "Julius Rosenwald Fund," 606. Rosenwald and Washington did not meet until May 18, 1911, when both attended the fifty-third anniversary celebration of the Chicago YMCA. YMCA, Chicago, Board of Managers, *Fifty-five Years: The Young Men's Christian Association of Chicago, 1858-1913* (Chicago: YMCA Board of Managers, [1913?]), 93. In 1912 Rosenwald became a trustee of Tuskegee Institute and began his support of rural schoolhouses for southern blacks. Harlan, *Wizard,* 140-42, 185, 197-99, 357, 433, 447, 449, 451; Belles, "Julius Rosenwald Fund"; Bachmann, "Julius Rosenwald," 101-2.

40. "Booker T. Washington on the Negro in the American City and His Needs," *Association Men,* Jan. 1911, p. 149; Julius Rosenwald to Chicago YMCA, Dec. 30, 1910, Julius Rosenwald Papers, Univ. of Chicago, Chicago, Illinois, microfilm, reel 85, hereinafter cited as JR Papers; Stanfield, *Philanthropy and Jim Crow,* 98; McCormick, "Julius Rosenwald Fund," 605-6.

41. McCormick, "Julius Rosenwald Fund," 606. For a discussion of black-Jewish cooperation during the early twentieth century, see David Levering Lewis, "Parallels and Divergences: Assimilationist Strategies of Afro-American and Jewish Elites from 1910 to the Early 1930s," *Journal of American History* 71 (Dec. 1984): 543-64; idem, "Shortcuts to the Mainstream: Afro-American and Jewish Notables in the 1920s and 1930s," in *Jews in Black Perspectives: A Dialogue,* ed. Joseph R. Washington, Jr. (Rutherford, N.J.: Fairleigh Dickinson Univ. Press, 1984), 83-97; Lenora E. Berson, *The Negroes and the Jews* (New

York: Random House, 1971), 63-95; and Hasia R. Diner, *In the Almost Promised Land: American Jews and Blacks, 1915-1935* (Westport, Conn.: Greenwood Press, 1977).

42. Julius Rosenwald address, Jan. 1, 1911, in *The Official Bulletin Supplement*, ca. 1911, Black YMCA Records, box 2, Miscellaneous Articles, Reports, and Historical Statements, 1910-50; *Chicago Defender*, Jan. 7, 1911, p. 1; "A Nation-Wide Benefaction," in *The Official Bulletin Supplement*, ca. 1911, Black YMCA Records, box 2, Misc. Articles, Reports, and Historical Statements, 1910-50.

43. Rosenwald contributed $625,000 to black YMCAs and YWCAs and an additional $20 million to other black institutions. *New York Times*, Jan. 7, 1932, p. 18.

44. "Press report of the dedication of the Wabash Avenue YMCA, June 15, 1913," JEM Papers, box 126-41, no. 869; Julius Rosenwald to Chicago YMCA, Dec. 30, 1910, JR Papers, reel 85; "To Give the City Negro a Fair Chance," *Association Men*, Feb. 1911, p. 199.

45. "A Nation-Wide Benefaction"; Booker T. Washington, "Remarkable Triple Alliance: How a Jew Is Helping the Negro through the YMCA," *Outlook*, Oct. 28, 1914, p. 485.

46. Jesse E. Moorland, "A Dream Come True," *Red Cross Magazine*, Feb. 1920, p. 49, Biographical Records, "Julius Rosenwald," no. 2; Werner, *Julius Rosenwald*, 119; Arthur, *Life on the Negro Frontier,* 36; L. Wilbur Messer to Moorland, June 11, 1907, Black YMCA Records, box 6, Colored Work Department—Local, State and Area Relationships, A-K, 1910-45; Moorland to Messer, Sept. 16, 1907, p. 5, Black YMCA Records, box 4, Studies, 1930s-70s. For studies of black Chicagoans during the late nineteenth and early twentieth centuries, see Allan H. Spear, *Black Chicago: The Making of a Negro Ghetto, 1890-1920* (Chicago: Univ. of Chicago Press, 1967); and James R. Grossman, *Land of Hope: Chicago, Black Southerners, and the Great Migration* (Chicago: Univ. of Chicago Press, 1989).

47. Werner, *Julius Rosenwald*, 119; Washington, "Remarkable Triple Alliance," 485; Julius Rosenwald to Chicago YMCA, Dec. 30, 1910, JR Papers, reel 85.

48. "Statement for Mr. Graves," ca. 1922, p. 1, Biographical Records, "Julius Rosenwald," no. 2; Julius Rosenwald, "A Fair Chance for the Colored Man," *Association Men*, Jan. 1914, pp. 192-93.

49. Rosenwald to Walter Wood, Oct. 29, 1913, JR Papers, reel 85; Rosenwald to Thomas E. Taylor, June 30, 1913, JR Papers, reel 84.

50. Stanfield, *Philanthropy and Jim Crow,* 98; "Dedication Chicago Y.M.C.A. for Colored Men, 6/15/13 (J.R.)," JR Papers, reel 85; Rosenwald, "Fair Chance," 192-93.

51. Moorland to William C. Graves, Feb. 12, 1915, Black YMCA Records, box 6, Colored Work Department—Local, State, and Area Associations, T-V, 1915-21 and 1940-42; Booker T. Washington to Moorland, Sept. 14, 1914, Booker T. Washington Papers, Library of Congress, Washington, D.C., microfilm, reel 378; hereinafter cited as BTW Papers; Jesse E. Moorland, "The Young Men's Christian Association among Negroes," *Journal of Negro History* 9 (April 1924): 130-31.

52. YMCA, Chicago, *Fifty-five Years*, 86. In December 1910 a group of blacks under the leadership of Ferdinand Barnett held a first fund-raising meeting. Spear, *Black Chicago*, 100.

53. YMCA, Chicago, *Fifty-five Years*, 86; Hopkins, *History of the YMCA*, 458; Spear, *Black Chicago*, 101.

54. Hopkins, *History of the YMCA*, 458; Channing H. Tobias, "Colored

YMCA," *Crisis,* Nov. 1912, p. 34; Washington, "Remarkable Triple Alliance," 488; "Colored People Who Have Made Large Individual Gifts to YMCA Buildings," p. 1, n.d., Black YMCA Records, box 1, History and Organization Reports, 1919-38.

55. Washington, "Remarkable Triple Alliance," 488; "Colored People Who Have Made Large Individual Gifts to YMCA Buildings," ca. 1914, BTW Papers, reel 378.

56. "Y.M.C.A. Colored, January 1911, letters from friends about the offer," JR Papers, reel 85; William Howard Taft to Rosenwald, Jan. 27, 1911, JR Papers, reel 86; William Howard Taft to L. Wilbur Messer, Jan. 9, 1911, reprinted in the *Chicago Defender*, Jan. 21, 1911, p. 2.

57. *Chicago Defender*, Jan. 7, 1911, p. 1; Washington, "Remarkable Triple Alliance," p. 485; Peabody to Rosenwald, Jan. 5, 1911, JR Papers, reel 85.

58. W.E.B. Du Bois, "Y.M.C.A.," *Crisis*, Dec. 1914, pp. 77, 80; "The Colored Young Men's Christian Association," *Chicago Broad Ax*, Jan. 28, 1911, p. 2.

59. While many black communities tried to match Rosenwald's offer, some blacks in Boston, Cleveland, and Detroit opposed the construction of black YMCAs as "a form of offensive segregation." Blacks in Boston never applied for Rosenwald funds, whereas in Detroit and Cleveland opposition to "Rosenwald YMCAs" decreased throughout the following decade. In 1925 Detroit opened a black YMCA with Rosenwald's support and in 1926 Cleveland applied for matching funds. Cleveland's black population, however, was unable to raise the necessary funds. This was the result of continued opposition to a segregated YMCA branch as well as the simultaneous fund-raising activities of the Phillis Wheatley Association. William C. Graves to Rosenwald, April 19, 1920, JR Papers, reel 84. For correspondence regarding the Cleveland and Detroit fund-raising campaigns see JR Papers, reel 84.

60. Reprint of editorial in "A Little Lay Sermon on the Negro," *Association Men*, March 1913, p. 293.

61. Moorland's salary was paid in part through the fund-raising campaigns. He received 1 percent of the funds raised, plus traveling and local entertainment expenses. Richard C. Morse, "Statement," Dec. 10, 1913, Black YMCA Records, box 1, Policy—Correspondence and Statements, 1913-41.

62. "Worker's Rules," ca. 1910s, JEM Papers, box 126-58, no. 1128. For a discussion of the YMCA's role in the development of fund-raising in the United States, see Scott M. Cutlip, *Fund Raising in the United States: Its Role in America's Philanthropy* (New Brunswick, N.J.: Rutgers Univ. Press, 1965), 38-53.

63. See appendix G. St. Louis conducted a successful campaign before the expiration of Rosenwald's 1910 offer, but the building was not completed until 1919. See also N. Webster Moore, "The Black YMCA of St. Louis," *Missouri Historical Society Bulletin* 36, no. 1 (1979): 35-40.

64. See appendix G, and Dreck Spurlock Wilson, "Druid Hill Branch, Young Men's Christian Association: The First Hundred Years," *Maryland Historical Magazine* 84 (Summer 1989): 135-46.

65. Rosenwald to George W. Browns, Nov. 17, 1915, JR Papers, reel 86.

66. "Statement for Mr. Graves," prepared by Jesse E. Moorland, March 20, 1916, and "Report by Mr. J.E. Moorland on the Progress of Colored Work," Jan. 15, 1920, both in JR Papers, reel 85.

67. William C. Graves to Rosenwald, May 2, 1920, JR Papers, reel 86.

68. William J. Parker to Rosenwald, March 15, 1920, JR Papers, reel 85; William C. Graves to Rosenwald, May 2, 1920, JR Papers, reel 86; Parker to Rosenwald, March 15, 1920, JR Papers, reel 85.

69. Moorland to William C. Graves, April 30, 1920, JR Papers, reel 85. In

1910, 89 percent of all black Americans lived in the South. Daniel O. Price, *Changing Characteristics of the Negro Population* (Washington, D.C.: GPO, 1969), 9.

70. For correspondence concerning Jacksonville, see JR Papers, reel 84; for Nashville and New Orleans, JR Papers, reel 85.

71. Moorland to William C. Graves, April 23, 1920, and Moorland to L. Wilbur Messer, April 23, 1920, both in JR Papers, reel 85.

72. Moorland suggested a fifteen-thousand-dollar donation from Rosenwald for every thirty-five thousand raised locally. "New Proposition to be submitted to Mr. Rosenwald," n.d., JR Papers, reel 85.

73. Rosenwald to Chicago YMCA, July 6, 1920, JR Papers, reel 85; *Year Book, 1921*, 16.

74. The Emerson Street branch in Evanston, Illinois, is frequently listed as a Rosenwald YMCA, although it was not subject to the conditions of the second offer. Rosenwald's donations to Evanston's black branch, totaling twelve thousand dollars, were personal contributions designed to help liquidate the debt of the branch. For correspondence concerning the black YMCA in Evanston, see JR Papers, reel 84.

75. See appendix G; Lillian S. Williams, "The Development of a Black Community: Buffalo, New York, 1900-1940," Ph.D. diss., State Univ. of New York at Buffalo, 1979; and idem, "To Elevate the Race: The Michigan Avenue YMCA and the Advancement of Blacks in Buffalo, New York, 1922-1940," in *New Perspectives on Black Educational History*, ed. Vincent P. Franklin and James D. Anderson (Boston: G.K. Hall, 1978), 129-48.

76. Werner, *Julius Rosenwald*, 120; Henry W. Hammonds to Booker T. Washington, Feb. 17, 1914, BTW Papers, reel 378; statement by Moorland for William C. Graves, March 20, 1919 (?), p. 2, JR Papers, reel 85; Channing H. Tobias, "Christian Work for Negro Youth," *Missionary Review of the World* 46 (March 1923): 202; Cary D. Wintz, *Black Culture and the Harlem Renaissance* (Houston: Rice Univ. Press, 1988), 23.

77. Arthur, *Life on the Negro Frontier*, 96, gives a membership of 19,296 for the year 1933.

78. YMCA of Chicago, "The Health Education Council," May 22, 1950, YMCA of Metropolitan Chicago Records, box 106, no. 4, Chicago Historical Society, Chicago; hereinafter cited as YMCA of Chicago.

79. Jesse E. Moorland, "Report on Colored YMCA Building," Jan. 15, 1920, YMCA of Chicago, box 92, no. 8; August Meier and Elliott Rudwick, *Black History and the Historical Profession, 1915-1980* (Urbana: Univ. of Illinois Press, 1986), 13-16.

80. "Colored People Who Have Made Large Individual Gifts to YMCA Buildings," ca. 1914, BTW Papers, reel 378; *Building a Christian Society*, ca. 1938, JEM Papers, box 126-67, no. 1296; "Washington's Modern Building for Colored Men," *Association Men* Jan. 1913, p. 203.

81. Wabash Avenue YMCA, "Service!" n.d., Alexander L. Jackson Papers, box 2, no. 8, Amistad Research Center, Tulane University, New Orleans.

82. African Americans contributed 14 percent, local whites 48 percent, and Rosenwald 21 percent to the black YMCAs. The remainder of the funds came from other sources outside the communities or from mortgages. William C. Graves to Rosenwald, March 20, 1920, JR Papers, reel 85; Moorland, "Colored People Who Have Made Large Individual Gifts to YMCA Buildings," n.d., Black YMCA Records, box 1, History and Organization Reports, 1919-38.

83. *New York Times*, April 8, 1928, pt. 2, p. 1; Channing H. Tobias, "Address

Delivered in Honor of the Memory of Julius Rosenwald over Station WEAF of New York and Broadcast over the NBS Network during the 'Southland Sketches' Hour," Feb. 7, 1932, JEM Papers, box 126-41, no. 871.

84. "Y.M.C.A. Holds Great Meeting at Ford Theatre," 1918, clipping, JEM Papers, box 126-73, no. 1385; William C. Graves to Rosenwald, March 20, 1920, JR Papers, reel 85; Moorland, "Colored People Who Have Made Large Individual Gifts to YMCA Buildings," n.d., Black YMCA Records, box 1, History and Organization Reports, 1919-38.

85. "Colored People Who Have Made Large Individual Gifts to YMCA Buildings," ca. 1914, BTW Papers, reel 378.

86. *Southern Workman* 43 (Jan. 1914): 6.

87. "Dedication Chicago Y.M.C.A. for Colored Men, 6/15/13 (J.R.)," JR Papers, reel 85; Wabash Avenue Department, YMCA, Minutes of Annual Meeting, Jan. 18, 1951, YMCA of Chicago, box 106, no. 4.

88. W.E.B. Du Bois, "The Y.M.C.A.," *Crisis*, Nov. 1925, p. 11.

89. Jesse E. Moorland, untitled manuscript, n.d., p. 2, JEM Papers, box 126-27, no. 561.

6. Serving African-American Soldiers in World War I

1. For a discussion of the YMCA's service with American soldiers in World War I, see Richard C. Lancaster, *Serving the U.S. Armed Forces, 1861-1986: The Story of the YMCA's Ministry to Military Personnel for 125 Years* (Schaumburg, Ill.: Armed Services YMCA of the USA, 1987), 46-84; and John R. Mott, "The War Work of the Young Men's Christian Associations of the United States," *Annals of the American Academy* 79 (Sept. 1918): 204-12. For a discussion of black soldiers in World War I, see Arthur E. Barbeau and Florette Henri, *The Unknown Soldiers: Black American Troops in World War I* (Philadelphia: Temple Univ. Press, 1974); Arthur E. Barbeau, "Thy Brother's Keeper," *Journal of the West Virginia Historical Association* 2, no. 1 (1978): 25-40; William B. White, "The Military and the Melting Pot: The American Army and Minority Groups, 1865-1924," Ph.D. diss., Univ. of Wisconsin, 1968; Jane Lang and Harry N. Scheiber, "The Wilson Administration and the Wartime Mobilization of Black Americans," *Labor History* 10 (Summer 1969): 433-58; Paul Thom Murray, Jr., "Blacks and the Draft: A History of Institutional Racism," *Journal of Black Studies* 2, no. 1 (1971): 57-76; idem, "Blacks and the Draft: An Analysis of Institutional Racism, 1917-1971," Ph.D. diss., Florida State Univ., 1972; Jack D. Foner, *Blacks and the Military in American History: A New Perspective* (New York: Praeger, 1974); Lowell Dwight Black, "The Negro Volunteer Militia Units of the Ohio National Guard, 1870-1954: The Struggle for Military Recognition and Equality in the State of Ohio," Ph.D. diss., Ohio State Univ., 1976; William W. Giffin, "Mobilization of Black Militiamen in World War I: Ohio's Ninth Battalion," *Historian* 40 (Aug. 1978): 686-703; Gerald W. Patton, *War and Race: The Black Officer in the American Military, 1915-1941* (Westport, Conn.: Greenwood Press, 1981); Theodore Kornweibel, Jr., "Apathy and Dissent: Black America's Negative Responses to World War I," *South Atlantic Quarterly* 80, no. 3 (1981): 322-38; Bernard C. Nalty, *Strength for the Fight: A History of Black Americans in the Military* (New York: Free Press, 1986); and Nina Mjagkij, "Behind the Lines: The Social Experience of Black Soldiers during World War I," M.A. thesis, Univ. of Cincinnati, 1986.

2. James Albert Sprenger and Franklin S. Edmonds, eds., *The Leave Areas of the American Expeditionary Forces, 1918-1919: Records and Memoirs* (Philadelphia: John C. Winston and Co., 1928), 33; William Howard Taft, ed., *Service*

with the Fighting Men: An Account of the Work of the American Young Men's Christian Associations in the World War, 2 vols. (New York: Association Press, 1922), 2:143; Charles H. Williams, "Negro Y.M.C.A. Secretaries Overseas," *Southern Workman* 49 (Jan. 1920): 34.

3. Enoch Crowder, *Second Report of the Provost Marshall General to the Secretary of War* (Washington, D.C.: GPO, 1919), 89; Charles H. Williams, *Sidelights on Negro Soldiers* (Boston: B.J. Brimmer Co., 1923), 139; Taft, *Service*, 1:344. Clarence S. Yoakum and Robert M. Yerkes estimate that illiterates constituted nearly 30 percent of the men tested (*Army Mental Tests* [New York: Henry Holt and Co., 1920], 12). The degree of illiteracy among World War I soldiers is difficult to estimate because the army kept no systematic records. Some data on individual camps exist, but most information has to be drawn from the army's intelligence examinations. The army used two tests to determine the intellectual capacities of drafted and enlisted men. The alpha examination was given to those soldiers able "to read and understand newspapers and write a letter," while the beta test was designed for illiterate and foreign-born men. Thus, the number and type of tests administered at each camp provide information about the degree of illiteracy. See also "Illiteracy in the Drafted Army," *School Life*, March 1, 1919, p. 12.

4. "Personal Experiences of a Black Veteran in World War I: An Interview with Eugene B. Bailey," New Castle, Indiana, May 19, 1982, p. 10, compiled and edited by Wayne L. Sanford, Indiana Historical Society, Military History Section, Indianapolis, Indiana; "The Attack on Illiteracy," *Independent*, March 22, 1919, p. 392; "Illiteracy and the War," *New York Age*, March 30, 1918, p. 4; U.S. Congress, House, *Hearing before the Committee on Education*, H.R. 6490, 65th Cong., 2d sess., March 4, 1918, p. 8.

5. YMCA, National War Work Council, Educational Bureau, "Educational Activities in the Training Camps," n.d., pp. 9-10, Armed Services Records Related to World War I, AS 8, Publications and Reports, Educational Bureau, 1914-18, YMCA Archives; hereinafter cited as Armed Services Records.

6. Quoted in Daniel R. Beaver, *Newton D. Baker and the American War Effort, 1917-1919* (Lincoln: Univ. of Nebraska Press, 1966), 220.

7. Beaver, *Newton D. Baker*, 220; YMCA International Committee, *General Pershing and the Young Men's Christian Association*, an address delivered at the annual dinner of the International Committee, New York City, May 10, 1921, (New York: YMCA International Committee, 1921), 5; Raymond B. Fosdick, *Chronicle of a Generation: An Autobiography* (New York: Harper, 1958), 147; Joseph Lee, "War Camp Community Service," *Annals of the American Academy* 79 (Sept. 1918): 193; Commission on Training Camp Activities, *Personnel of the War and Navy Department Commission on Training Camp Activities* (Washington, D.C.: GPO, 1918), 3-4, 19-20. For a discussion of venereal disease in America, see Allan M. Brandt, *No Magic Bullet: A Social History of Venereal Disease in the United States since 1880* (New York: Oxford Univ. Press, 1985). As a result of the high incidence of venereal disease among the drafted men, Congress passed the Chamberlain-Kahn bill, creating a division of venereal diseases in the Public Health Service in 1919. Wilbur A. Sawyer, "Venereal Disease Control in the Military Forces," *American Journal of Public Health* 9 (1919): 338.

8. Commission on Training Camp Activities, *Personnel*, 3; Beaver, *Newton D. Baker*, 221; Jesse E. Moorland to Newton D. Baker, June 25, 1919, Black YMCA Records, box 1, Fundraising Pamphlets, 1920s.

9. Barbeau and Henri, *Unknown Soldiers*, 40; YMCA, *Summary of the World War Work of the American YMCA: With the Soldiers and Sailors of America at Home, on the Sea, and Overseas. With the men of the Allied Armies and*

with the Prisoners of War in All parts of the World (N.p.: For private distribution, 1920), 409.

10. YMCA, *Summary*, 112; Caroll L. Miller, "The Negro and Volunteer War Agencies," *Journal of Negro Education* 12 (Summer 1943): 442. According to these figures, the YMCA provided one secretary for every 279 white soldiers and one secretary for every 1,267 black soldiers. Emmett J. Scott, special assistant to the secretary of war, recorded an even smaller number: 268 black secretaries. Scott, *Scott's Official History of the American Negro in the World War* (N.p., 1919), 399. The YMCA and the army had agreed on a ratio of one secretary for every 217 soldiers. Lancaster, *Serving*, 53.

11. The African-American secretarial force in France consisted of sixty-one men and twenty-three women, but there were never more than seventy-five black secretaries in France at any time. Lancaster, *Serving*, 79; Moorland to Newton D. Baker, June 25, 1919, Black YMCA Records, box 1, Fundraising Pamphlets, 1920s; Williams, "Negro Y.M.C.A. Secretaries," 25.

12. YMCA, *Summary*, 150; Educational Bureau of YMCAs of the U.S., "Manual of YMCA Educational Work, Army and Navy," May 1918, p. 3, Armed Services Records, AS 8, Publications and Reports, Educational Bureau, 1914-18; Jesse E. Moorland, "The 'Y' Working with Colored Troops," p. 4, JEM Papers, box 126-27, no. 557.

13. *First United War Work Drive: Mississippi Asked to Raise 1,000,000.00 Dollars 30% or 300,000 Dollars of It to Be Raised by the Colored People,* undated pamphlet, W.E.B. Du Bois Papers, Fisk University, Nashville, box 58, microfilm ed., Amistad Research Center, New Orleans, reel 4; hereinafter cited as Du Bois Papers.

14. *Southern Workman* 47 (July 1918): 367-68; 47 (Oct. 1918): 509. Irving H. Hart, "Keeping up Morale: At Camp Alexander, Virginia," *Southern Workman* 48 (May 1919): 228; "Draft of a History of the Black Man in World War I," p. 6, Du Bois Papers, box 54, reel 2.

15. Taft, *Service*, 1:349; John Duncan Spaeth, *Camp Reader for American Soldiers: Lessons in Reading, Writing, and Spelling* (Atlanta: National War Work Council, YMCA, 1918), 33.

16. Cora Wilson Stewart, *Soldier's First Book* (New York: Association Press, 1918), 37.

17. For a discussion of physicians' perceptions of syphilis among African Americans during the early twentieth century, see James H. Jones, *Bad Blood: The Tuskegee Syphilis Experiment—A Tragedy of Race Relations* (New York: Free Press, 1981); and War Department, *Annual Report, 1919, pt. 2, Report of the Surgeon General* (Washington, D.C.: GPO, 1919), 2350.

18. Arthur B. Spingarn, "The War and Venereal Disease among Negroes," *Social Hygiene* 4 (July 1918): 334.

19. Ibid., 342.

20. "Memorandum for Mr. Arthur B. Spingarn on the Moral Conditions Surrounding Cantonments Where Colored Soldiers Are Assembled," n.d., p. 2, Du Bois Papers, box 64, reel 7; "Intelligence Report," n.d., Walter Howard Loving Papers, Moorland-Spingarn Research Center, Howard University, Washington, D.C., box 113-1, no. 11; hereinafter cited as WHL Papers.

21. Spingarn, "War and Venereal Disease," 333, 340-41, 338; "Report of Dr. M.J. Exner on Work for Moral Conservation in the Army, June to December [1917?]," pp. 3, 5, RF Archives, RG 2, JDR, Jr.—Welfare Interests—Youth, box 31, YMCA—International Committee—Sex Lectures.

22. Taft, *Service*, 1:348, 411; *School Life*, Nov. 16, 1918, p. 3; Theodore W.

Koch, *Books in the War: The Romance of Library War Service* (Boston: Houghton Mifflin Co., 1919), 10, 52; Charles E. Arnold to W.E.B. Du Bois, July 12, 1918, Du Bois Papers, box 54, reel 2; *Southern Workman* 47 (July 1918): 368.

23. John B. Cade, *Twenty-two Months with "Uncle Sam": Being the Experiences and Observations of a Negro Student Who Volunteered for Military Service against the Central Powers from June, 1917 to April, 1919* (Atlanta: Robinson-Cofer Co., 1929), 26-27, 31; Williams, *Sidelights*, 94; Harrison J. Pinkett to Miss Ovington, Jan. 19, 1918, Du Bois Papers, box 56, reel 4.

24. *Southern Workman* 47 (May 1918): 250; 46 (Dec. 1917): 656. Williams, *Sidelights*, 97.

25. *Southern Workman* 46 (Dec. 1917): 656; Williams, *Sidelights*, 97.

26. Anson Phelps Stokes, *Educational Plans for the American Army Abroad* (New York: Association Press, 1918), 44; YMCA, *Summary*, 152.

27. Stokes, *Educational Plans*, 54, 33.

28. Occasionally white secretaries served black soldiers in their huts. As Joshua E. Blanton, a black entertainer traveling among the troops in France, observed, however, the white secretaries "were doing just enough to get by, nothing more than they had to do." Joshua E. Blanton to R.B. DeFrantz, Sept. 9, 1919, Black YMCA Records, box 6, WW I—War Work Council, 1919.

29. Taft, *Service,* 1:410; M.W. Bullock to Moorland, May 31, 1918, and Thomas M. Clayton to Moorland, Oct. 18, 1918, both in Black YMCA Records, box 3, Colored Work Department—WW I—Letters, 1917-19.

30. Thomas M. Clayton to Moorland, Oct. 18, 1918, and James Garfield Wiley to Moorland, April 6, 1918, both in Black YMCA Records, box 3, Colored Work Department—WW I—Letters, 1917-19; Ridgely Torrence, *The Story of John Hope* (New York: Macmillan, 1948), 209.

31. Torrence, *John Hope*, 198, 207; Rayford W. Logan, "Hope, John," in *Dictionary of American Negro Biography*, ed. Rayford W. Logan and Michael R. Winston (New York: Norton, 1982), 321-25; Clarence A. Bacote, "John Hope," *Journal of Negro History* 21 (April 1936): 240-44. Moorland was unable to go to France and supervise the work of the black secretaries because he could not obtain a passport. Some government officers of the Intelligence Division had charged him with disloyalty because of "his sympathy with people thought to be seditious and by his appointment to war service of those of radical temper." Following the war the YMCA investigated Moorland and cleared him of all charges. "The Report to the Committee on Colored Work of the Sub-Committee Appointed to Investigate the Charges against Dr. Moorland," n.d., JEM Papers, box 126-60, no. 1155.

32. Moorland to John Hope, Oct. 28, 1917, Hope Papers, reel 12; Torrence, *John Hope*, 198, 208; Hope to Channing H. Tobias, Nov. 6, 1917, Hope Papers, reel 12.

33. John Hope, report, Sept. 24, 1919, in Torrence, *John Hope*, 220-21; Hope to Moorland, Sept. 16, 1918, Hope Papers, reel 12.

34. Williams, "Negro Y.M.C.A. Secretaries," 32; Tod B. Galloway to Lucy (Mrs. William F.) Black, March 25, 1918, Tod Buchanan Galloway Letters, March 6, 1918-Feb. 14, 1919, Ohio Historical Society, Columbus, Ohio.

35. Addie W. Hunton and Kathryn M. Johnson, *Two Colored Women with the American Expeditionary Forces* (Brooklyn, N.Y.: Brooklyn Eagle Press, 1920), 204. The other black women who served with the YMCA in France during the war were Helen Curtis and Kathryn M. Johnson.

36. *Southern Workman* 47 (Oct. 1918): 507. The *Stars and Stripes* even contended that some African Americans from Louisiana had linguistic advan-

tages in learning French because, being used to Creole, they were "more or less familiar with the language." *Stars and Stripes*, Aug. 8, 1918.

37. Stokes, *Educational Plans*, 50, 61.

38. Williams, "Negro Y.M.C.A. Secretaries," 28-31; Moses A. Davis to Moorland, Aug. 21, 1918, Black YMCA Records, box 3, Colored Work Department—WW I—Letters, 1917-19.

39. Koch, *Books*, 94; Hunton and Johnson, *Two Colored Women*, 214; "Exhibits to Report of Investigation of the YMCA," vol. 5, p. 967, Record Group 120, box 3464, E 445, National Archives, Washington, D.C.; Williams, "Negro Y.M.C.A. Secretaries," 31.

40. Koch, *Books*, 83-84 (officer quoted), 317.

41. Taft, *Service*, 1:354; Lancaster, *Serving*, 81; General Order no. 9, General Headquarters, AEF, France, Jan. 13, 1919, in Department of the Army, Historical Division, *US Army in the World War, 1917-1919: Bulletins, G.H.Q., A.E.F.* (Washington, D.C.: GPO, 1948), 605-7.

42. General Order no. 30, "Educational Work in the A.E.F.," General Headquarters, AEF, France, Feb. 13, 1919, in Department of the Army, Historical Division, *US Army in the World War*, 653; National War Work Council, YMCA, Educational Bureau, "Conference of Departmental Educational Directors, January 23-26, 1919," p. 3, Armed Services Records, box 135, Army and Navy Department, Historical to 1929; Max Yergan to Moorland, Jan. 31, 1919, adjusted due to bad orthography in the original, JEM Papers, box 126-69, no. 1219; *Outlook*, April 30, 1919, p. 733; Stokes, *Educational Plans*, 1.

43. Hunton and Johnson, *Two Colored Women*, 208-9, 210.

44. Following the Armistice, the army authorized the YMCA to recruit secretaries among the members of the AEF. A.G. Bookwalter to H.H. Booth, Dec. 11, 1918, Hope Papers, reel 4.

45. Williams, "Negro Y.M.C.A. Secretaries," 28-29; "YMCA Army Educational Commission: Organization," JEM Papers, box 126-69, no. 1219. At times of departure and arrival, as many as seven thousand black soldiers were at Montoir. *New York Age*, Sept. 13, 1919, p. 1.

46. Joseph L. Whiting, "A Letter to the Mothers of Soldier-Teachers," undated; "YMCA Army Educational Commission: Organization," and Commanding Officer Co. B, 308th Labor Battalion, to Joseph L. Whiting, Jan. 1, 1919, all in JEM Papers, box 126-69, no. 1219. American soldiers were entitled to a seven-day furlough every four months. Throughout the war and the period of demobilization, the YMCA operated nineteen holiday resorts for the American soldiers in France, five in the Rhine Valley, two in Italy, and one in England. Taft, *Service*, 2:143; YMCA, *Summary*, 169.

47. Robert G. Paterson, "The Leave Areas Draft," Sept. 17, 1920, p. 3, Armed Services Records, AS 19, Leave Areas—Robert G. Paterson, 1920; Taft, *Service*, 2:144. In July 1917 E.C. Carter, chief secretary of the YMCA in France, suggested a plan for the supervision of the soldiers' furloughs. After the YMCA investigated the possibilities and drew up a tentative plan, General Pershing authorized the establishment of leave areas on November 13, 1917.

48. Paterson, "Leave Areas Draft," 3-4; Taft, *Service*, 2:143; George Walker, *Venereal Disease in the A.E.F.* (Baltimore: Medical Standard Book Co., 1922), 178.

49. Taft, *Service*, 2:162, 143; Paterson, "Leave Areas Draft," 25, 37-38; Williams, "Negro Y.M.C.A. Secretaries," 34.

50. Taft, *Service*, 2:147; General Order no. 38, General Headquarters, AEF,

France, March 9, 1918, in Department of the Army, Historical Division, *US Army in the World War*, 239-40; YMCA, *Summary*, 175; Paterson, "Leave Areas Draft," 16.

51. YMCA, *Summary*, 170. Despite the relative freedom the soldiers enjoyed in the leave areas, they were still members of the AEF and subjected to some rules. For example, the men had to be in their hotels by midnight, they had to dress properly, and they were reminded that "drunkenness and intoxication will not be tolerated while noisy, boisterous or disorderly conduct and the use of profane or obscene or of the German language are prohibited." Headquarters, Savoie Leave Areas, A.P.O. 730, Aix-les-Bains, France, March 18, 1919, Armed Services Records, AS 25, F.S. Edmonds Leave Area Materials, ca. 1919-28.

52. W.L. Anderson, "Colored Leave Area: Chambéry—Savoie," p. 1, Armed Services Records, AS 19, Final Report of Leave Area Department—YMCA—AEF, 1919; John Hope to George F. Peabody, April 2, 1919, Hope Papers, reel 4; J.B. Howarth, "Entertaining the American Colored Troops in the Savoie Leave Area," pp. 1, 3, Armed Services Records, AS 25, F.S. Edmonds—Leave Area Materials, ca. 1919-28.

53. John Hope to George F. Peabody, April 2, 1919, Hope Papers, reel 4; Anderson, "Colored Leave Area," 1.

54. Torrence, *John Hope*, 221; Anderson, "Colored Leave Area," 2.

55. Torrence, *John Hope*, 221, 215; Howarth, "Entertaining the American Colored Troops in the Savoie Leave Area," 3.

56. Miller, "The Negro and Volunteer War Agencies," 442. Chambéry served black soldiers between January 15 and May 21, 1919. Anderson, "Colored Leave Area," 10. Challes-les-Eaux served them between January 17 and May 23, 1919. William Stevenson, "Challes les Eaux—Savoie," pp. 1, 6, Armed Services Records, AS 19, Final Report of Leave Area Department—YMCA—AEF, 1919.

57. Anderson, "Colored Leave Area," 2-3. The black secretaries who served in Chambéry were Helen Curtis, Garrie Moore, J. Harry Scroggins, J.E. Parks, N. Ousley, W.H. Kindle, Laura Williamson, Madeline P. Childs, and N. Fairfax Brown.

58. Stevenson, "Challes les Eaux," 1. The black secretaries at Challes-les-Eaux were Addie W. Hunton, William Stevenson, M.W. Bullock, H.E. Dunn, A.W. Shockley, W.E. Watkins, Kathryn M. Johnson, Florence K. Thoms, and Meta V. Evans.

59. "Exhibits to Report of Investigation of the Y.M.C.A.," vol. 5, pp. 967, 970, 969, National Archives, RG 120, box 3464, E 445; Stevenson, "Challes les Eaux," 2, 3; Williams, "Negro Y.M.C.A. Secretaries," 34.

60. Hunton and Johnson, *Two Colored Women*, 170, 171; Anderson, "Colored Leave Area," 9; Taft, *Service*, 2:154.

61. Anderson, "Colored Leave Area," 6; Stevenson, "Challes les Eaux," 3; Hunton and Johnson, *Two Colored Women*, 170.

62. Anderson, "Colored Leave Area," 8, 7.

63. Ibid., 8; Stevenson, "Challes les Eaux," 5; John Hope to George F. Peabody, April 2, 1919, Hope Papers, reel 4.

64. Taft, *Service*, 1:411.

65. Jesse E. Moorland, "The Y.M.C.A. with Colored Troops," *Southern Workman* 48 (April 1919): 173; Hunton and Johnson, *Two Colored Women*, 253.

66. "Signal for Applause Wins Ready Response," undated clipping, JEM Papers, box 126-73, no. 1385.

67. Hunton and Johnson, *Two Colored Women*, 145, 207; James W. Mance to editor of *Crisis*, undated, Du Bois Papers, box 55, reel 3.

68. Ruby M. English to Addie W. Hunton, July 4, 1921, Papers of the NAACP, Library of Congress, Washington, D.C., Group I, ser. C, container 65, "Hunton, Addie W., 1921-33."

69. *Southern Workman* 47 (July 1918): 339-40; Ralph D. Taylor, 372d Infantry, interview by author, Dayton, Ohio, July 15, 1985; *Southern Workman* 48 (Feb. 1919): 95.

7. Interracial Dialogue and Cooperation in the 1920s

1. "Report of the Commission on Colored Work," 1920, p. 4, Black YMCA Records, box 2, Colored Work Department—Committees and Semi-Centennial Committee.

2. See "The Twentieth National Conference, Colored Men's Department, YMCA of North America," Cincinnati, Dec. 4, 1921, pp. 4-5, Hope Papers, reel 12.

3. Galen M. Fisher, *Public Affairs and the Y.M.C.A.: 1844-1944, with Special Reference to the United States* (New York: Association Press, 1948), 71-74.

4. C. Howard Hopkins, *History of the YMCA in North America* (New York: Association Press, 1951), 541; "Report of the Colored Men's Department for International Convention—1920," p. 1, Black YMCA Records, box 3, Colored Work Department—Secretary Reports, 1910-24; Commission on Interracial Cooperation, "Review of Ten Years' Work," ca. 1929, Laura Spelman Rockefeller Memorial, Rockefeller Archive Center, ser. 3, subser. 8, box 96, no. 976; hereinafter cited as LSRM.

5. Commission on Interracial Cooperation, "A Sane Approach to the Race Problem, 1930," p. 5, LSRM, box 97, no. 977.

6. Commission on Interracial Cooperation, "Review of Ten Years' Work"; Du Bois quoted in Elliott Rudwick, *W.E.B. Du Bois: Voice of the Black Protest Movement* (Urbana: Univ. of Illinois Press, 1960), 238.

7. Walter Howard Loving to director, Military Intelligence, March 18, 1919, WHL Papers, box 113-1, no. 12.

8. Commission on Interracial Cooperation, "Review of Ten Years' Work." Weatherford served as international student secretary between 1901 and 1919. For biographical information, see George P. Antone, Jr., "Willis Duke Weatherford: An Interpretation of His Work in Race Relations, 1906-1946," Ph.D. diss., Vanderbilt Univ., 1969; and idem, "The Y.M.C.A. Graduate School, Nashville, 1919-1936," *Tennessee Historical Quarterly* 32, no. 1 (1973): 67-82.

9. Antone, "Willis Duke Weatherford," 91.

10. Ibid., Willis Duke Weatherford, *Negro Life in the South: Present Conditions and Needs* (New York: Association Press, 1910); Jesse E. Moorland, "The Young Men's Christian Association among Negroes," *Journal of Negro History* 9 (April 1924): 136.

11. Clarence P. Shedd, *Two Centuries of Student Christian Movements: Their Origin and Intercollegiate Life* (New York: Association Press, 1934), 396; Commission on Interracial Cooperation, "Commission on Interracial Cooperation, 1922," p. 11, LSRM, box 96, no. 974; Jesse E. Moorland, "The Colored Men's Department," ca. 1920, p. 14, JEM Papers, box 126-59, no. 1132.

12. Will W. Alexander to W.S. Richardson, Aug. 17, 1922, LSRM, box 96, no. 974; Wilma Dykeman and James Stokely, *Seeds of Southern Change: The Life of Will Alexander* (New York: Norton, 1962), 97, 112.

13. Willis Duke Weatherford, "The Colored YMCA, the Interracial Commit-

tee and Related Subjects," June 13, 1949, pp. 33-34, Black YMCA Records, box 1, History and Organization Reports, 1919-38; "Reports on the Work of the National Council of the YMCAs of the United States of America for the Year 1924-1925," Washington, D.C., Oct. 27, 1925, p. 33, LSRM, box 24, no. 248.

14. Channing H. Tobias to John R. Mott, Jan. 28, 1919, Black YMCA Records, box 3, Colored Work Department—Secretary Reports, 1910-24.

15. Ibid.

16. Weatherford, "Colored YMCA, the Interracial Committee and Related Subjects," 35-36; Antone, "Willis Duke Weatherford," 123; Tobias to Mott, Jan. 28, 1919, Black YMCA Records, box 3, Colored Work Department—Secretary Reports, 1910-24.

17. Tobias to Mott, Jan. 28, 1919, and "The Training of Colored Community Workers of the Southeast by the National War Work Council, in Connection to C.H. Tobias Therewith," n.d., pp. 7, 10, both in Black YMCA Records, box 3, Colored Work Department—Secretary Reports, 1910-24.

18. Tobias to Lucien T. Warner, April 11, 1919, Black YMCA Records, box 3, Colored Work Department—Secretary Reports, 1910-24; Weatherford, "Colored YMCA, the Interracial Committee and Related Subjects," 35; Antone, "Willis Duke Weatherford," 114-15; Hopkins, *History of the YMCA*, 341; Dykeman and Stokely, *Seeds of Southern Change*, 67; "Service for Returned Soldiers," n.d., JEM Papers, box 126-73, no. 1386.

19. Tobias to Mott, Jan. 28, 1919, Black YMCA Records, box 3, Colored Work Department—Secretary Reports, 1910-24; Commission on Interracial Cooperation, "Review of Ten Years' Work," 3.

20. Commission on Interracial Cooperation, "Commission on Interracial Cooperation, 1922," 12; idem, "Review of Ten Years' Work," 3; "Reports on the Work of the National Council of the YMCAs of the United States of America for the Year 1924-1925," 33; Dykeman and Stokely, *Seeds of Southern Change*, 8.

21. Weatherford, "Colored YMCA, the Interracial Committee and Related Subjects," 39; Fisher, *Public Affairs*, 87; Jesse E. Moorland, "Statement," March 1, 1919, Black YMCA Records, box 3, Colored Work Department—Secretary Reports, 1910-24; Gunnar Myrdal, *An American Dilemma: The Negro Problem and Modern Democracy* (New York: Harper and Brothers, 1944), 847.

22. Commission on Interracial Cooperation to Beardsley Ruml, Feb. 1, 1930, LSRM, box 96, no. 976; Will W. Alexander to Frank B. Stubbs, Nov. 12, 1923, LSRM, box 96, no. 975; Commission on Interracial Cooperation, "Progress in Race Relations: A Survey of the Work of the Commission on Interracial Co-operation for the Year 1923-24," pp. 18-19, LSRM, box 97, no. 978.

23. Alfred G. Bookwalter to William J. Parker, Feb. 3, 1920, JR Papers, reel 85; Fisher, *Public Affairs*, 79; Harry L. Senger, *The Story of the Young Men's Christian Association of Cincinnati and Hamilton County, 1853-1953* (N.p.: Parthenon Press, 1953), 90. In 1924 Nelson was a delegate to the first YMCA National Council meeting and became its vice-president. He also served as vice-president of the Ohio State YMCA Committee.

24. "Statement of Encouragements and Discouragements and the 1925 Objective of the Colored Work of the Y.M.C.A.," p. 1, Black YMCA Records, box 1, Addresses, 1893-1935.

25. Bookwalter to Parker, Feb. 3, 1920, JR Papers, reel 85.

26. Fisher, *Public Affairs*, 88; Shedd, *Two Centuries*, 398-99.

27. Cooper to Mott, March 2, 1923, reprinted in *Crisis,* Sept. 1924, p. 201.

28. Ibid., 202, 201.

29. "Report of the YMCA Commission on Work among Colored Men and

Boys," Nov. 1919, JEM Papers, box 126-59, no. 1145; "Report of the Commission on Colored Work," 1920, pp. 4-5.

30. "Report of the Commission on Colored Work," 1920, pp. 1, 5-6; Dykeman and Stokely, *Seeds of Southern Change*, 71.

31. "Report of the Commission on Colored Work," 1920, p. 9.

32. Ibid., 15-16.

33. Hopkins, *History of the YMCA*, 438-41.

34. Moorland, "Colored Men's Department," 18; "Twentieth National Conference, Colored Men's Department, YMCA of North America," 4-5. See appendix C.

35. YMCA National Council, *Negro Youth in City YMCAs: A Study of YMCA Services among Negro Youth in Urban Communities* (New York: Association Press, 1944), 11; Hopkins, *History of the YMCA*, 441-51.

36. Tobias served as student secretary until 1923 and then as senior secretary until his retirement in 1946. During his service with the YMCA, he was associate director of the Commission on Interracial Cooperation between 1935 and 1942. In World War II Tobias served on the National Advisory Committee on Selective Service and the Joint Army and Navy Committee on Welfare and Recreation. Following the war Tobias was appointed to President Truman's Committee on Civil Rights, and in 1951-52 he was an alternate to the Sixth General Assembly of the United Nations in Paris. Between 1946 and 1953 he was the first black director of the Phelps-Stokes Fund, and he subsequently became chairman of the board of directors of the NAACP. Tobias held honorary degrees from the Jewish Institute of Religion, Morehouse College, Gammon Theological Seminary, the New School for Social Research, and New York University. In 1928 he received the Harmon Award for Religious Services, and in 1948, the NAACP's Spingarn Medal. For biographical information about Tobias, see Rayford W. Logan, "Tobias, Channing H[eggie]," in *Dictionary of American Negro Biography*, ed. Rayford W. Logan and Michael R. Winston (New York: Norton, 1982), 593-95; Louis Finkelstein, *Thirteen Americans: Their Spiritual Autobiographies* (New York: Institute for Religious and Social Studies, n.d.), 179-92; and Biographical Records, "Channing H. Tobias."

37. Tobias to S. Parkes Cadman, Jan. 3, 1929, JEM Papers, box 126-39, no. 828; Channing H. Tobias, "Service to Colored Men and Boys by the Young Men's Christian Association," Jan. 11, 1928, Black YMCA Records, box 1, Policy—Correspondence and Statements, 1913-41; Tobias to Moorland, Oct. 13, 1929, JEM Papers, box 126-39, no. 828.

38. Finkelstein, *Thirteen Americans*, 182; Tobias quoted in Robert F. Martin, *Howard Kester and the Struggle for Social Justice in the South, 1904-77* (Charlottesville: Univ. Press of Virginia, 1991), 22.

39. Addie W. Hunton, "Report," Jan. 3-Feb. 7, 1923, Papers of the NAACP, Library of Congress, Washington, D.C., Group I, ser. C, container 65, "Hunton, Addie W., 1921-33"; Jackson to Mott, Nov. 5, 1919, JR Papers, reel 85; Channing H. Tobias, "Visits to Central, Western and Southern Region," Cleveland, Oct. 17, 1930, JEM Papers, box 126-67, no. 1294.

40. Jackson to Mott, Nov. 5, 1920, JR Papers, reel 85; Jackson to Mott, Nov. 5, 1920, YMCA of Chicago, box 92, no. 7; Jackson to L. Wilbur Messer, Dec. 9 and June 28, 1919, Alexander L. Jackson Papers, box 1, no. 1, Amistad Research Center, Tulane University, New Orleans.

41. "Report of Findings Committee of National Conference on Colored Work of the YMCA," Oct. 21-23, 1925, p. 2, JEM Papers, box 126-58, no. 1120.

42. Shedd, *Two Centuries*, 396-97.

43. Hopkins, *History of the YMCA*, 635-36, 642; Martin, *Howard Kester*, 23.

44. Martin, *Howard Kester*, 25.

45. Ibid., 22, 26-27.

46. Benjamin E. Mays, *Born to Rebel: An Autobiography* (Athens: Univ. of Georgia Press, 1971), 127.

47. "Statement and Resolutions of the Middle Atlantic YMCA Association of Negro Colleges and Schools," March 20-April 1, 1928; "Problems Facing the Negro Student YMCA: Financial, Staff and Organizational Status," Feb. 19, 1928; and "Statement and Resolution of Recommendation by the Georgia Student Council for the YMCAs Relative to the Present Status and Problems Facing Negro Student Associations of Georgia and the Nation in re the Student Division," Feb. 6, 1928, all in Black YMCA Records, box 1, Interagency Relationships—Correspondence and Reports, 1928-40.

48. Report by Campbell C. Johnson, May 1, 1928, Black YMCA Records, box 1, Interagency Relationships—Correspondence and Reports, 1928-40.

49. Ibid.

50. Channing H. Tobias, "Colored Work Department in Its Relation to Student Associations," May 9, 1928, JEM Papers, box 126-60, no. 1156; report by Campbell C. Johnson, May 1, 1928.

51. "Minutes, Meeting of Special Committee to Consider the Organizational Status of Negro Students as They Relate Themselves to the Student Division and the Colored Men's Department of the Home Division," Oct. 20, 1929, Black YMCA Records, box 1, Interagency Relationships—Correspondence and Reports, 1928-40.

52. "Statement Concerning the Relations of Colored Student Associations to the Colored Work Department and the Student Division," ca. 1929, Black YMCA Records, box 1, Interagency Relationships—Correspondence and Reports, 1928-40; Frank T. Wilson to Robert R. Moton, April 29, 1933, Robert R. Moton Papers, Moton Family Papers, Library of Congress, Washington, D.C., Subject File: YMCA 1933, May-June; hereinafter cited as Moton Papers; Shedd, *Two Centuries*, 397.

8. From Depression to Desegregation, 1929-1946

1. On the condition of African Americans during the Great Depression, see Harvard Sitkoff, *A New Deal for Blacks: The Emergence of Civil Rights as a National Issue, vol. 1, The Depression Decade* (Oxford: Oxford Univ. Press, 1978); John B. Kirby, *Black Americans in the Roosevelt Era: Liberalism and Race* (Knoxville: Univ. of Tennessee Press, 1980); and William H. Harris, *The Harder We Run: Black Workers since the Civil War* (Oxford: Oxford Univ. Press, 1982), 95-122.

2. Sitkoff, *New Deal for Blacks*, 35.

3. "Plans of Celebration of the 50th Anniversary of the Founding of the First Regular YMCA for Colored Men and Boys in the U.S.," 1937, p. 3, Black YMCA Records, box 1, History and Organization Reports, 1919-38; Minutes, National Conference of Laymen and Secretaries, Bordentown, New Jersey, July 11-12, 1936, Moton Papers, Subject File: YMCA 1936, Sept.-Oct.

4. Ralph W. Bullock, "A Study of Special Services Rendered by Twenty-Six Local YMCA's to Unemployed Colored Men and Boys," June 1932, p. 1, Moton Papers, Subject File: YMCA 1932, May-Aug.; J.H. McGrew to George F. Peabody, Oct. 21, 1932, Moton Papers, Subject File: YMCA 1932, Sept.-Dec.; "Christian Street Building YMCA Emergency Fund Campaign," Feb. 28-March 7, 1933, Moton Papers, Subject File: YMCA 1933, March-April.

5. Tobias to Robert R. Moton, ca. 1938, Moton Papers, Subject File: YMCA 1938, Jan.-Aug.; Lyman Pierce to YMCA Student Division, Oct. 26, 1933, Moton Papers, Subject File: YMCA 1933, July-Oct.; Francis A. Honson [*sic*] to David R. Porter, Feb. 2, 1932, Moton Papers, Subject File: YMCA 1932, Jan.-April.

6. "A Report of the Work of the National Council—Staff and Committees—In Carrying Out the 1932 Policy of Service," Jan. 1932, p. 7, Moton Papers, Subject File: YMCA 1933, Jan.-Feb.

7. Packard memo to files, "Colored Work Division YMCA (Conversation with Mr. Tobias)," June 20, 1933, RF Archives, RG 2, JDR, Jr.—Welfare Interests—Youth, box 33, YMCA—National Council, envelope no. 1; F.S. Harmon and J.A. Urice to Rockefeller, Jr., June 27, 1932, p. 2, RF Archives, RG 2, JDR, Jr.—Welfare Interests—Youth, box 34, YMCA—July 1932 Appeal—National and International Council.

8. "International Committee of YMCAs," Nov. 15, 1938, Davison Fund, Inc., II, box 21, no. 165, Rockefeller Archive Center.

9. Robert R. Moton to Adrian Lyon, Feb. 6, 1933, and R.H. King to John E. Manley, Feb. 22, 1933, both in Moton Papers, Subject File: YMCA 1933, Jan.-Feb.

10. R.H. King to John R. Mott, May 4, 1932, Moton Papers, Subject File: YMCA 1932, May-Aug.

11. Frank T. Wilson to Robert R. Moton, April 17, 1933, and "Excerpt from Minutes of the National Council of Student Christian Associations Meeting," Columbus, Ohio, April 6-10, 1933, both in Moton Papers, Subject File: YMCA 1933, March-April; Galen M. Fisher, *Public Affairs and the Y.M.C.A.: 1844-1944, with Special Reference to the United States* (New York: Association Press, 1948), 86.

12. John E. Manley, general secretary of the National Council, to Robert R. Moton, Jan. 3, 1934, Moton Papers, Subject File: YMCA 1934, Jan.-March; Ralph W. Bullock, "A Study of the Effect of the Present Economic Depression upon the Operating Efficiency and Program Service of Local Associations Serving Colored Boys," June 1932, p. 1, Moton Papers, Subject File: YMCA 1932, May-Aug.; *Secretarial Letter,* Oct. 1931, vol. 8, no. 4, p. 1, Black YMCA Records, box 3, Colored Work Department—Periodicals—*Secretarial News Letter*, 1930-36; Lillian S. Williams, "The Development of a Black Community: Buffalo, New York, 1900-1940," Ph.D. diss., State Univ. of New York at Buffalo, 1979, p. 224.

13. Bullock, "Study of the Effect of the Present Economic Depression," p. 1; R.P. Hamlin to Robert R. Moton, Sept. 16, 1932, Moton Papers, Subject File: YMCA 1932, Sept.-Dec.

14. Bullock, "Study of Special Services," 1; *Secretarial Letter,* Oct. 1931, vol. 8, no. 4, p. 1, Black YMCA Records, box 3, Colored Work Department—Periodicals—*Secretarial News Letter*, 1930-36.

15. Bullock, "Study of Special Services," 1.

16. Ralph W. Bullock and Boyd W. Overton, "A Study of the Sources of Income and Problems of Financing YMCAs Serving Colored Men and Boys," Dec. 1937, pp. 9-10, Black YMCA Records, box 4, Studies, 1930s-70s.

17. Bullock, "Study of Special Services"; idem, "Study of the Effect of the Present Economic Depression"; Minutes, National Conference of Laymen and Secretaries, Bordentown, New Jersey, July 11-12, 1936, p. 7, Moton Papers, Subject File: YMCA 1936, Sept.-Oct.; A.Q. Martin to Jesse E. Moorland, April 17, 1929, JEM Papers, box 126-20, no. 267.

18. Minutes, National Conference of Laymen and Secretaries, Bordentown, New Jersey, July 11-12, 1936, p. 2, Moton Papers, Subject File: YMCA 1936, Sept.-Oct.; Harlem YMCA, New York City, "Activities Week Celebration, April 24-May 1, 1938," Black YMCA Records, box 4, Studies, 1930s-70s.

19. Ralph W. Bullock, "A Report Based upon a Study of the Financial Condition and Administration of the Butler Street YMCA," Aug. 3, 1938, Black YMCA Records, box 4, Studies, 1930s-70s.

20. Ralph W. Bullock, "A Survey of the Work of the YMCA among Colored Men and Boys, 1938," p. 61, Black YMCA Records, box 4, Studies, 1930s-70s.

21. "Appendix to Monthly Narrative Report, New York City, National Youth Administration, November 1938," p. 3, National Archives, RG 119, National Youth Administration—Records of the Director—Director's File of Representatives of State Directors of Negro Affairs, 1936-39, box 2, New Mexico, New York State, New York City, 1937-38, hereinafter cited as RG 119, NYA, Director's File. Harlem YMCA, "Activities Week Celebration."

22. "Appendix to Monthly Narrative Report, New York City, National Youth Administration, November 1938," 3; "Projects," n.d., RG 119, NYA, General Subject File of the Director, 1936-41, box 2, Proposed Negro Projects; "October Report for Tennessee," ca. 1936, RG 119, NYA, Director's File, box 2, Tennessee, 1936-37.

23. "Report of Project 36-1Y-28, Camden, New Jersey," ca. 1936; "Camden Workshop Project October Report, 1937"; and "Monthly Report, July and August 1938," all in RG 119, NYA, Director's File of Reports of State Directors of Negro Affairs, 1936-39, box 1, New Jersey, 1936-37.

24. "District of Columbia, Month of November, 1938 and December 1938," RG 119, NYA, Director's File, box 2, District of Columbia, 1937-38; and "Purpose, Montclair Health Projects," 1936, RG 119, NYA, Director's File, box 1, New Jersey, 1936-37.

25. *The Y's Man*, Oct. 17, 1936, Black YMCA Records, box 4, Miscellaneous Local Materials, 1920s-40s; Harlem YMCA, "Activities Week Celebration."

26. Channing H. Tobias, "Report of Colored Work," ca. 1936, p. 1, Black YMCA Records, box 6, Colored Work Department—Reports—1940-49; "NYA: City, State, Nation for Negro Youth," ca. 1936, and "NYA Monthly Report, December 1937," both in RG 119, NYA, Director's File, box 1, New Jersey, 1936-37.

27. *Trenton State Gazette*, June 7, 1937, RG 119, NYA, Director's File, box 1, New Jersey, 1936-37; "August Report, Kansas City, Missouri, August 1936," RG 119, NYA, Final Report of the Division, 1943, box 1, Missouri, 1936-37; NYA Michigan, "August Report," ca. 1936, RG 119, NYA, Final Report of the Division, 1943, box 1, Michigan, Minnesota, 1936-37.

28. Ralph W. Bullock, "A Survey of the Work of the YMCA," 1938, p. 61, Black YMCA Records, box 4, Studies, 1930s-70s; "Final Report, NYA Division of Negro Affairs," ca. 1943, p. 220, RG 119, NYA, Final Report of the Division, 1943, box 1, Final Report, NYA, Division of Negro Affairs, 1943.

29. "The YMCA and Churches: A Report on YMCA Relations with Churches to the 1934 Meeting of the National Council," Moton Papers, Subject File: YMCA 1934, Aug.-Dec.

30. Herbert Shapiro, *White Violence and Black Response: From Reconstruction to Montgomery* (Amherst: Univ. of Massachusetts Press, 1988), 205; Commission on Interracial Cooperation, "Depression Intensifies Race Problem," 1931, p. 8, and Commission on Interracial Cooperation, "Some Recent Trends in Race Relations Together with a Brief Survey of the Work of the Commission on Interracial Cooperation," 1932, p. 8, both in LSRM, box 97, no. 978.

31. Arthur P. Moor and Frank Olmsted to J.R. Stevenson, Aug. 13, 1930, and James A. Fairley to Carlton Harrison, Oct. 9, 1930, both in Black YMCA Records, box 6, Colored Work Department—Local, State and Area Associations, L-R, 1916-42.

32. Fairley to Harrison, Oct. 9, 1930, and Moor and Olmsted to Stevenson, Aug. 13, 1930, both in Black YMCA Records, box 6, Colored Work Department—Local, State and Area Associations, L-R, 1916-42.

33. Moor and Olmsted to Stevenson, Aug. 13, 1930, Black YMCA Records, box 6, Colored Work Department—Local, State and Area Associations, L-R, 1916-42.

34. "Resolution on Race Relations," Oct. 20-23, 1930, Black YMCA Records, box 6, Colored Work Department—Local, State and Area Associations, L-R, 1916-42; Willis Duke Weatherford, "The Colored YMCA, the Interracial Committee and Related Subjects," p. 47, Black YMCA Records, box 1, History and Organization Reports, 1919-38; YMCA National Council, *Negro Youth in City YMCAs: A Study of YMCA Services among Negro Youth in Urban Communities* (New York: Association Press, 1944), 11.

35. William B. West to Channing H. Tobias, Nov. 5, 1930, and Channing H. Tobias to Jay A. Urice, Oct. 3, 1930, both in Black YMCA Records, box 6, Colored Work Department—Local, State and Area Associations, L-R, 1916-42; Channing H. Tobias to Howard Kester, Nov. 12, 1937, Biographical Records, "Channing H. Tobias," no. 24; *Ebony*, Feb. 1, 1951, pp. 15-21; Channing H. Tobias to Carl Murphy, April 23, 1936, Black YMCA Records, box 6, Colored Work Department—Local, State and Area Associations, L-R, 1916-42.

36. Channing H. Tobias, "Christ and Negro Youth," Helsinki, Finland, 1926, p. 2, JEM Papers, box 126-39, no. 830.

37. Clarence P. Shedd, *History of the World's Alliance of the YMCAs* (London: World's Committee of YMCAs, 1955), 506.

38. Fisher, *Public Affairs*, 88.

39. Channing H. Tobias, "Interracial Ideal of the Y.M.C.A. Movement," Feb. 3, 1933, p. 2, Black YMCA Records, box 1, Policy—Correspondence and Statements, 1913-41.

40. Ibid; *Secretarial Letter,* Oct. 1931, vol. 8, no. 4, Black YMCA Records, box 3, Colored Work Department—Periodicals—*Secretarial News Letter*, 1930-36.

41. "Interracial Relations: Problems and Solutions in Recent Association Experience," June 5, 1936, Black YMCA Records, box 1, Various Interracial Reports, 1930s-60s.

42. Ibid.

43. Quoted in Rayford W. Logan, "Tobias, Channing H[eggie]," in *Dictionary of American Negro Biography,* ed. Rayford W. Logan and Michael R. Winston (New York: Norton, 1982), 593; "Biographical Sketch of Dr. Channing H. Tobias, Chairman of NAACP, Board of Directors," n.d., in Biographical Records, "Channing H. Tobias," no. 2; Shedd, *History of the World's Alliance*, 506-7.

44. Shedd, *History of the World's Alliance*, 507.

45. National Study Commission on Interracial Practices in the YMCA, *Interracial Practices in the YMCA: A Guide for Officers and Leaders of Local YMCAs* (New York: Association Press, 1953), 7.

46. YMCA National Council, *National Council Bulletin*, Nov.-Dec. 1935, p. 7, and Nov.-Dec. 1936, p. 6; YMCA National Council, "Let's Think—and Work—Together," Record of the twelfth annual meeting of YMCAs of the United States, Cincinnati, Oct. 21-24, 1936, p. 10.

47. For a discussion of African-American protest during World War II, see John Hope Franklin, *From Slavery to Freedom: A History of Negro Americans* (New York: Knopf, 1988), 385-410; John Morton Blum, *V Was for Victory: Politics and American Culture during World War II* (New York: Harcourt Brace Jovano-

vich, 1976), 182-220; Neil A. Wynn, *The Afro-American and the Second World War* (New York: Holmes and Meier, 1975); Richard M. Dalfiume, "The 'Forgotten Years' of the Negro Revolution," *Journal of American History* 55 (June 1968): 90-106; Herbert Garfinkel, *When Negroes March: The March on Washington Movement in the Organizational Politics of FEPC* (Glencoe, Ill.: Free Press, 1959); Harvard Sitkoff, "Racial Militancy and Interracial Violence in the Second World War," *Journal of American History* 58 (Dec. 1971): 661-81; Lee Finkle, "The Conservative Aims of Militant Rhetoric: Black Protest during World War II," *Journal of American History* 60 (Dec. 1973): 692-713; idem, *Forum for Protest: The Black Press during World War II* (Rutherford, N.J.: Fairleigh Dickinson Univ. Press, 1975); A. Russell Buchanan, *Black Americans in World War II* (Santa Barbara, Calif.: Clio Books, 1977); and B. Richard Skinner, "The Double 'V': The Impact of World War II on Black America," Ph.D. diss., Univ. of California, Berkeley, 1978; Shapiro, *White Violence*, 301-48; and Richard Polenberg, *One Nation Divisible: Class, Race, and Ethnicity in the United States since 1938* (New York: Penguin Books, 1984), 69-78.

48. Alain Locke, "The Unfinished Business of Democracy," *Survey Graphic* 31 (Nov. 1942): 458.

49. *New Sign*, Feb. 15, 1941, p. 2, Papers of the NAACP, Group II, ser. E, container 61, YMCA, 1940-54; Perry B. Jackson to W.H. McKinney, March 4, 1942, Biographical Records, "Channing H. Tobias," no. 24; Henry W. Pope, "Report of the Resolutions and Findings Committee," Bordentown, New Jersey, July 12, 1942, Black YMCA Records, box 6, Colored Work Department—Reports, 1940-49.

50. Campbell C. Johnson, "Facing the War and Planning for the Peace," Bordentown, New Jersey, July 12, 1942, p. 19, Black YMCA Records, box 4, Surveys and Studies, 1926-47; Pope, "Report of the Resolutions and Findings Committee," July 12, 1942; Channing H. Tobias, "The YMCA of Tommorrow," June 6, 1944, Black YMCA Records, box 2, Miscellaneous Articles, Reports and Historical Statements, 1910-50.

51. Tobias to Edwin R. Embree, Nov. 2, 1944, Black YMCA Records, box 2, Colored Work Department, Budget Rosenwald.

52. Tobias to Jay A. Urice, July 14, 1941, Black YMCA Records, box 2, Staff and Lay Conferences—Minutes and Reports, 1899-1945; "National YMCA Lay Conference, July 10 and 11, 1943," Papers of the NAACP, Group II, ser. A, container 676, YMCA National Laymen's Conference, 1943.

53. Henry W. Pope, "Report of the Resolutions and Findings Committee," July 12-13, 1941, Black YMCA Records, box 2, Staff and Lay Conferences—Minutes and Reports, 1899-1945; Channing H. Tobias, "The Negro in Our Democracy," March 23, 1943, Papers of the NAACP, Group II, ser. A, container 147, Board of Directors, Channing Tobias, 1943-49.

54. YMCA National Council, *Negro Youth in City YMCAs*, 14; Kendall Weisiger, *Background for Brotherhood* (New York: Association Press, 1944), 31; *Survey* 80 (May 1944): 171; Eugene E. Barnett quoted in Channing H. Tobias to Edwin R. Embree, Nov. 2, 1944, Black YMCA Records, box 2, Colored Work Department, Budget Rosenwald.

55. "Resolution Approved by the National Council and Adopted by the International Convention, Atlantic City, New Jersey, March 17 and 18, 1946," Black YMCA Records, box 6, Commission on Interracial Policies and Program—Minutes, 1950-51; Commission on Interracial Policies and Program, *Steps Taken to Improve Racial Practices in the YMCA, 1946-1959* (New York: National Board of the YMCA, [1960?]), 4.

56. Yorke Allen, Jr., to Rockefeller Brothers Fund, Nov. 30, 1954, Rockefeller Brothers Fund, Rockefeller Archive Center, box 116, YMCA—National Board, 1953-59.

57. "Chart Showing Areas and States; Territory Served by Each Number of Y.M.C.A. Units in Each Area and State; Number of Units in Each Area and State with Complete and Partial Interracial Practices and Policies, with Totals of Each Category," Sept. 23, 1950, Black YMCA Records, box 6, Commission on Interracial Policies and Program, 1950-51; "Some A.B.C.'s for Improving Human Relationships in Y.M.C.A.'s Having Branches Primarily Serving Negroes and Other Minorities, November 1950," Black YMCA Records, box 1, Addresses, 1893-1935.

58. Eugene E. Barnett to Rockefeller, Jr., Nov. 7, 1952, p. 3, RF Archives, RG 2, box 34, YMCA—National Council, envelope no. 2.

Conclusion

1. Eugene E. Barnett quoted in Channing H. Tobias to Edwin R. Embree, Nov. 2, 1944, Black YMCA Records, box 2, Colored Work Department, Budget Rosenwald; Channing H. Tobias to Carl Murphy, April 23, 1936, Black YMCA Records, box 6, Colored Work Department—Local, State and Area Associations—L-R, 1916-42.

2. B.F. Hathaway, "Trends in Community Relationships of YMCAs," July 8-9, 1935, JEM Papers, box 126-28, no. 591.

3. Channing H. Tobias to Carl Murphy, April 23, 1936, Black YMCA Records, box 6, Colored Work Department—Local, State and Area Associations—L-R, 1916-42; Channing H. Tobias, "Visits in the Central, Western and Southern Region," Oct. 17, 1930, JEM Papers, box 126-67, no. 1294.

4. "Minutes, Joint Meeting of the Colored Work Department Committee and Executive Committee of the Semi-Centennial Celebration," Oct. 19, 1941, Biographical Records, "Channing H. Tobias," Colored Work Department—Minutes, 1919-43, no. 10; Jesse E. Moorland, "The Work of the YMCA among Colored Young Men," ca. 1901, p. 5, JEM Papers, box 126-27, no. 554.

5. Booker T. Washington, "The Future of the Negro Race," *Men*, March 27, 1897, p. 1.

6. Ibid.

7. Clipping, *New York Times*, Sept. 8, 1948, and James E. Allen to Henry L. Moon, Oct. 19, 1948, both in Papers of the NAACP, Library of Congress, Washington, D.C., Group II, ser. A, container 676, YMCA, 1945-55; Channing H. Tobias, "The YMCA and Negro Youth," March 19, 1939, Black YMCA Records, box 3, Miscellaneous Reports and Publications, 1917-56; idem, "The Contribution of the YMCA to the Progress of the American Negro," Oct. 9, 1932, Black YMCA Records, box 2, Miscellaneous Articles, Reports and Historical Statements, 1910-50.

8. Tobias, "Contribution of the YMCA to the Progress of the American Negro."

9. C.M. Potts to Moorland, July 23, 1922, JEM Papers, box 126-21, no. 290.

Selected Bibliography

For more than a century the YMCA has been an integral part of American society, yet historians have largely ignored the association and its leadership. The only book tracing the institutional development of the YMCA in the United States is C. Howard Hopkins, *History of the YMCA in North America*. Since its publication in 1951, historians have displayed little interest in the YMCA.

In articles, George P. Antone has examined the YMCA Graduate School in Nashville, and Lawrence W. Fielding and Clark F. Wood have studied the Louisville YMCA's gymnasium. David I. Macleod, Clifford Putney, and Jodi Vandenberg-Daves have explored the issues of gender, masculinity, and social control in the YMCA. In addition to these scholarly studies, Richard C. Lancaster's *Serving the U.S. Armed Forces, 1861-1986* (1987) offers important insights into the YMCA's service to military personnel.

African Americans in the YMCA have received even less scholarly attention. Historians of the postemanicipation period have all but ignored black YMCAs and their leadership. Those studying African Americans in cities have mainly focused on the forces shaping the emergence of the ghetto. They have examined residential segregation, the impact of migration, and race relations and their effects on family and kin relationships. They have neglected the role of YMCAs as African-American community centers. Only a few urban historians even mention the existence of African-American YMCAs.

Similarly, studies of nineteenth- and twentieth-century African-American leaders have failed to include black YMCA officials. There are no biographies or biographical essays assessing the leadership of the three highest ranking African-American YMCA officials: William A. Hunton, Jesse E. Moorland, and Channing H. Tobias. Instead, the historical discussion of black leadership continues to be dominated, and at times even paralyzed, by Booker T. Washington's advocacy of vocational training and W.E.B. Du Bois's espousal of academic education.

More than forty years after the publication of Hopkins's *History of the YMCA in North America*, historians still know very little about the YMCA's work among African Americans. Only three article-length scholarly studies have examined aspects of the black YMCA experience: Frank N. Schubert's "The Fort Robinson YMCA, 1902-1907: A Social Organization in a Black Regiment"; Lillian S. Williams's "To Elevate the Race: The Michigan Avenue YMCA and the Advancement of Blacks in Buffalo, New York, 1922-1940"; and her "Black Communities and Adult Education: YMCA, YWCA, and Fraternal Organizations." In addition, three YMCA officials, Thomas B. Hargrave, Jr., N. Webster Moore, and Dreck S. Wilson, provide some information about the African-American YMCAs in Washington, D.C., St. Louis, and Baltimore. Their studies, however, are of limited use to historians since they frequently do not document their sources.

The paucity of YMCA histories is surprising, considering that associations provided many black communities with important and otherwise unavailable services. The largest and most important collection of YMCA documents can be found in the YMCA of the USA Archives, University of Minnesota Libraries, Minnesota. The YMCA Archives contain a wealth of material illustrating all aspects of YMCA history. The records are national in scope and include financial records, statistics, correspondence, annual reports, minutes of meetings, and statements of policy decisions. The YMCA Archives are also the largest repository of YMCA publications, such as monographs, yearbooks, periodicals, newspapers, pamphlets, newsletters, and photographs. Moreover, the Biographical Records at the YMCA Archives contain important information about YMCA leaders whose personal papers have not survived, such as Anthony Bowen, Henry E. Brown, William A. Hunton, and Channing H. Tobias.

The Jesse E. Moorland Papers at the Moorland-Spingarn Research Center at Howard University are essential for the study of African-American YMCAs and their leadership. Moorland was instrumental in creating a network of black associations during the late nineteenth and early twentieth centuries and he was responsible for the recruitment and training of association secretaries. His well indexed papers contain the draft of a history of the African-American YMCA, fund-raising statistics, newspaper clippings, photographs, and local, regional, and national reports, as well as personal and business correspondence between various black and white YMCA officials. Smaller, yet useful, collections in the Moorland-Spingarn Research Center are the personal papers of Benjamin E. Mays, president of Morehouse College and a member of the YMCA's World Committee, and Campbell C. Johnson, who served as executive secretary of the African-American association in Washington, D.C., from 1923 to 1940.

The collaboration between white philanthropists and black YMCAs is best documented in the George Foster Peabody Papers, the Rockefeller Family Archives, and the Julius Rosenwald Papers. The Rosenwald Papers are particularly useful for the study of African-American YMCAs in urban communities in the North. The papers contain rich files on all black communities that applied for Rosenwald's financial assistance.

Documents illustrating the YMCA's service with African-American troops in World War I can be found in the Armed Services and Education Records of the YMCA Archives, the Jesse E. Moorland Papers, the Papers of John and Lugenia Burns Hope, and the W.E.B. Du Bois Papers. The Armed Services Records and Education Records at the YMCA Archives consist of official reports of black YMCA secretaries who served with the soldiers in the United States and France. The Moorland and John Hope papers contain reports as well as letters from African-American secretaries and soldiers. Du Bois, who planned to write a book about black troops in World War I, compiled a wealth of information about the racism and discrimination the soldiers experienced. His opinion of African-American YMCA leaders, however, is better documented in the editorial pages of the *Crisis*. Important sources for an understanding of the YMCA's postwar interest in interracial dialogue and cooperation are located in the YMCA Archives, the Moorland Papers, and the Laura Spelman Rockefeller Memorial and Rockefeller Family Archives at the Rockefeller Archive Center.

The impact of the Depression and the subsequent desegregation of the YMCA during World War II can be traced through the holdings of the YMCA Archives, the Rockefeller Archive Center, the Moorland Papers, the Robert R. Moton Papers, and the records of the Office of Negro Affairs of the National Youth Administration at the National Archives. Moton's papers in particular illustrate the devastating effect the depression had on African-American YMCAs, while the records of the National Youth Administration highlight the collaboration between the YMCA and the New Deal agencies. The Papers of the National Association for the Advancement of Colored People at the Library of Congress contain important information on the post-World War II period and the ensuing struggle to desegregate local associations.

Manuscripts

American Expeditionary Force (World War I), 1917-1923. Record Group 120, National Archives, Washington, D.C.

Armed Services Records Related to World War I. YMCA of the USA Archives, Univ. of Minnesota Libraries, St. Paul.

Biographical Records: Anthony Bowen, Cephas Brainerd, Henry E. Brown, William A. Hunton, William Chauncey Langdon, Jesse E. Moorland, Channing H. Tobias. YMCA Archives, Univ. of Minnesota, St.Paul.

Du Bois, W.E.B. Papers. Microfilm, Amistad Research Center, Tulane Univ., New Orleans, Louisiana.

Education Records, 1889-1980. YMCA of the USA Archives, Univ. of Minnesota Libraries, St.Paul.

Hope, John, and Lugenia Burns. Papers. Robert A. Woodruff Library, Atlanta Univ. Center, Atlanta, Georgia. Microfilm, University Publications of America.

Johnson, Campbell C. Papers. Moorland-Spingarn Research Center, Howard Univ., Washington, D.C.

Julius Rosenwald Fund Archives. Fisk Univ., Nashville, Tennessee.

Laura Spelman Rockefeller Memorial. Rockefeller Archive Center, Pocantico Hills, North Tarrytown, New York.

Loving, Walter Howard. Papers. Moorland-Spingarn Research Center, Howard Univ., Washington, D.C.

Mays, Benjamin E. Papers. Moorland-Spingarn Research Center, Howard Univ., Washington, D.C.

Moorland, Jesse E. Papers. Moorland-Spingarn Research Center, Howard Univ., Washington, D.C.

Moton, Robert R. Papers. Moton Family Papers. Library of Congress, Washington, D.C.

National Association for the Advancement of Colored People. Papers. Library of Congress, Washington, D.C.

National Youth Administration, Office of Negro Affairs. Record Group 119, National, Archives, Washington, D.C.

Peabody, George Foster. Papers. Library of Congress, Washington, D.C.

Records Relating to YMCA Work with Blacks, 1891-1979. YMCA of the USA Archives, Univ. of Minnesota Libraries, St.Paul.

Rockefeller Family Archives. Rockefeller Archive Center, Pocantico Hills, North Tarrytown, New York.

Rosenwald, Julius. Papers. Univ. of Chicago, Chicago, Illinois. Microfilm, Hebrew Union College, Cincinnati, Ohio.

Washington, Booker T. Papers. Library of Congress, Washington, D.C.

Books

Ames, J. Quincy. *The Advance in Professional Standards of the Secretaryship of the Young Men's Christian Associations*. Chicago: YMCA College, 1929.

Arthur, George R. *Life on the Negro Frontier: A Study of the Objectives and the Success of the Activities Promoted in the YMCA's Operating in "Rosenwald" Buildings*. New York: Association Press, 1934.

Atwood, Jesse H. *The Racial Factor in YMCA's: A Report on Negro-White Relationships in 24 Cities*. New York: Association Press, 1946.

Bowen, Trevor, *Divine White Right: A study of Race Segregation and Interrracial Cooperation in Religious Organizations and Institutions in the United States*. New York: Harper & Brothers, 1934.

Bullock, Ralph W. *In Spite of Handicaps*. New York: Association Press, 1927.

Cade, John B. *Twenty-Two Months with "Uncle Sam": Being the Experiences and Observations of a Negro Student who Volunteered for Military Service against the Central Powers from June, 1917 to April, 1919*. Atlanta: Robinson-Cofer Co., 1929.

Doggett, Laurence L. *History of the Young Men's Christian Association*. New York: Association Press, 1922.

———. *Life of Robert R. McBurney*. Cleveland: F.M. Barton, 1902.

Donoghue, Terry. *An Event on Mercer Street: A Brief History of the YMCA of the City of New York*. New York: n.p., ca. 1952.

Dykeman, Wilma. *Prophet of Plenty: The First Ninety Years of Willis Duke Weatherford*. Knoxville: Univ. of Tennessee Press, 1966.

———, and James Stokely. *Seeds of Southern Change: The Life of Will Alexander*. New York: W.W. Norton, 1962.

Eddy, Sherwood. *A Century with Youth: A History of the YMCA from 1844 to 1944*. New York: Association Press, 1944.

Embree, Edwin R., and Julia Waxman. *Investment in People: The Story of the Julius Rosenwald Fund*. New York: Harper and Bros., 1949.

Fisher, Galen M. *Public Affairs and the Y.M.C.A.: 1844-1944, With Special Reference to the United States*. New York: Association Press, 1948.

Hargrave, Thomas B., Jr. *Private Differences--General Good: A History of the YMCA of Metropolitan Washington*. Washington, D.C.: YMCA of Metropolitan Washington, 1985.

Hopkins, C. Howard. *History of the YMCA in North America*. New York: Association Press, 1951.

Hunton, Addie W. *William Alphaeus Hunton: A Pioneer Prophet of Young Men*. New York: Association Press, 1938.

———, and Kathryn M. Johnson. *Two Colored Women with the American Expeditionary Forces*. Brooklyn: Brooklyn Eagle Press, 1920.

Hunton, William A. *Colored Young Men: History, Methods and Relationships of Association Work Among Them*. New York: YMCA International Committee, ca. 1900.

Lancaster, Richard C. *Serving the U.S. Armed Forces, 1861-1986: The Story of the YMCA's Ministry to Military Personnel for 125 Years*. Schaumburg, Ill.: Armed Services YMCA of the U.S.A., 1987.

Macleod, David I. *Building Character in the American Boy: The Boy Scouts, YMCA, and Their Forerunners, 1870-1920*. Madison: Univ. of Wisconsin Press, 1986.

Martin, Robert F. *Howard Kester and the Struggle for Social Justice in the South, 1904-77*. Charlottesville: Univ. Press of Virginia, 1991.

Mays, Benjamin E. *Born to Rebel: An Autobiography*. Athens: Univ. of Georgia Press, 1971.

McMillen, T.C. *The Springfield, Ohio, YMCA, 1854-1954*. Springfield, Ohio: Springfield Tribune Printing Co., 1954.

Morse, Richard C. *History of the North American Young Men's Christian Associations*. New York: Association Press, 1913.

———. *My Life with Young Men: Fifty Years in the YMCA*. New York: Association Press, 1918.

Moss, Lemuel. *Annals of the U.S. Christian Commission*. Philadelphia: J.B. Lippincott, 1868.

Moton, Robert Russa. *Finding a Way Out: An Autobiography*. College Park, Maryland: Doubleday, Page, 1920.

Pence, Owen E. *The Professional Boy's Worker in the YMCA: An Occupational Study*. New York: Association Press, 1932.

———. *The YMCA and Social Need: A Study of Institutional Adaptation*. New York: Association Press, 1939.

Pontius, John W. *The Educational Function of the YMCA*. New York: Association Press, 1927.

Ross, Murray G. *The YMCA in Canada: The Chronicle of a Century*. Toronto: Ryerson Press, 1951.

Senger, Harry L. *The Story of the Young Men's Christian Association of Cincinnati and Hamilton County, 1853-1953*. N.p.: Parthenon Press, 1953.

Shedd, Clarence P. *Two Centuries of Student Christian Movements: Their Origins and Intercollegiate Life*. New York: Association Press, 1934.

———. *History of the World's Alliance of the YMCAs*. London: World's Committee of YMCAs, 1955.

Spaeth, John Duncan. *Camp Reader for American Soldiers: Lessons in Reading, Writing, and Spelling*. Atlanta: National War Work Council, YMCA, 1918.

Sprenger, James Albert, and Franklin S. Edmonds, eds. *The Leave Areas of the American Expeditionary Forces, 1918-1919: Records and Memoirs*. Philadelphia: John C. Winston & Co., 1928.

Stewart, Cora Wilson. *Soldier's First Book*. New York: Association Press, 1918.

Stokes, Anson Phelps. *Educational Plans for the American Army Abroad*. New York: Association Press, 1918.

Super, Paul. *What Is the YMCA: A Study in the Essential Nature of the YMCA*. New York: Association Press, 1922.

Taft, William Howard, ed. *Service with the Fighting Men: An Account of the Work of the American Young Men's Christian Associations in the World War*. 2 vols. New York: Association Press, 1922.

Torrence, Ridgely. *The Story of John Hope*. New York: Macmillan, 1948.

Ware, Louise. *George Foster Peabody: Banker, Philanthropist, Publicist*. Athens: Univ. of Georgia Press, 1951.

Weatherford, Willis Duke. *Negro Life in the South: Present Conditions and Needs*. New York: Association Press, 1910.

———. *Present Forces in Negro Progress*. New York: Association Press, 1912.

———. *Interracial Cooperation: A Study of the Various Agencies Working in the Field of Social Welfare*. N.p.: Interracial Committee of the War Work Council of the YMCA, 192?.

———. *A Survey of the Negro Boy in Nashville, Tennessee*. New York: Association Press, 1932.

Weisiger, Kendall. *Background for Brotherhood*. New York: Association Press, 1944.

Werner, Morris Robert. *Julius Rosenwald: The Life of a Practical Humanitarian*. New York: Harper and Bros., 1939.

Whiteside, William B. *The Boston Y.M.C.A. and Community Need: A Century's Evolution, 1851-1951*. New York: Association Press, 1951.

Williams, Charles H. *Sidelights on Negro Soldiers.* Boston: B.J. Brimmer, 1923.
Williams, J.E. Hodder. *The Father of the Red Triangle: The Life of Sir George Williams, Founder of the Y.M.C.A.* New York: Hodder and Stoughton, 1918.
Worman, E. Clark. *History of the Brooklyn and Queens Young Men's Christian Association, 1853-1949.* New York: Association Press, 1952.

YMCA Publications

Commission on Interracial Policies and Program. *Steps Taken to Improve Racial Practices in the YMCA--1946-1959.* New York: National Board of YMCA, 1960?
"Constitution of the Colored Young Men's Christian Association, Washington, D.C., organized December 26, 1866." Washington, D.C.: R.O. Polkinhorn, 1879. In the possession of Thomas B. Hargrave, Jr., president of the YMCA of Metropolitan Washington, D.C.
National Study Commission on Interracial Practices in the YMCA. *Interracial Practices in the YMCA: A Guide for Officers and Leaders of Local YMCAs.* New York: Association Press, 1953.
New York City YMCA. "The War Correspondence between the Young Men's Christian Associations of Richmond, Virginia, and of the City of New York." New York: G.P. Putnam, 1861.
YMCA. *Summary of the World War Work of the American YMCA: With the Soldiers and Sailors of America at Home, on the Sea, and Overseas. With the Men of the Allied Armies and with the Prisoners of War in All Parts of the World.* N.p.: For Private Distribution, 1920.
YMCA, Chicago, Board of Managers. *Fifty-Five Years: The Young Men's Christian Association of Chicago, 1858-1913.* Chicago: YMCA Board of Managers, 1913?
YMCA, International Committee. *Proceedings of the Conventions.* Annually 1854-1877; biennially 1878-1901; triennially since 1902.
———. *Year Book and Official Roster.* Annually since 1875.
———. "The Colored Men's Department of the YMCA." New York: YMCA International Committee, 1894.
———. "General Pershing and the Young Men's Christian Association." An Address Delivered at the Annual Dinner of the International Committee, New York City, May 10, 1921. New York: YMCA, International Committee, 1921.
YMCA, National Council. *Negro Youth in City YMCAs: A Study of YMCA Services among Negro Youth in Urban Communities.* New York: Association Press, 1944.
———. "Let's Think-and Work-Together." Record of the 12th Annual Meeting of the YMCAs of the United States, Cincinnati, Ohio, Oct. 21-24, 1936.
YMCA, National Council, Bureau of Records, Studies and Trends. *Negro Youth in City YMCA's: A Study of YMCA Services Among Negro Youth in Urban Communities.* New York: International Committee YMCA, 1944.

Theses

Antone, George P., Jr. "Willis Duke Weatherford: An Interpretation of His Work in Race Relations, 1906-1946." Ph.D. diss., Vanderbilt Univ., 1969.
Belles, A. Gilbert. "The Julius Rosenwald Fund: Efforts in Race Relations, 1928-1948." Ph.D. diss., Vanderbilt Univ., 1972.

Boom, Kathleen Williams. "The Julius Rosenwald Fund's Aid to Education in the South." Ph.D. diss., Univ. of Chicago, 1949.

Dunn, Frederick Roger. "The Central Y.M.C.A. Schools of Chicago: A Study in Urban History." Ph.D. diss., Univ. of Chicago, 1940.

Hardy, A.W. "A Study of the Organization and Operation of Rosenwald YMCA's for the Period 1917-1927." M.A. thesis, Ohio State Univ., 1928.

Harlow, Harold C., Jr. "Racial Integration in the YMCA: A Study of the Closing of Certain Negro YMCAs with Special Reference to the Role of Religious Factors." Ph.D. diss., Hartford Seminary, 1961.

Holland, Ira H. "A Study of Interracial Relationships and Practices in Selected YMCA's." Ph.D. diss., Columbia Univ., 1953.

Macleod, David I. "Good Boys Made Better: The Boy Scouts of America, Boys Brigades, and the YMCA Boy's Work, 1880-1920." Ann Arbor: University Microfilms, 1976.

Perlman, Daniel. "Stirring the White Conscience: The Life of George Edmund Haynes." Ph.D. diss., New York Univ., 1972.

Articles

"Agenda for Advance in Inter-Racial Practice." *National Council Bulletin,* Aug.-Sept. 1946, pp. 4-5.

Allen, Cleveland G. "Work of the Y.M.C.A. of the New York City." *Colored American Magazine,* May 1908, pp. 272-77.

Allen, Sarah A. "A New Profession: The First Colored Graduate of the Y.M.C.A. Training School, Springfield, Massachusetts." *Colored American Magazine,* Sept. 1903, pp. 661-63.

Angell, Pauline K. "Julius Rosenwald." *American Jewish Yearbook* 34 (Oct. 1, 1932 to Sept. 20, 1933): 141-76.

Antone, George P. "The YMCA Graduate School, Nashville 1919-1936." *Tennessee History Quarterly* 32, no. 1 (1973): 67-82.

Arthur, George R. "The Young Men's Christian Association Movement among Negroes." *Opportunity,* March 1923, pp. 16-18.

Atkins, S.G. "The Mental Improvement of Colored Men." *Men,* Dec. 18, 1897, pp. 252-53.

Bachmann, Lawrence P. "Julius Rosenwald." *American Jewish History Quarterly* 66, no. 1 (1976): 89-105.

Bacote, Clarence A. "John Hope." *Journal of Negro History* 21 (April 1936): 240-44.

Barbeau, Arthur E. "Thy Brother's Keeper." *Journal of the West Virginia Historical Association* 2, no. 1 (1978): 25-40.

Boorstin, Daniel J. "Transforming the Charitable Spirit." In *The Julius Rosenwald Centennial,* pp. 5-33. Chicago: Univ. of Chicago, 1962.

Bowen, J.W.E. "Bishop Bowen on the Colored Association." *Association Men.* Jan. 1902, p. 156.

Brown, Evelyn S. "The Harmon Awards: Association Secretaries Win Recognition for their Services." *Association Men,* Feb. 1927, pp. 255-56.

Brown, John Smith, Jr. "The New York Branch of the YMCA." *Colored American Magazine,* June 1904, pp. 409-14.

Bullock, Ralph W. "Adult Education Program of the YMCA Among Negroes." *Journal of Negro Education* 14 (Summer 1945): 385-89.

Busbee, F.D. "The Y.M.C.A. Work at Hampton." *Southern Workman* 35 (Oct. 1906): 569-71.

Cannon, M. Hamlin. "The United States Christian Commission." *Mississippi Valley Historical Review* 38 (1951-1952): 61-80.
"The Christian Association Conference." *Southern Workman* 33 (Jan. 1904): 7.
"Colored Associations." *Association Men,* Oct. 1917, p. 128.
"Colored Boys Gain a New Physique, Ideals and Outlook." *Association Men,* Oct. 1915, p. 29.
"The Colored Department." *Association Men,* Aug. 1912, p. 583.
"The Colored Department." *Association Men,* Sept. 1912, p. 645.
"The Colored Department." *Association Men,* Dec. 1912, p. 149.
"Colored Department." *Association Men,* Oct. 1913, p. 35.
"The Colored Department." *Association Men,* March 1914, pp. 318-19.
"The Colored Department." *Association Men,* Feb. 1914, p. 258.
"The Colored Department." *Association Men,* May 1914, p. 427.
"The Colored Department." *Association Men,* Feb. 1916, p. 272.
"Colored Department." *Association Men,* March 1916, p. 331.
"Colored Department." *Association Men,* June 1917, p. 519.
"Colored Department Briefs." *Association Men,* March 1912, p. 304.
"A Colored Man and His Problem." *Association Men,* Jan. 1911, p. 181.
"Colored Men." *Association Men,* Jan. 1906, p. 147.
"Colored Men." *Association Men,* Jan. 1912, p. 163.
"The Colored Men." *Association Men,* Feb. 1913, p. 240.
"Colored Men." *Association Men,* June 1914, p. 495.
"Colored Men and Boys." *Association Men,* Nov. 1915, p. 87.
"Colored Men at Work." *Association Men,* Dec. 1911, pp. 129-30.
"The Colored Men Gaining." *Association Men,* Nov. 1912, p. 85.
"Colored Men Make Progress." *Association Men,* April 1912, p. 351.
"The Colored Men of North America." *Association Men,* Jan. 1908, p. 173.
"The Colored Men's Advance." *Association Men,* Oct. 1911, p. 33.
"The Colored Men's Department." *Association Men,* Jan. 1903, p. 161.
"Colored Men's Department." *Association Men,* Nov. 1909, p. 86.
"The Colored Men's Department." *Association Men,* May 1911, p. 354.
"Colored Men's Department." *Association Men,* June 1912, p. 471.
"Colored Men's Department News." *Association Men,* Oct. 1908, p. 33.
"The Colored Men's Work." *Association Men,* Sept. 1914, p. 660.
"Colored Y.M.C.A. Conference." *Voice of the Negro,* Jan. 1904, p. 9.
"The Colored YMCA Conference." *Southern Workman* 36 (Jan. 1907): 5-6.
Craver, William Curtis. "The Y.M.C.A. in Negro Schools." *Southern Workman* 56 (Feb. 1927): 80-82.
"Dr. Tobias . . . on the YMCA." *Brown American,* Fall-Winter 1944-45, pp. 2-3, 16.
Dodson, N. Barnett. "Carlton Avenue Branch of the Brooklyn, N.Y., Young Men's Christian Association." *Colored American Magazine,* Feb. 1904, pp. 117-19.
Du Bois, W.E.B. "The Negro and the Y.M.C.A." *Horizon,* March 1910, pp. 1-5.
———. "Y.M.C.A." *Crisis,* Dec. 1914, pp. 77, 80.
———. "The YMCA." *Crisis,* Nov. 1925, pp. 10-11.
———. "The Proportion of Christians." *Crisis,* March 1931, p. 101.
Embree, Edwin R. "The Business of Giving Away Money." *Harper's Magazine,* Aug. 1930, pp. 320-29.
Fielding, Lawrence W., and Clark F. Wood. "From Religious Outreach to Social Entertainment: The Louisville YMCA's First Gymnasium, 1876-1880." *Filson Club History Quarterly* 60, no. 2 (1986): 239-56.
"For a $50,000 Colored Association Building." *Association Men,* Nov. 1906, pp. 71-72.

"For Colored Men." *Association Men,* Nov. 1911, p. 73.

"For Colored Men." *Association Men,* July 1912, p. 514.

"For Colored Men of the Cities." *Association Men,* April 1911, p. 306.

"For the Good of the Negro and the City." *Association Men,* March 1911, pp. 253-54.

Foster, A.L. "The Spring Street Branch Y.M.C.A. of Columbus, Ohio." *Competitor* 2, no. 1 (July 1920): 9-12.

Hamlin, Robert H. "Work of the Y.M.C.A. among the Young Colored Men of Brooklyn, N.Y." *Colored American Magazine,* June 1908, pp. 337-39.

Hart, Irving H. "Keeping up Morale: At Camp Alexander, Virginia." *Southern Workman* 48 (May 1919): 225-30.

Hope, John. "Colored Y.M.C.A." *Crisis,* Nov. 1925, pp. 14-17.

Hunton, William A. "The Association among Colored Men." *Men,* Dec. 18, 1897, p. 249.

———. "Colored Men's Department of the Young Men's Christian Association." *Voice of the Negro,* June 1905, pp. 388-94.

Hutson, Jean Blackwell. "Hunton, Addie D. Waites." *Dictionary of American Negro Biography,* pp. 337-38.

"The Indianapolis 'Y'." *Crisis,* March 1924, pp. 205-8.

Johnson, Campbell C. "Negro Youth and the Educational Program of the Y.M.C.A." *Journal of Negro Education* 9 (April 1940): 354-62.

Johnson, Charles S. "Julius Rosenwald." *Opportunity,* April 1935, pp. 110-12, 122.

"Julius Rosenwald and the Negro." *Crisis,* Sept. 1922, pp. 203-10.

"A Little Lay Sermon on the Negro." *Association Men,* March 1913, pp. 292-93.

Logan, Rayford W. "Hunton, William A." *Dictionary of American Negro Biography,* pp. 338-40.

———. "Tobias, Channing H[eggie]." *Dictionary of American Negro Biography,* pp. 593-95.

McCormick, J. Scott. "The Julius Rosenwald Fund." *Journal of Negro Education* 3 (Oct. 1934): 605-26.

MacFarland, Henry B.F. "The Man by Man Rise of a Race of Men." *Association Men,* Jan. 1915, pp. 200-201.

Macleod, David. "A Live Vaccine: The YMCA and Male Adolescence in the US and Canada, 1870-1920." *Social History* (Canada), 11, no. 21 (1978): 5-25.

McMillan, L.K., Jr. "Anthony Bowen and the YMCA." *Negro History Bulletin* 21 (April 1958): 159-60.

Miller, Caroll L. "The Negro and Volunteer War Agencies." *Journal of Negro Education* 12 (Summer 1943): 438-51.

Miller, Kelly. "The Negro Young Men's Christian Association." *Southern Workman* 33 (Feb. 1904): 93-99.

Moore, N. Webster. "The Black YMCA of St. Louis." *Missouri Historical Society Bulletin* 36, no. 1 (1979): 35-40.

Moorland, Jesse E. "Work among Colored Men." *Association Men,* Jan. 1901, pp. 124-25.

———. "Educational Work of the Colored Young Men's Christian Association." *Southern Workman* 35 (April 1906): 244-46.

———. "The YMCA and the War." *Crisis,* Dec. 1917, pp. 65-68.

———. "The Y.M.C.A. with Colored Troops." *Southern Workman* 48 (April 1919): 171-75.

———. "Julius Rosenwald, Friend to Man." *Association Men,* Sept. 1920, pp. 15, 41.

———. "The Young Men's Christian Association among Negroes." *Journal of Negro History* 9 (April 1924): 127-38.

Mott, John R. "The War Work of the Young Men's Christian Associations of the United States." *Annals of the American Academy* 79 (Sept. 1918): 204-12.
"National Conference Y.M.C.A." *Southern Workman* 54 (Dec. 1925): 531-32.
"Needs of Colored Boys in Small Cities is Problem." *Association Men,* Dec. 1925, p. 174.
"The Negro and the Association." *Association Men* (July 1902), pp. 455-56.
"The New International Y.M.C.A. Secretary." *Voice of the Negro,* Oct. 1905, p. 676.
Overton, B.W. "The Cincinnati 'Y'." *Opportunity,* Feb. 1923, p. 14.
"President Taft Appeals for Colored Men." *Association Men,* July 1911, pp. 460-61.
Putney, Clifford. "Character Building in the YMCA, 1880-1930." *Mid-America* 73, no. 1 (1991): 49-70.
"A Race on the Road to Self-Realization." *Association Men,* Jan. 1917, p. 203.
Roberts, Samuel K. "George Edmund Haynes: Advocate for Interracial Cooperation." In *Black Apostles: Afro-American Clergy Confront the Twentieth Century,* ed. Randall K. Burkett and Richard Newman, pp. 97-127. Boston: G.K. Hall, 1978.
Rosenwald, Julius. "The Burden of Wealth." *Saturday Evening Post,* Jan. 5, 1929, pp. 12-13, 136.
———. "A Fair Chance for the Colored Man." *Association Men,* Jan. 1914, pp. 192-93.
———. "Principles of Public Giving." *Atlantic Monthly,* May 1929, pp. 599-606.
———. "A New Chapter in Philanthropy." *Whitman College Quarterly,* Jan. 1931, pp. 3-19.
Sanders, Frank K. "A New Perspective for Colored Men and Boys." *Association Men,* Jan. 1916, p. 198.
Schubert, Frank N. " The Fort Robinson YMCA, 1902-1907: A Social Organization in a Black Regiment." *Nebraska History* 55, no. 2 (1974): 165-79.
Scott, Emmett J. "Fifty Years of 'Y' Work." *Crisis,* June 1938, pp. 209-11.
Segal, Ben. "Color and the Chicago YMCA." *Crisis,* July 1945, pp. 197, 206.
"Student Y.M.C.A. Conference." *Southern Workman* 54 (Aug. 1925): 347-48.
"The Ten Years' Record of Colored Men." *Association Men,* Jan. 1910, p. 167.
"This Is the Colored Department's Day." *Association Men,* June 1911, p. 406.
Tobias, Channing H. "Colored YMCA." *Crisis,* Nov. 1912, pp. 32-36.
———. "Decade of Student YMCA Work." *Crisis,* Oct. 1922, pp. 265-67.
———. "Christian Work for Negro Youth." *Missionary Review of the World* 46 (March 1923): 200-203.
———. "YMCAs in American Negro Colleges." *Student World* 16 (April 1923): 58-62.
———. "Epoch in Race Relations." *Association Men,* Aug. 1924, p. 555.
———. "The Work of the YM and YWCA with Negro Youth." *Annals of the American Academy* 140 (Nov. 1928): 283-86.
———. "--in the hearts of men." *Association Men,* Feb. 1932, pp. 174, 188-89.
———. "YMCA." *Journal of Negro Education* 2 (April 1933): 246-47.
———. "Max Yergan." *Crisis,* July 1933, pp. 155, 166.
Vandenberg-Daves, Jodi. "The Manly Pursuit of a Partnership between the Sexes: The Debate over YMCA Programs for Women and Girls, 1914-1933." *Journal of American History* 78, no. 4 (March 1992): 1324-46.
"To Give the City Negro a Fair Chance." *Association Men,* Feb. 1911, pp. 199-201.
"To Help the Negro to Help Himself." *Association Men*, Feb. 1911, pp. 196-97.
Walker, C.T. "For 10,000 Negroes." *Association Men,* Dec. 1910, p. 105.
Washington, Booker T. "The Future of the Negro Race." *Men,* March 27, 1897, p. 1.

———. "Booker Washington's Address." *Association Men,* July 1901, p. 374.

———. "The Future of 10,000 Negroes." *Association Men,* March 1909, pp. 258-59.

———. "Booker T. Washington on the Negro in the American City and His Needs." *Association Men,* Jan. 1911, p. 149.

———. "Remarkable Triple Alliance: How a Jew Is Helping the Negro through the YMCA." *Outlook,* Oct. 28, 1914, pp. 485-92.

"Washington's Modern Building for Colored Men." *Association Men,* Jan. 1913, p. 203.

Weatherford, Willis Duke. "Changing Attitudes of Southern Students." *Journal of Negro Education* 2 (April 1933): 147-50.

Weaver, Frank G. "An Adventure in Brotherliness." *Association Men,* Dec. 1920, pp. 157-58, 180.

West, Earle H. "Moton, Robert Russa." *Dictionary of American Negro Biography,* pp. 459-61.

Williams, Charles H. "Negro Y.M.C.A. Secretaries Overseas." *Southern Workman* 49 (Jan. 1920): 24-35.

Wilson, Dreck Spurlock. "Druid Hill Branch, Young Men's Christian Association: The First Hundred Years." *Maryland Historical Magazine* 84 (Summer 1989): 135-46.

Williams, Lillian S. "To Elevate the Race: The Michigan Avenue YMCA and the Advancement of Blacks in Buffalo, New York, 1922-1940." In *New Perspectives on Black Educational History*, ed. Vincent P. Franklin and James D. Anderson, pp. 129-48. Boston: G.K. Hall, 1978.

———. "Black Communities and Adult Education: YMCA, YWCA, and Fraternal Organizations." In *Education of the African American Adult: An Historical Overview*, ed. Harvey G. Neufeldt and Leo McGee, pp. 135-62. New York: Greenwood, 1990.

Wilson, P. Whitwell. "The Negro." *Association Men,* April 1925, pp. 345-46, 383-86.

Winston, Michael R. "Moorland, Jesse E." *Dictionary of American Negro Biography,* pp. 448-52.

"With Colored Men." *Association Men,* May 1920, p. 570.

"Work among Colored Boys Shows Steady Growth." *Association Men,* Oct. 1925, pp. 70, 83.

Wright, John C. "The Red Triangle in Harlem." *Southern Workman* 49 (July 1920): 315-21.

"The Young Men's Christian Association." *Voice of the Negro,* March 1906, p. 172.

"The YMCA and the Negro." *Crisis,* Jan. 1923, p. 120.

"YMCA Makes Progress in Inter-Racial Practice." *National Council Bulletin,* June 1945, p. 7; Jan. 1946, p. 10.

"YMCA Senior Secretary." *Southern Workman* 52 (Nov. 1923): 524-25.

"YMCA Student Conference." *Southern Workman* 50 (Aug. 1921): 340-42.

Index